Agriculture, Food Security, Poverty, and Environment

Agriculture, Food Security, Poverty, and Environment

Essays on Post-reform India

C.H. Hanumantha Rao

OXFORD
UNIVERSITY PRESS

OXFORD
UNIVERSITY PRESS

YMCA Library Building, Jai Singh Road, New Delhi 110001

Oxford University Press is a department of the University of Oxford. It furthers the University's objective of excellence in research, scholarship, and education by publishing worldwide in

Oxford New York
Auckland Cape Town Dar es Salaam Hong Kong Karachi
Kuala Lumpur Madrid Melbourne Mexico City Nairobi
New Delhi Shanghai Taipei Toronto

With offices in
Argentina Austria Brazil Chile Czech Republic France Greece
Guatemala Hungary Italy Japan Poland Portugal Singapore
South Korea Switzerland Thailand Turkey Ukraine Vietnam

Published in India
by Oxford University Press, New Delhi

First published 2005

ISBN-13: 978-0-19-567195-7
ISBN-10: 0-19-567195-3

This work has grown out of the research undrtaken at the Centre for Economic and Social Studies, Hederabad

Typeset in Times New Roman 10/12 by InoSoft Systems, Noida
Printed by Sai Printopack Pvt Ltd., New Delhi 110 020
Published by Manzar Khan, Oxford University Press
YMCA Library Building, Jai Singh Road, New Delhi 110 001

To

Professor Waheeduddin Khan
(1934–85)
Founder-Member and First Director of the Centre for Economic and Social Studies

Contents

RURAL POVERTY

SUSTAINABLE RURAL DEVELOPMENT

CONCLUSIONS

Tables

Foreword

In the post-economic reform period in India, there has been a lively debate about the impact of economic reforms on important sectors of the economy as well and on the standard of living of the population. In this book, C.H. Hanumantha Rao examines developments in the interrelated areas like agriculture, food security, poverty, and environment in India in the post-reform period. He also examines the pre- and post-reform trends in agriculture and rural development in East and South-east Asian countries and compares them with the Indian experience. The author concludes that the performance in terms of economic growth, agricultural development, rural non-farm sector, poverty reduction, and demographic transition in East and South-east Asian countries has been much superior as compared to the Indian experience. The superior performance in East and South-east Asia is attributed not only to the liberalization and market driven economy but significantly to the high rate of savings, capital formation, physical infrastructure, implementation of land reforms, and high priority accorded to education and health in the pre-reform period. India's achievements are lower in all these indicators. This could be the main reason for the slow progress in economic growth and poverty reduction despite reforms in the 1990s.

The author examines, in detail, the performance and policies in agricultural sector, food security, rural poverty, and sustainable rural development. The last chapter of the book provides an overview of the findings as well as the agenda for further reform. To improve the performance of agriculture, the author suggests strengthening of infrastructure, agriculture research and extension, credit and removing restrictions on agriculture trade and processing. He strongly advocates for reducing input subsidies not only to improve public investments in agriculture but also to provide incentives for more efficient use of scarce resources to achieve sustainability. According to him, food security does not mean food grain security as consumption patterns are shifting towards non-foodgrains. This indicates the need for diversifying agriculture to increase employment and reduce poverty.

Throughout the book, C.H. Hanumantha Rao suggests policies for achieving growth with equity. Thus, policies that reduce disparities across regions, classes, social groups would improve both growth and equity. The study emphasizes that economic reforms should have a human face. The author also stresses the need for more meaningful globalization that is 'in line with' the socio-political factors. According to him, the success of economic reforms in a democratic polity depends on the support from wider sections of population.

I am happy to note that most of the work for this study has been done during C.H. Hanumantha Rao's association with our Centre as an Honorary Professor since the early 1990s. His earlier books were well received by professionals and policy makers. I am sure that this book on post-economic reform developments in agriculture and rural economy will be equally well received. The relevance of issues and the manner in which these are analysed would make this book extremely useful for the research community and policy makers.

S. Mahendra Dev
Director
Centre for Economic and Social Studies
Hyderabad

Preface

This book is the outcome of my explorations, over the last decade, to understand the rationale for the paradigm shift and the economic reforms that ensued in the hitherto centrally planned economies, and to design a reform package for India which would reconcile the goals of efficiency with those of equity. The experience of the East and South-east Asian countries underscores that economic reforms—their content as well as sequencing—need to take due account of the initial or pre-reform conditions in India, viz., socio-economic inequalities, insufficient infrastructure, inadequate social development and also the imperatives of pursuing development within a democratic polity. Many of the shortfalls in achieving the avowed objectives of growth with social justice in the post-reform period are attributable to the failure to take due account of these unfavourable initial conditions in framing the reform agenda. This book attempts to spell out a reform strategy and agenda for agriculture, food security, poverty alleviation and management of natural resources in India in the light of the pre-reform conditions as well as the post-reform experience.

A number of my papers prepared for different occasions in the course of the last decade form the basic source material for this book. These are listed in the Annexure. These papers have been substantially revised by sifting and rearranging the material and by updating the findings. The initial stimulus for this effort was provided by my work, jointly with Ashok Gulati, as a Visiting Fellow at the International Food Policy Research Institute, Washington, D.C., for two months in 1994. I pursued this work at the CESS as a National Fellow of the Indian Council of Social Science Research during 1994–6. My work as a Consultant for the Rural Development Division of the ESCAP, United Nations, Bangkok, for a few months during 1995–6 provided me opportunities to study the East and South-east Asian experience with economic reforms. I also had an opportunity to work on WTO and

Agriculture as a Visiting Fellow at the Department of Economics, Free University, Amsterdam, during the summer in 1999, supported by the Indo-Dutch Programme on Alternatives in Development.

The comments and suggestions made on the manuscript by the anonymous referee, at the Oxford University Press, were quite helpful in revising the manuscript. I am indebted to several of my colleagues at the CESS for their help. B.P.R. Vithal read the first chapter on The Political Economy of Economic Reforms and gave valuable comments. S. Mahendra Dev provided some of the useful material for the book. He also carefully read through the whole manuscript and suggested several alterations for tightening the presentation. C. Ravi helped me with the statistical analysis for the section on Food Security. G.K. Mitra consolidated, at one place on the computer, the scattered material from various papers and rendered technical help. I have also received useful suggestions and help from S. Subrahmanyam, V. Ratna Reddy, N. Sreedevi and K. Chandrasekhar. G. Vijay Kumar, the Librarian and P. Sudhakar, the Assistant Librarian gave their full cooperation. I also received competent assistance from B. Sankara Reddy and V.M. Sarma. I am grateful to all.

C.H. Hanumantha Rao
Centre for Economic and Social Studies
Hyderabad

Abbreviations

APL	Above Poverty Line
AMS	Aggregate Measure of Support
APCE	Average Per Capita Consumption Expenditure
APMA	Agricultural Produce Marketing Act
BPL	Below Poverty line
CSO	Central Statistical Organization
CMIE	Centre for Monitoring Indian Economy
CACP	Commission for Agricultural Costs and Prices
CESS	Centre for Economic and Social Studies
CGIAR	Consumer Group on International Agricultural Research
DPAP	Drought Prone Area Programme
DWCRA	Development of Women and Children in Rural Areas
ESCAP	Economic and Social Commission for Asia and the Pacific
EAS	Employment Assurance Scheme
ECA	Essential Commodities Act
FAO	Food and Agricultural Organization
FCI	Food Corporation of India
FDI	Foreign Direct Investment
FGT	Foster-Greer-Thorbecké
GATT	General Agreement on Trade and Tariff
GDP	Gross Domestic Product
GOI	Government of India
GCFA	Gross Capital Formation in Agriculture
HYV	High Yielding Variety
HP	Horse Power
HCR	Head-count Ratio
IT	Information Technology
IARC	International Agricultural Research Centre
ICAR	Indian Council of Agricultural Research
IFPRI	International Food Policy Research Centre

IRDP	Integrated Rural Development Programme
IMF	International Monetary Fund
IMT	Irrigation Management Transfer
IWMI	International Water Management Institute
IAAE	International Association of Agricultural Economists
JRY	Jawahar Rozgar Yojana
JFM	Joint Forest Management
LDB	Land Development Bank
MSP	Minimum Support or Procurement Price
MFA	Multi-fibre Agreement
NABARD	National Bank for Agriculture and Rural Development
NAS	National Account Statistics
NPK	Nitrogen Phosphorous Potassium
NSS	National Sample Survey
NSSO	National Sample Survey Organization
NGO	Non-governmental Organization
NCAER	National Council of Applied Economic Research
NWDPRA	National Watershed Development Programme for Rain-fed Areas
NEP	New Economic Policy
NREP	National Rural Employment Programme
OECD	Organization for Economic Cooperation and Development
PRI	Panchayati Raj Institution
PDS	Public Distribution System
PSE	Producer Support Estimate
PAC	Primary Agricultural Cooperative
PIM	Participatory Irrigation Management
PAP	Poverty Alleviation Programme
RBI	Reserve Bank of India
RIDF	Rural Infrastructure Development Fund
RRB	Regional Rural bank
RPDS	Revamped Public Distribution System
RLEGP	Rural Landless Employment Guarantee Programme
SHG	Self-help Group
SGSY	Swarnajayanti Gram Swarozgar Yojana
SSI	Small Scale Industry
SPS	Sanitary and Phyto-sanitary
SDP	State Domestic Product
SC	Schedule Caste
ST	Schedule Tribe

TFP	Total Factor Productivity
T&V	Travel and Visit
TRIPS	Trade Related Intellectual Property Rights
TRYSEM	Training of Rural Youth for Self-employment
UNDP	United Nation Development Programme
UNCTAD	United Nations Conference on Trade and Development
WTO	World Trade Organization
WUA	Water Users' Association
WDP	Watershed Development Programme

Section I

Economic Reforms and Agriculture

1

The Political Economy of Economic Reforms

Introduction

In this book we look at the developments in the highly interrelated areas like agriculture, food security, rural poverty, and environment in India in the post-economic reform period of the 1990s. These reforms have significantly affected agriculture and the related sectors, although the full impact of the reforms undertaken so far is yet to be felt, not to speak of the considerable potential from reforms yet to be initiated. The economic reforms launched in the early 1990s in India represent a major paradigm shift in the management of the economy and are, in a sense, an extension of the historic changes witnessed in the former socialist countries and other developing countries practising centralized economic planning. To trace out the implications of these far-reaching global changes in economic systems for the sectors under review in India, it is necessary to understand the origin and the nature of these systemic changes in their totality in a political economy perspective. We propose to make such an attempt in this chapter before we examine specifically the possible impact of these reforms on the sectors under study.

The Demise of Centralized Bureaucratic Planning

In the last few years there have been far-reaching changes in economic systems as well as the political framework in the former socialist world. What do these changes signify? Do they represent the victory of the capitalist system over the socialist system? Do they signify the victory of pluralist democracy over one-party rule? One can, perhaps, give a clearer answer to the second question. The urge for freedom and political democracy has won the day at least in a large part of the socialist world and it is only a matter of time before it can establish itself in the rest of the former socialist territory. Individual freedom in economic decision making within a market setting is incompatible, in the long run, with the denial of individual freedom in the political sphere (Chakravarty 1993). There can be little doubt about it, considering the historical experience, even though it would be difficult to predict whether the process of change towards democracy would be as smooth as it has been in eastern Europe and in the former Soviet Union.

However, what is important even with respect to the change towards political democracy is that, unlike in many of the so-called Third World Countries, the democratic system once established in the former socialist countries is likely to ensure a genuinely wider and effective participation of the people in the body politic rather than being twisted and moulded by vested interests. This is because of the thorough-going changes made in the property relationships and the relative economic equality achieved in these societies even before they embarked upon economic development in the post-revolution period. The educational and awareness levels of people at large are also quite high in the former socialist countries, as against the very slow improvement in literacy and awareness levels in several other developing countries despite pursuing economic planning for decades.

With regard to the first question, many have been asserting that the recent changes represent a triumph of capitalism over the socialist system. However, classical capitalism, that is, the capitalism the working of which had, in fact, prompted socialist revolutions, does not exist today anywhere in the world. After the October Revolution, the classical capitalism was called into question in the West on account of the recurring depressions resulting in widespread unemployment and human misery. The climax of this was seen in the Great Depression of the 1930s which gave birth to Keynesianism, and which indeed was applauded as a via media between the Soviet type of socialism and the then functioning capitalism. J.M. Keynes exposed the inherent weaknesses of the then existing capitalism and made out a strong case for public intervention in the form of public investments and regulation of macroeconomic activity within which capitalism is to function.

Keynesianism influenced powerfully the growth models of many of the so-called capitalist countries as well as the mixed economies which embarked upon economic planning following their independence after the Second World War. Today, in many of the Western economies, particularly in Europe, the public expenditure on economic infrastructure and welfare activities as a proportion to their national income is much greater than that in several of the mixed economies which have taken to economic planning (Dreze and Sen 2002). Indeed, many of the so-called western capitalist economies will collapse the moment their governments stop expenditures on the welfare programmes. Apart from contributing to the expansion of effective demand, the governments in these countries ensure macroeconomic stability, protect their trading interests and also undertake long-range or strategic planning in the key sectors of the economy. Capitalism has thus done a lot of introspection and has learnt a great deal from the socialist experiment.

The question that arises in this context is whether 'socialism', as practised in the former socialist or centrally planned economies has done similar introspection and learnt from the market economies in order to lend dynamism to itself. Unfortunately, it had not done so until the late 1970s when China embarked upon market-oriented reforms. Capitalism had been affected and modified more by the socialist experiment than socialism had learnt from the functioning of the market economies. This self-righteousness on the part of socialism is rooted in its strong moral appeal, rigid doctrines, closed nature of such economies, and the authoritarian political system which kept it isolated from the rest of the world and prevented feed-back from its own people. This has basically been responsible for the lack of resilience in the socialist system. However, ironically, the Peoples Republic of China with its authoritarian political system still intact has readily incorporated, in the last two decades, several features of the market economy. The growth rate of the Chinese economy has been phenomenal in the last two decades. Yet, the wonder is that it is more a state-driven market economy than a market-driven economy with a diminishing role for the state.

Centralized economic planning in the former socialist and other developing countries yielded positive results in the initial stages when the role of the state was important for mobilizing large resources for investing in infrastructure, which, in any case, was beyond the capacity of the private sector in these countries. This success coupled with the reduction of social and economic inequalities at the dawn of revolution in socialist countries provided inspiration and held out great promise for development and improvement in the standards of living for several developing economies, which won freedom from colonial rule after the Second World War. This was a phase when consumer demands were limited to fewer essential items, the prevailing technology favoured large-scale enterprises and the workers belonging to the immediate post-revolution generation were willing to put in their best for social good without making excessive demands on the system.

Certain basic changes occurred within a couple of decades in the sphere of technology and management in the developed capitalist economies which revolutionized their production systems but the socialist countries and other mixed economies practising economic planning remained insulated from these far-reaching changes because of the closed nature of their economies. The most important development in the Western capitalist economies was that technological change became extremely important in bringing about growth when compared to savings and capital formation (Abramovitz 1956, Solow 1957). Very high growth rates were being achieved even with lower saving rates and capital formation. Of course, there were economies, which had the advantage of a high rate of technological advance as well as a high rate of capital formation. On the other hand, the centrally planned economies typically depended on high rates of savings by squeezing even essential consumption in a phase when the consumerism of the West was exerting a powerful demonstration effect through mass media which itself experienced a phenomenal technological advance. Thus, the dominant paradigm of development in the post-war years—which emphasized savings and investment, surpluses from agriculture, import substitution, and the dominant role of the state in economic activity having shown positive results in the first few decades—began to flounder in the later period.

The basic reason for technological retrogression in the centrally planned economies was the absence of incentives for modernizing and updating their production systems. Apart from the absence of competition among the public enterprises, there were no incentives for cost reduction by adopting improved methods as the costs actually incurred were generally underwritten by the state. Excepting perhaps in the area of defence, much of the advanced technology evolved in Soviet laboratories seems to have been more readily adopted in the Western economies than in the Soviet Union itself. In particular, despite radical land reforms, agriculture invariably proved to be a drag on the economies of the former socialist countries because of the failure to appreciate the role of the peasant proprietorship in providing incentives for raising productivity.

Despite the high educational levels and skills and better access to health facilities, the productivity of workers in terms of effort put in began to decline among the later generation of workers. Neither exhortation based on appeals to 'socialist ethics' nor strict enforcement of discipline could deliver the goods. Guarantee of employment and wages unrelated to performance left very little incentive for greater effort and improvement in the quality of performance. It was readily assumed that unlike the 'economic man' of the capitalist world, the workers under socialism would be prompted entirely by a sense of social responsibility and subordinate their individual interests to social good. This was a highly moralistic and unrealistic position. At one stage, the leadership in China even thought that the socialist principle of paying each according to one's work was already outdated and the time had come for leap-frogging into communism and paying each according to her/his needs, regardless of the nature of work put in. What constituted 'needs' was, of course, defined by the leadership under communes! This turned out to be a disaster and, as they admit now with great regret, the people were called upon to eat from the same pot. The total disregard of human nature and of the need for material incentives led to frustration among workers. In view of low productivity, ideological exhortation for satisfying only the basic needs regardless of the work put in, was at best landing them into primitive communism. The position became much worse in the Soviet Union where out of frustration, the workers had taken to heavy drinking even in the offices and workplaces. The situation became so serious that Mikhail Gorbachev had to virtually introduce prohibition for some time and convert distilleries into units for extracting fruit juice in order to protect employment!

In a nutshell, the demise of centralized bureaucratic planning can be attributed to the inefficiency and low productivity that the system had perpetuated for a long time. The system collapsed under its own weight without any outside intervention. However, it goes to the credit of the Chinese leadership, that once they realized that they had been left behind by a few decades in respect of modern technology and productivity, they engineered a big change in their economic system after the late 1970s and, within a decade, placed themselves in a position from where they could dictate terms to the international financial institutions rather than being twisted by them as happened in the case of some other countries. Those opposed even to the broad direction of change towards economic liberalization in India need to ask this simple question as to why the centralized planning, as it was practised in the former socialist countries, collapsed on its own.

Changing Roles of Planning and Markets in Development

What role should be assigned to the state in relation to market is perhaps the most important issue in development today. However, the controversy today is not so much about 'statist' versus 'market friendly' approach. There is a consensus now about the need to redefine the role of the state in relation to markets. The choice is really in regard to the content of economic reform, its sequencing and the speed with which it is to be carried out. In order to arrive at a proper conclusion, it would be necessary to understand the strengths and weaknesses of the markets and the state. Indeed, it would be necessary to know why the centrally planned economies did exceedingly well for quite some time after they embarked upon planning and began to show weaknesses and infirmities after a certain stage of development.

A purely capitalist or market economy suffers from three major defects. All the three deficiencies arise from its main driving force, that is, the single-minded pursuit of profit. First, it is short-sighted and has a narrow time horizon when compared to the society as a whole. Therefore, where long-term and heavy investments in infrastructure are required, with low and uncertain returns for individual investors the state has to step in to provide the long-range perspective and mobilize the large resources needed for such investments. Second, the market-oriented decisions betray insensitivity to the adverse external effects on the economy such as on environment. The state has to step in to discourage certain socially harmful enterprises and the overuse of limited natural resources through the system of taxes and subsidies or through banning outright certain activities and business practices.

The third major drawback of the capitalist system which has always invited social resentment and continues to render this system unpopular is its persistent tendency to economize on the use of labour and on welfare expenditures. Its pursuit of efficiency and productivity has been directed, among other things, towards saving on labour. Whereas from the social point of view, the ultimate goal of development is human welfare, for an individual capitalist entrepreneur human labour is a mere factor of production. In mature capitalist economies, the state has taken the brunt of this capitalist ethos by providing unemployment insurance and by undertaking other welfare measures on a large-scale. State action on all these three fronts has been found to be indispensable to mitigate the adverse effects of the free-play of market forces and indeed such state action accounts for the survival of capitalism in the developed capitalist as well as the developing economies.

What lessons does one draw from the recent changes in the economic systems and policies in the socialist countries, which were undoubtedly a source of inspiration for many of the developing economies when they embarked upon the path of planned economic development fifty years ago? Perhaps, the foremost lesson is that as an economy gets rich and sophisticated, markets have to play a greater role for transmitting signals from the consumers regarding their tastes and preferences. Bureaucracy cannot perform this function. It can only try to impose on consumers goods and services of low quality produced at a high cost. Markets also convey signals regarding the costs of resources to be used in production in an environment of competition among the producers at home and abroad.

A major failure of the markets or the private enterprise is in respect of employment generation and social welfare. This is basically attributable to the highly unequal distribution of income and wealth in societies where the private sector operates through the market mechanism. In an unequal society the price signals in the marketplace favour the production of luxury goods even where the resources are not sufficient for producing essential goods of mass consumption. On the cost side, the markets put a low price on labour where the poor are without assets and lack bargaining power. It is often said that markets bypass the poor and the underprivileged, who cannot participate in the market-driven development. This is not an accurate statement. The poor and the underprivileged are very much driven into the market. The child labour and the bonded labour are all participating in the market but at very unequal or unfavourable terms (Rao 1995). Therefore, markets can be expected to perform their efficiency function without harming equity only when the initial distribution of income and wealth is favourable. On this score, markets can do less harm in the former socialist and East Asian countries than in countries where the social and economic inequalities are greater. In such situations various strategies and policies have to be evolved to counter the harmful effects of the operation of markets.

Therefore, it has rightly been said that the market can be a good servant when it is intelligently utilized but a bad master when it is allowed free play. The concept of 'market socialism' purported to be followed in China conveys the message that the market mechanism and the private sector would be allowed to operate within the broad parameters set by the state. It would be interesting to recall that the term 'market socialism' was first coined by the late Polish economist Oscar Lange in the 1950s when he was actively engaged in planning and wanted to incorporate certain features of the market in order to make the working of socialism more efficient. But he was apparently overruled by the authorities at that time. The rebirth of this concept after 30 years in the communist mainland is, therefore, a fitting tribute to this great economist.

The foremost lesson from the development experience of the last 50 years is that the state should support rather than supplant markets by investing in physical infrastructure and human capital and by letting the markets function. The achievements in terms of growth as well as equity have been impressive in situations where the state has supplemented markets, leading to the efficient use of resources through technological change and development of human capital (World Bank 1991).

The ongoing economic reforms to effect a paradigm shift rightly assign overriding importance to macroeconomic stabilization, as a prerequisite for the success of other reforms such as domestic deregulation, and trade reform. The reform package is also right in implying that one reform without the other does not yield optimum results (World Bank 1991). However, the reformers in general opt for proceeding fast simultaneously on all the fronts, instead of following a gradualistic approach.

The World Development Report, 1991, for example, outlines the case for 'shock treatment' as follows:

> Bold changes are especially necessary if a government lacks credibility.... Adjustment usually occurs in a climate of crisis. Governments do well to capitalise on the broad, potentially short-lived mandate for reform that crisis confers by frontloading the reform programme.... Erring on the side of speed appears to be the best. Speed also makes sense if political opportunity for reform is unlikely to last.... (p. 117).

Such a course of action would close the options for learning from doing and expose the economy to various risks. Such an approach is not in the interests of reform itself because, if problems arise, some of these reforms can be reversed or one can go slow, defeating the very objectives of reform. Such a frontloading can discredit governments further, if they already lack credibility.

The Indian Experience

Unlike the former socialist countries, India opted for economic planning within the framework of a mixed economy where the private sector and markets have always had a strong presence. Again, unlike in the socialist economies, India's multi-class and multi-caste social structure has remained intact. Further, India opted for the parliamentary form of democracy but without a democratic revolution or thorough-going social transformation preceding it as in the Western democracies. It is true that while adopting planning for economic development and social transformation, India was powerfully influenced by the then ruling Keynesian ideas as well as the Soviet experiment where the state played a key role. But, because of the basic differences in the initial conditions outlined above, the similarities of planning experience between India and the former socialist countries are only of a superficial nature.

Contrary to the initial expectations, the content of planning and, especially, the manner of its implementation in India were powerfully influenced by the prevailing social structure and the vested interests. For example, in respect of land reforms, even though India succeeded in arresting the further concentration of land holdings through the imposition of ceiling on such holdings, there was a failure to provide land to the landless in the measure envisaged. On the other hand, the institution of peasant proprietorship has contributed to the success of the Green Revolution and stood in strong contrast to the collectives and communes of the socialist economies in the corresponding period. In the industrial sector too, private enterprise has been strong ever since independence. However, the rate of protection that Indian industry enjoyed from competition within and outside was among the highest in the world. On account of such pressures and pulls, it has neither been possible to mobilize resources required for speedy development, nor to enforce the discipline needed for effective implementation of programmes.

The rates of saving and capital formation in the former socialist countries have been much higher than in our case, so that they are embarking upon liberalization with strong physical infrastructure, whereas we have to step up investment in such infrastructure to derive the full benefit from liberalization. In China, for example, agricultural growth accelerated from 2.5 per cent per annum to a little over 7 per cent per annum in the 1980s following price reforms and the introduction of household responsibility system in place of communes (ESCAP 1996). But this high growth could be realized due to the existence of tremendous slack, as capital formation was very high and its utilization was inefficient before reform. It was not possible to realize such a high growth in Indian agriculture in the post-reform period mainly because there was no such slack. We did not introduce collectives or communes nor was capital formation sufficiently high.

Further, the level of human resource development in the case of the former socialist countries was of a very high order and we have to go a long way to achieve those levels. Finally, despite the initial social disruption being reported from certain former socialist countries, especially from the former Soviet Union, their social structure, as it has historically evolved, could well prove to be conducive to the more equitable sharing of benefits from development than in many developing countries. Therefore, the characterization of alternative paradigms almost implying that economies hitherto practising central planning have either to start on a clean slate or to build the 'new' on the ruins of the past is not wholly objective. The very high growth in per capita income achieved in China in the 1980s and the1990s is no doubt attributable to the efficient allocation of resources, but, as mentioned, it also arises not in the least from the high saving rate achieved in the pre-reform period (Rao 1991).

It would, therefore, be more objective to follow the 'stages' approach in discussing alternative paradigms. That is, it should not imply that the paradigm suggested now would have been a preferred one even in the early 1950s in developing economies when there was hardly any physical and institutional infrastructure for markets to function efficiently or in the 1920s in the USSR, when the problems and challenges faced were quite different from those faced now. Instead, it would be illuminating to know at what stage the command economies began to flounder and for what reasons.

The stronger side of the Indian experience is that when compared to fifty years ago, we have been able to build up infrastructure of irrigation, power, transport, and financial and social services sufficient to integrate a large and diversified country into a single national market where resources such as capital, labour, and skills flow more or less freely across the country. The working of our democracy and the system of transfer of financial resources provided under our Constitution have so far prevented the emergence of sharp inequalities in the levels of development as between different regions, although the position is by no means such as to justify complacency. Our agriculture has, by and large, been a success story and we have not only achieved self-sufficiency in food grains but are in a position to export them. Our pool of scientific and technical manpower ranks among the top few in the world. The saving rate in the economy rose steeply from about 9 per cent in 1950–1 to around 23 per cent in 1990–1 when we were not particularly 'market-friendly' and stagnated around this level, despite some rise in the private corporate sector saving, in the post-reform decade of the 1990s (Government of India, *Economic Survey 2003*).

But, the major deficiencies of our development experience are: (a) the neglect of trade with other countries and the consequent insulation from the beneficial effects of competition such as technological upgradation of our economy; (b) excessive bureaucratization of economic activity, especially the management of public sector enterprises leading to gross inefficiency in the use of resources; and (c) the failure to ensure social justice through effective implementation of land reforms, expansion of employment opportunities, and provision of universal primary education and primary health facilities.

The economic reforms undertaken so far have yielded impressive results mainly in respect of the external sector; but only moderate impact on growth, welfare, and poverty; negligible impact on savings from the household sector; and negative results in respect of savings from the public sector (Government of India 2003). No serious attempt has so far been made to de-bureaucratize the management of public enterprises, despite the recommendations to this effect made by several expert committees. There have been moves towards privatization of public enterprises but considering the size of our public sector, there is no alternative to improving the management within the framework of public ownership for quite some time to come. The experience of China is relevant in this context. It has considerably liberalized the working of public enterprises and has been able to achieve very high growth rates consistently for over two decades within the framework of public ownership.

The weakest aspect of our reforms so far is the insufficient attention given to the social sectors and poverty alleviation. It is true that considerably large resources have been allocated to rural development. Yet, social development, through the provision of universal primary education and primary health services, housing and other minimum needs, requires massive effort from several ministries, particularly from state governments. But these efforts are considerably undermined by the slow growth of tax revenues of the Centre, in which poorer states have a substantial share, as well as the decline in the share of central assistance for state plans consequent to fiscal compression (see Chapter 14). Moreover, social development and poverty alleviation is not merely a matter of financial allocation but of social engineering with a strong political commitment. Reservation in jobs for the weaker sections and activization of Panchayati Raj institutions do hold promise for change but, the experience so far shows that economic reforms have been concerned basically with industry and trade, and the attention being given to social sectors has not been adequate to provide the much needed 'safety net' for the poor with a view to protecting them from the adverse effects of economic reforms.

Whereas economic reforms have so far enthused the business community, the upper income groups, and the rising middle classes, we have not been able to impart a social content to these reforms which could inspire the common people in a way the Nehruvian model did in the early years of planning in the 1950s or Indira Gandhi's policy orientation towards poverty eradication did in the 1970s. For example, employment guarantee, abolition of child labour, and universal primary education are highly interdependent. Strong time-bound programmes for achieving these are essential not only to ensure wider sharing of benefits from development but to step up productivity itself, as future growth is going to be increasingly dependent on the educational levels and the technical skills of the labour force. Moreover, liberalization and privatization are going to immediately favour the developed regions, which are adequately served with infrastructure. Unless the development of backward regions where poverty is extensive gets a high priority in the package of reforms, the accentuation of regional disparities in development is almost a certainty, as is already borne out by the post-reform experience of the 1990s (Ahluwalia 2000; Deaton and Dreze 2002; Dreze and Sen 2002; and Bhattacharya and Sakthivel 2004).

The moral of all this is clear. People in the modern age, especially in a democracy, will never accept the inequalities of opportunity arising from the mere accident of having been born in households with differences in wealth and status. The foremost challenge before us, therefore, is to reconcile the goals of economic efficiency with social justice. In a democratic polity like ours, economic liberalization can succeed only in the measure in which it is able to win the support of the large majority of our people who still suffer from various social and economic disabilities.

Economic Reforms in India: The Underlying Socio-political Factors

The rationale for the ongoing economic reforms in the country, their consequences and prospects have generally been discussed in the parlance of economics. However, these 'economic' phenomena represent largely a superstructure, which is profoundly influenced by the underlying socio-political factors. Failure to understand these factors is responsible for the false perception of 'consensus' behind reforms, and for the reluctance to see that the 'burden' of reforms is being borne disproportionately by the poor and that the prospects for further reforms now rest on harder decisions calling for sacrifices from the better-off sections of the society.

In our socio-political setting, a package of economic reforms, to be balanced and equitable, has to be concerned with four major tasks, viz., deregulating economic activity to promote enterprise and efficiency; reducing open as well as hidden subsidies by targeting them only to the deserving sections; de-bureaucratizing the management of public enterprises and privatizing them where necessary; and speeding up rural transformation by pursuing programmes for socio-economic development within a decentralized or participatory framework.

Economic reforms in India have so far been focused on deregulation, particularly in industry and trade. The successful reforms so far are those, which could be implemented with a stroke of pen, so to say, without encountering much resistance from the vested interests, even though these tasks have been highly demanding in terms of expertise and diligence. This is because, economic reforms in India were not prominent on the political agenda through the process of mass politics but remained essentially the concern of the political elite (Varshney 1999). Removal of controls has released the initiative and latent energy of our entrepreneurs endowed with resources, talent, and status. Likewise, liberalization of the economy has excited the imagination of resourceful farmers, professionals, and the elite in general, who see greater prospects for earnings and for more productive use of their resources and talents. Economic reforms have thus become highly popular among these visible and articulate sections.

The collapse of centralized planning in the former socialist countries in this period reinforced the self-confidence of our reformers and demoralized even some of the staunch critics of reform. In the initial stages, the government underestimated the latent support for reforms.

However, when the support for reforms gathered momentum from the vocal sections, the government was overtaken by a feeling that consensus around reforms had already been built up, making it insensitive to the adverse consequences for the poor.

The harder tasks of cutting down subsidies for the better-off sections, de-bureaucratizing the management of public enterprises, and decentralizing rural development have barely been touched, as the resistance from the vested interests in these areas is quite strong (Varshney 1999). The tardy progress on these fronts is responsible for the rising revenue deficits of both the Centre and states, slow reduction in poverty, and hence a lack of support for reforms from the poor and the underprivileged.

Unlike in the western democracies and the former socialist countries, our iniquitous social structure has largely remained intact with an uneasy coexistence between different classes and castes, albeit, in a democratic setting. Whereas centralized planning may have curbed the creative energies of certain enterprising sections, it has not been able to resist the pressures from the affluent sections in general for larger subsidies. The amount of subsidies on fertilizers, irrigation, power, transport, benefiting those who can afford to pay is several times higher than that going to the poor by way of food subsidies. These subsidies resulted in unsustainable fiscal deficits, overuse of scarce resources like water and electricity, and shortfalls in resources for public investment.

Further, given the inequities in our system, releasing market forces without simultaneously widening opportunities for gainful employment for the poor and improving their capabilities to avail of such opportunities can lead to lopsided development and social tensions. Tensions can be contained, even with increasing inequality, if the incomes of the poorer sections rise significantly. However, despite a step-up in outlays on rural development, the ongoing economic reforms could not carry credibility with the poor and created serious misgivings. The idiom, which gave prominence to globalization and privatization while calling for austerity on the part of the common people has contributed further to their alienation from reforms.

Therefore, the question is not how the reforms need to be 'projected'. The problem basically concerns the appropriate mix of measures for the liberalization of the economy and the democratization of the social structure at the grass roots level, which can result in high growth as well as wider sharing of benefits. The cases of success with economic reforms in East Asia show that the social conditions prior to reforms were far more egalitarian than in India. Successful land reforms, greater attention to agriculture and rural development, and achievement of universal primary education led to slow population growth, high saving rates, and thus to high economic growth with wider sharing of benefits (ESCAP 1996; Dreze and Sen 2002).

Confiscatory land reforms may not be feasible in a democratic polity like ours. But this only reinforces the need for effective alternative measures for example, employment guarantee, minimum needs programmes, public distribution system (PDS). Thus the elements of a package suited to our conditions cannot be entirely new or original. Nor do the common people expect any such dramatic formula. The concern for the poor and the earnestness as well as the will to implement the package of measures, even if modest, would be decisive in carrying credibility with the people. The concerns, commitments, and actions have a way of communicating themselves.

The credibility of the programmes depends not so much on the fine-tuning of elements in the package as on the effectiveness of the instruments—institutions and the persons manning them—chosen for implementation. The Finance Ministry, Planning Commission, and the Prime Minister's Secretariat need to be evenly placed, so that a balance can be struck between the financial angle, the requirements of overall development on equitable lines and the compulsions of a democratic polity. At present, there is a widespread feeling that in shaping the economic policy of the country, the role of the Planning Commission has been marginalized. Apart from sending wrong signals to the common people, this has undermined the lateral as well as the reverse communication to the powers that be. The quality of the policy package as well as the effectiveness of its implementation need to be enhanced by restoring balance between the relevant institutions.

Whenever the Finance Ministers in their budgets proposed measures for social development and poverty alleviation with a view to rectifying the imbalance in the existing package of economic reforms, such as those proposed in the budget for 1995–6, fears have been expressed that such proposals represent a revival of 'populism'. Such fears arise, at best, from an inadequate understanding of our social structure and insufficient appreciation of the contribution of social development to growth and equity. At worst, these arise from the 'elitist' outlook and the alienation from the common people. It is this mindset, which has been responsible for missing the opportunities to evolve an integrated package of reforms consisting of an appropriate mix of measures for the liberalization of economy and for the democratization of the social structure at the grass roots level. Such a package would have enthused the poor and the downtrodden and brought forth their willing support for the reforms even as it would have whetted the 'animal instincts' and released the creative energies of our entrepreneurs.

Fiscal policy has been unable to raise the tax–gross domestic product (GDP) ratio which has fallen by over 2 percentage points when compared to the pre-reform level, despite the acceleration in the GDP growth rate and hence the rise in taxable capacity (see Chapter 14). As a result, the reduction in fiscal deficit has been lower than envisaged. However, it is the continued rise of revenue deficit, which is a matter of greater concern.

In view of the stickiness of expenditures on revenue account in the short-run, due essentially to rising interest payments and the salary bill, mopping up of purchasing power through better collection of revenues offers a more promising route for reducing revenue deficit. Reduction in tax rates, up to a point, is integral to the reform process. There is evidence to show that the reduction in the rates of direct taxes has resulted in larger revenues on account of better compliance. However, there is considerable scope for raising revenues further from direct taxes by broadening the base and improving collections.

Two alternative scenarios for the rise in saving–investment and growth rates can be visualized. If there is a significant increase in direct foreign investment and if the efficiency of resource-use improves dramatically in the immediate future on account of economic reform, then there may be a step-up in the growth rate of GDP which may set in motion a cycle of higher savings–investment and growth. If this is considered unlikely owing to very little underutilized capacities, infrastructural bottlenecks, human capital deficiencies, and other hindrances to the reform process itself, then a major policy thrust to raise saving rates and improve the investment climate would become inevitable. The reformers seem to be leaning on the prospect of the first scenario materializing.

Thus the incentives offered for household savings are marginal. There is no major initiative to raise public savings (which turned negative for the first time consecutively for four years since 1998–9) by improving the management of public enterprises. The budgetary decline in capital and plan expenditures is no doubt in keeping with the philosophy of ongoing reforms. But unless the private sector is in a position to make good the gap immediately, growth may suffer especially because the complementarity between public and private investment in India is still quite high (Government of India 2000).

Vertical communication from the lower social ladder to the ruling elite at the top is blocked in the normal course owing to iniquitous social structure, illiteracy, and lack of organization among the poor. Unfortunately, electoral verdicts seem to be the only effective mechanism for such communication. It is now abundantly clear that the true consensus around the ongoing economic reforms is yet to be built by enlisting the support of the common people. This would require determined action to step up investment and growth by reducing subsidies for the well-off sections and decentralize the management of public enterprises as well as of rural development.

If subsidies on irrigation, power, and transport cannot be reduced in a democratic polity under the existing system of management owing to the resistance from those affected, an alternative effective course, short of wholesale privatization of such services, is to promote participatory management of services like irrigation and rural electricity. Many state governments are already moving in this direction. However, in the case of public enterprises where such resistance from the users of services is not encountered, ideological considerations favouring immediate and wholesale privatization seem to be coming in the way of de-bureaucratizing their management. As for decentralization of rural development, the unwillingness of state governments to devolve the necessary functions, resources, and power over administration to the Panchayati Raj institutions is the main hurdle (Rajiv Gandhi Foundation 2000). All these measures would require great political will. It is clear, however, that without such bold measures, it would be difficult to carry forward the economic reforms, much less to muster the necessary support from the wider sections of our population.

2

Economic Reforms and Agricultural Growth

The Relevance of East and South-east Asian Experience for India

Introduction

Many of the East and South-east Asian economies, being land-scarce and labour-surplus, have had structural similarities with India at different stages of development in post-war years. As such, their experience with structural adjustment through economic reforms would be more relevant to India than the corresponding experience of, say, countries of Latin America or sub-Saharan Africa. In particular, the socio-political structures under which economic reforms were implemented in many of the South-east Asian countries are such that the lessons emerging from their experience seem even more relevant for a country like India. The objective of this chapter is to understand the experience of the East and South-east Asian countries with agricultural development under economic reforms in the 1980s and the 1990s with a view to draw possible lessons for agricultural development strategy and policy in India.

Pre-reform Achievements and the Initial Conditions

The experience of several countries undertaking measures aimed at stabilization and structural adjustment shows that the consequences of such measures on balance of payments, investment and growth, employment, inflation, and poverty vary considerably between these countries depending on the initial conditions in terms of prevailing socio-economic structures as well as the inner dynamism of the economies before undertaking reforms, the severity of crises faced, and the quality of measures adopted to cope with the crises.

The East and South-east Asian countries have to their credit substantial achievements in respect of infrastructure and institution building in the pre-reform period, which not only helped them to sustain the momentum of growth over a long period by simultaneously enabling a large number of the poor to cross the poverty line but also enabled them to withstand the external economic shocks as well as those arising from the internal efforts at economic reform and adjustment to the changing economic environment. For example, already in 1980, the saving rate in East Asia at 30 per cent of gross domestic product (GDP) was much higher than that in most countries of the world (World Bank 1990). The growth rates in GDP in East Asia over the pre-reform period of 1960s and 1970s at 7.9 per cent and 6.5 per cent, respectively represented the highest recorded in the world. Further, agricultural growth rates in the post-green revolution but pre-adjustment period, that is, during 1965–80, were far above population growth rates in this region ranging between 3.2 per cent for East Asia and 4.6 per cent for Thailand and Philippines (World Bank 1990, p. 181).

The impressive performance of several countries of South and South-east Asia in respect of growth as well as poverty alleviation, cutting across socio-economic systems, in the post-adjustment period could be attributed, in a significant measure, to the infrastructures built and institutions organized and restructured in the pre-reform period, whose full potential could not be realized earlier on account of certain defects in the policy environment. In this respect, the region's performance stands in sharp contrast with, for example, the situation in the countries of sub-Saharan Africa where serious deficiencies in infrastructure and institutions rendered them particularly vulnerable to the shocks of adjustment.

Thorough-going land reforms were implemented under such diverse socio-political systems as in China and Republic of Korea. Even in countries where radical land reforms could not be implemented owing to socio-political constraints, as in many parts of South and South-east Asia, the ceiling on the ownership of land became effective which prevented further concentration of land in a few hands. Thus the access to land, on the whole, is less unequal in these countries when compared, for example, to the several developing countries in Latin America—contributing to a more egalitarian pattern of development. Land reforms, where effective, did facilitate broad-based human development resulting in a speedy demographic transition with favourable consequences for overall development.

Development of irrigation, rural electrification, and rural roads and transport received a high priority in the development plans of the countries in the region which gave an impetus to the growth of agriculture and rural industries, thus raising the incomes of small farmers and artisans and increasing the employment opportunities for the rural poor in general. For example, already in 1983, when most countries in the region had initiated policies for the liberalization of their economies, the percentage of irrigated area to agricultural land stood at 45.4 per cent in China, 60.7 per cent in Republic of Korea, and 76.5 per cent in Pakistan (FAO 1995, p. 10).

Rural credit from institutional sources was expanded significantly at concessional rates of interest in order to ensure that farmers had access to vital inputs at affordable cost. The governments of the region also played a key role in strengthening agricultural research and extension which revolutionized farming through the widespread use of high yielding seeds and fertilizers—even by the small and marginal farmers who increasingly became science and technology conscious. The use of mineral fertilizers in terms of plant nutrients per ha. of agricultural land in 1983 was as high as 331 kg in Republic of Korea, 184 kg in China, and 117 kg in Malaysia as compared to the world average of 88 kg (FAO 1995, p. 12).

Distortions in the Prevailing Strategies

However, these tasks were pursued, in general, within the broad framework of an inward-looking and import-substituting development strategy which had an in-built bias against agriculture. Besides, the prevailing strategy through its protective policies promoted capital-intensive pattern of development which was out of line with the factor endowments of the economies in the region. Further, it inhibited direct foreign investment and technological upgradation of the economy. These deficiencies in the policy framework and the consequent inefficiencies in resource allocation resulted in a lower than feasible rate of overall economic growth and employment generation, including that in agriculture. Since the transfer of labour force from agriculture to the more remunerative non-agricultural activities is a necessary consequence of economic growth, the slow growth and its high capital-intensity resulted in a sluggish reduction in rural poverty.

The prevailing development strategy through various barriers on trade discriminated against agriculture directly by keeping the producer prices lower than what would have prevailed under liberalized trade with the official exchange rate, and indirectly through industrial protection and over-valued exchange rates. The terms of trade were thus deliberately kept unfavourable to agriculture in keeping with the prevailing wisdom to 'extract' surpluses from this sector for promoting industrialization. Beyond a point, however, both industry and agriculture suffered—the former on account of undue protection from competition, the resulting technological lag and the inefficiencies in resource allocation, and the latter on account of 'disprotection' denying it resources as well as the avenues for technological upgradation in a liberalized trading environment.

Undoubtedly, the lower food prices by themselves favoured the poor, as they spend a larger proportion of their income on food than the rich. However, given the initial access to productive assets, the overall growth rate of the economy seems to have been the most important factor accounting for the alleviation of poverty across countries (Quibria and Srinivasan 1994). This may be partly explained by the fact that opening up trade and correction of overvalued exchange rates have favoured the tradeable goods characterized by greater labour-intensity in production. This is demonstrated by devaluation benefiting the small farmers producing commercial crops and even those producing foodgrains partly for the market. Besides, governments in quite a few countries have subsidized food purchased by the poorer sections. On balance, therefore, the poor seem to have suffered under the earlier development strategy, especially in its later stages, on account of the opportunities lost by way of increased employment and higher wages associated with speedy transformation of economies. The net result was the higher incidence of rural poverty than would have been the case under a liberalized policy framework.

Crises and the Post-adjustment Experience

The development paradigms and strategies followed earlier by the countries of the region came under severe strain and proved to be unsustainable as the economies of the region were exposed to external shocks in the 1970s and the 1980s, for example, the successive oil crises and the economic depression in the developed countries resulting in unfavourable terms of trade for the developing economies.

The countries of the region responded, by and large, on their own to the emerging economic crises through short-term measures for macroeconomic stabilization such as devaluation of currencies and bringing down public expenditures by reducing fiscal deficits, as well as by undertaking long-term measures for structural adjustment such as opening up their economies through liberalization of trade and investment, deregulating industry and trade, liberalizing the exchange rate regime, and reducing the role of the state in economic activity by privatizing public enterprises.

In general, the countries of the region have experienced smoother adjustment than the economies of Latin America, sub-Saharan Africa, the former socialist countries in East Europe, and the former Soviet Union. This is partly on account of the relatively low vulnerability of the economies in the region to the crises, which itself is traceable, in no small measure, to the achievements of the pre-reform period discussed earlier. Thus, the combined impact of external shocks—terms of trade and interest rate shocks—in the 1980s in terms of the percentage of GDP, was lowest in China (–1.2 per cent), followed by East Asia excluding China (–8.1 per cent), South Asia excluding India (–10.2 per cent), and India (–5.66 per cent). On the other hand, this shock was highest in sub-Saharan Africa (–14.4 per cent), the next highest being –10.3 per cent for Latin America and the Caribbean (World Bank 1990, p.107). But, the smoother transition is basically explained by the timely and flexible responses carefully tailored to the individual country situations.

Republic of Korea and China have shown a very high rate of growth and a speedy alleviation of poverty in the 'post-liberalization' period of the 1980s and 1990s, even though no two countries could perhaps be more dissimilar in respect of their ideologies and socio-political systems. Republic of Korea has basically been a market-oriented economy from the very beginning, whereas China staunchly followed and strictly implemented the inward-looking, import substitution strategy for nearly three decades. However, in both the countries radical land reforms were implemented at the very start and their achievements in respect of rural physical infrastructure such as irrigation as well as social development like health and education were impressive. Also, both countries displayed great political will and lent resolute state support in implementing their policies. Thus, Chinese 'market socialism' cannot be equated with 'market-led' development with a passive role for the state. Rather, it has increasingly become a 'state-led', 'market-oriented' economy. On the other hand, the basically 'market-led' economic development of Korea has been characterized by active state intervention to subserve the goals of a market economy.

Next in order of performance come a group of countries in South-east Asia, for example, Indonesia, Malaysia, and Thailand. Their record on land reforms as well as infrastructure building in the 'pre-liberalization' period was not as impressive as in the first group of countries. However, there was increased access to land for the poor in certain situations on account of government support for the expansion of area under cultivation, even though at the cost of forests. Their adherence to the inward looking, import-substitution strategy was neither strong nor protracted as in the case of China. They have been relatively flexible throughout in adjusting their policies to suit the domestic interests by responding to the changing international environment (Chakravarty 1993). Also, the governments in these countries have shown a consistent and strong commitment to the goals of development with wider sharing of benefits and the alleviation of poverty. In the Philippines, however, land reforms have been a failure and sharp inequalities in land holdings persist. Levels of social development have been comparatively low and population growth has been quite high. Despite the initial spurt in agricultural output following the green revolution, agricultural and overall economic growth has been slow for long periods resulting in the persistence of high levels of poverty. Its performance is more akin to that of countries of South Asia.

The performance of the countries of South Asia, viz., Bangladesh, India, Nepal, Pakistan, and Sri Lanka in respect of growth as well as poverty alleviation has been modest, although variations in performance within this group are substantial. Sri Lanka, for example, made significant strides in respect of social development and reducing population growth rates. These countries opted for economic planning within the framework of mixed economies with a significant role assigned for the private sector. Yet, their adherence to the earlier paradigm of development continued for a longer period than in the other two groups of countries. Land reforms did not succeed in ensuring access to land for the poor and landlessness is widespread among them. Although the green revolution has enabled these countries to achieve high levels of self-sufficiency in foodgrains, the supply constraints to agricultural growth in terms of infrastructural and institutional bottlenecks and lags in agricultural research and extension continue to be severe.The available evidence points to a rise in hardships for the rural poor in the countries of the region, especially in the early years of reform, as a result of the manner in which stabilization measures have been pushed through in a situation of high inequalities in the access to productive assets and low levels of social development.

Agricultural Growth

The green revolution of the 1970s and the 1980s was sustained basically by the physical and institutional infrastructure built during the 1950s and the 1960s. On the other hand, productivity gains from the macroeconomic reforms implemented in the 1980s and the 1990s are traceable, to a significant extent, to the infrastructure built and the green revolution technology introduced in the pre-reform period. However, macroeconomic reforms have in turn opened up opportunities and created incentives for further investment by the private sector as well as for the widespread adoption of new technology.

Thanks to the infrastructure development and green revolution, the South-east Asian countries had already achieved in the decade of 1970s, a high rate of agricultural growth of around 4 per cent per annum (Table 2.1), which was well above their population growth rates. In the 1980s, China experienced an exceptionally high agricultural growth of 5.3 per cent per annum basically on account of economic reforms which favourably affected agriculture enabling it to reap the benefits from infrastructure development and agricultural research and extension put in place in the pre-reform period. Countries in South Asia in general experienced an acceleration in their agricultural growth rates in the 1980s, even though macroeconomic reforms were yet to be initiated. This achievement is attributable mainly to the spread of green revolution facilitated by the availability of physical and institutional infrastructure developed earlier.

However, agricultural growth in most of the countries under study decelerated during the 1990s (Table 2.1). This is surprising as there was a positive correlation between the overall GDP growth rates and agriculture growth rates over the periods of 1970s and 1980s, and the GDP growth rates continued to be high in the 1990s, which in fact accelerated in most cases when compared to the 1980s. This deceleration in agricultural growth, despite a favourable macroeconomic environment, raises the questions of green revolution fatigue, inadequacy of infrastructure, and the unfavourable trading environment for

Table 2.1: GDP Growth Rates, Overall and from Agriculture in Selected Economies, in Asia-Pacific Region

(*per cent per annum*)

	GDP Growth Rate			GDP Growth Rate Originating from Agriculture		
	1970–80	1981–90	1990–2001	1970–80	1980–90	1990–2001[1,2]
	(1)	(2)	(3)	(4)	(5)	(6)
East Asia						
China	6.4[3]	10.3	10.0	2.8[3]	5.3	4.3
Rep. of Korea	9.6	9.1	5.7	2.7	2.7	1.0
South-east Asia						
Indonesia	7.2	5.8	3.8	4.1	3.2	2.9
Malaysia	7.9	5.2	6.5	–	3.5	1.7
Philippines	6.0	1.0	3.3	4.0	1.2	2.1
Thailand	7.1	7.9	3.8	4.4	3.8	3.4
South Asia						
Bangladesh	2.3	4.1	4.9	0.6	2.6	1.4
India	3.4	5.6	5.9	1.8	3.0	2.6
Nepal	2.7	4.7	4.9	0.5	3.6	2.5
Pakistan	4.9	6.2	3.7	2.3	4.4	4.8
Sri Lanka	4.1	3.8	5.1	2.8	2.1	2.4

Notes: [1] Average of annual growth rates; [2] Growth rate of value-added in agriculture; [3] Relates to the period 1965–80.

Sources: 1. For columns 1, 4 and 5: ESCAP, United Nations, 1996, *Rural Poverty Alleviation and Sustainable Development in Asia and the Pacific*, pp. 7, 35.

2. For columns 2: Asian Development Bank, 1997–8, *Asian Development Outlook*, pp. 223, 225, Oxford University Press.

3. For columns 3 and 6: The World Bank, 2003, *World Development Report*.

agro-products, in the context of growing diversification of agriculture. These questions assume importance as many of these countries are known to enjoy comparative advantage in agricultural and agro-processed products. A related and important issue is whether the manner in which macroeconomic reforms have been implemented in some of these countries has adversely affected public investment in agriculture, or alternatively, failed to provide sufficient incentives for private investment.

On account of high growth in GDP, as expected, there has been a rapid decline in the share of agriculture in the GDP, especially in countries of East and South-east Asia, where it ranged between 10–20 per cent in 1996 (Table 2.2). However, the decline in the share of labour force dependent on agriculture has been slow in these countries. The share of agricultural labour force in mid-1990s was over 3.5 times the agriculture's share of GDP in China and Republic of Korea and as high as 6 times this share for Thailand (Col. 6, Table 2.2). These facts indicate growing disparity in labour productivity between the farm and non-farm sectors at higher levels of development even in a situation of a slow down in population growth and labour force. In this context, the concepts underlying the estimates of labour force dependent on agriculture need to be looked into, as a substantial proportion of rural labour force is engaged in both farm and non-farm activities. The educational and skill levels of the labour force, labour market flexibility, and other related issues of labour absorption including the nature of export demand for goods and services also need to be investigated.

Some Individual Country Experiences

It would be interesting to discuss more specifically some of the individual country experiences in the region. The discussion is restricted to China in East Asia, and Indonesia and Thailand in South-east Asia. The chapter concludes with a summary of experience of the East and South-east Asian countries.

China

Rapid agricultural growth in China in the post-reform period of the 1980s and 1990s is explained by the high levels of infrastructure, particularly irrigation, achieved in the pre-reform period, which, however, remained severely underutilized on account of the distortions in the development

Table 2.2: Share of Agriculture in GDP and Employment

(per cent)

	Share in GDP			Share in Employment		
	1970	1980	1996	1965	1993	(5)/(3)
	(1)	(2)	(3)	(4)	(5)	(6)
East Asia						
China	42.2	25.6	18.1	81.0	64.4	3.6
Rep. of Korea	29.8	14.2	6.0	–	21.7	3.6
South-east Asia						
Indonesia	35.0	24.4	15.2	70.0	45.8	3.0
Malaysia	–	22.9	12.2	58.0	29.5	2.4
Philippines	28.2	23.5	21.0	58.0	45.4	2.2
Thailand	30.2	20.2	10.4	82.0	61.5	5.9
South Asia						
Bangladesh	–	49.4	31.9	84.0	66.6	2.1
India	44.5	38.1	26.1	73.0	65.5	2.5
Nepal	–	61.8	41.4	94.0	91.2	2.2
Pakistan	40.1	30.6	24.8	60.0	48.2	1.9
Sri Lanka	30.7	26.6	19.1	56.0	51.5	2.7

Sources: 1. For columns 1, 2, and 3: Asian Development Bank, 1997–8, *Asian Development Outlook*, p. 228, Oxford University Press.
2. For columns 4 and 5: ESCAP, United Nations, 1996, *Rural Poverty Alleviation and Sustainable Development in Asia and the Pacific*, pp. 8, 34.

strategy and defective institutional framework. Agriculture in China was heavily taxed by turning the terms of trade against it and the organization of production through communes led to severe misallocation of resources by sapping the incentives for farmers. The dismantling of communes and the introduction of production responsibility system following liberalization greatly improved the allocation of resources and released the creative energies of the farmers. Further, the terms of trade were turned in favour of agriculture significantly by raising farm procurement prices by more than 7 per cent per annum, on an average, which was more than twice the growth rate of rural consumer prices during 1978–84 (World Bank 1992). As a result of these reforms, agricultural sector experienced a real average annual growth rate of 6.6 per cent during 1978–84.

Even though agriculture seems to have grown at over 4 per cent per annum during the 1990s, there are serious doubts about sustaining this growth rate. There is clear evidence of a significant deceleration in investment in agriculture by the local governments as well as individual farmers after 1984 when there was a breakthrough in the growth of the rural non-farm sector (Saith 1993; Fan 1990). The dismantling of communes resulted in the erosion of a major source of capital formation in agriculture by the rural communities. Besides, the savings and investments by the individual peasants are showing a decline on account of continued uncertainty regarding tenurial rights under the Household Responsibility System. Further, unlike in the pre-reform period, there is evidence of a significant net transfer of capital resources from agricultural sector to non-farm rural enterprises (Saith 1993; Fan 1990).

Indonesia

Unlike in India, the development strategy in Indonesia in the late 1960s and the 1970s was almost entirely focused on agriculture and rural development which included a rice intensification campaign and expansion of rural infrastructure. Like China, Indonesia was much ahead of India in moving away from the inward-looking import-substituting strategy of development which discriminated against agriculture towards an export-oriented, labour intensive manufacturing. The economy grew at the rate of 7 per cent per annum during this period. As in China, the agriculture sector also grew rapidly during 1978–83 with rice growing by about 6.5 per cent per annum. Rural areas experienced a faster rate of growth than urban areas.

However, with public revenues under strain, the large subsidies on irrigation and fertilizers, which mainly benefit rice, are becoming unsustainable. A shift in public policy towards diversification of agriculture with an accent on the export of agro-processed products, in line with their comparative advantage, is strongly indicated with greater support for the lagging regions and the small farmers (ESCAP 1996).

Thailand

Like other Asian countries, Thailand followed import substituting industrialization until the late 1970s, but it was only to a moderate degree. Even so, the industrial protection policies including export tax on rice were, on balance, biased against agricultural and labour-intensive activities.

Owing to the abundance of land, agricultural growth in Thailand was characterized by the expansion of land under cultivation, so that agricultural research for raising crop yields through the application of seed-fertilizer technology did not receive adequate attention (Siamwalla 1991). Thus, the high agricultural growth of the 1960s and the 1970s is explained basically by the rapid expansion of area under cultivation which came to a halt later resulting in the deceleration of agricultural growth. Also, this extensive pattern of agricultural growth explains, to a large extent, the comparatively greater dependence of labour on agriculture.

Thailand has built a good transport infrastructure and the level of primary schooling in rural areas is quite high. There is thus considerable potential for stepping up agricultural growth, if agricultural research is focused on yield-increasing technology, especially in unfavourable production environments.

Summary of East and South-east Asian Experience

The contrasting performance of the countries of the East, South-east, and South Asia can not be explained fully in terms of the variables discussed in this chapter, viz., land reforms, infrastructure and education, levels of capital formation, degree of openness, sequencing of reforms, and the quality of response of the governments to the emerging post-reform scenario. Economic gowth, income distribution, and poverty also depend on factors such as attitudes to and strategies for technology acquisition and improvement, the quality of entrepreneurial response to the favourable incentive regimes, and the configurations of power in the state and how it is used to mediate relations between different segments of society. These aspects could not be addressed, as this would take us much beyond the scope of this chapter.

The experience of East and South-east Asian countries, analysed in this chapter, shows that the impact of development on rural poverty reduction has been the greatest in situations where land reforms have been implemented effectively, and a high priority has been accorded to infrastructure development, agriculture, and human resource development within a liberalized economic policy framework (Rao 1996, Chapter 11). These facts suggest, in the first place, that in a country like India where the physical and social infrastructure inherited from the pre-liberalization period is not strong and the redistribution of land on a significant scale is not feasible, public investment needs to be stepped up significantly for human resource development and for expanding physical infrastructure in the less developed areas.

Second, measures for structural transformation of the rural economy by significantly raising agricultural growth and by strengthening rural industries for greater labour-absorption have to be given high priority in the development strategy in India. This would require improving access to infrastructure, technology, and credit, especially for the resource-poor sections. In other words, development policy has to be more inclusive, concerned not merely with 'structural adjustment' to make the economy market-friendly, but also with 'structural change' with a view to simultaneously making markets friendly to the poor, basically by strengthening their socio-economic position.

Third, the experience shows that 'disprotection' of agriculture under the pre-liberalization strategy and the implied subsidy to the consumers of food failed to reduce rural poverty significantly by weakening the socio-economic position of the landed interests. Economic liberalization for raising agricultural and overall growth is now the only feasible option open for reducing the pressure on land both from the landless and the landed sections. This may indeed open up opportunities for turning the land market in favour of the poor if there is a conscious policy to enable them to purchase land. Even in many of the South-east Asian economies this opportunity needs to be explored to further reduce poverty and inequality.

Fourth, the experience of the East and South-east Asian countries underlines the changing and not the diminishing role of the state in economic activity. Instead of directly managing infrastructure and enterprises already in place, the state is getting increasingly involved in the creation and promotion of new infrastructure. With the reduction of rural poverty to low levels in many East and South-east Asian countries, inequality or relative poverty is surfacing as a major area of concern. Public policy has become important in such situations for the development of infrastructure in the less developed regions, supporting agricultural research and extension focused on the resource-poor regions, human resource development, particularly in the area of education and skills, and for ensuring decentralized development. Such a role for the state is even more compelling in a country like India.

Finally, the political commitment of the leadership to change and its ability to win public support for change has been an extremely important factor in many of the East and South-east Asian countries. Such a commitment and ability seems to depend not only on the nature of the political system, that is, whether it is a democracy or a dictatorship but also on a variety of historical, political, and socio-cultural factors. In India, where there is a competitive coexistence of different classes, castes, and ethnic groups within a democratic polity, consensus building around any desirable policy package is not an easy task. Even so, there is no alternative to political leadership mustering the necessary political will to evolve a coherent strategy for redirecting the economy on to a sustained path of growth and poverty alleviation by winning popular support for economic reforms.

3

Liberalization of Agriculture in India

Some Major Issues

Introduction

The purpose of this chapter is to raise certain major issues and approaches concerning the liberalization of agriculture as a part of the ongoing economic reform process in India. In doing so, we draw upon the experience of the East and South-east Asian countries with economic reforms discussed in the previous chapter. There are three major areas of interest, in this context, which have a direct bearing on agriculture: Impact of macroeconomic reforms including liberalization of agricultural trade; domestic reforms, bearing especially on input subsidies; and institutional framework, for example, farm size and tenure. The issues raised here are probed in greater detail in the subsequent chapters on agriculture.

Possible Impact of Macroeconomic Reforms including Trade Liberalization

A sector as large as agriculture cannot remain insulated from the ongoing economic reform process in India for a long period. There are strong reasons why market reforms in India should be extended to agriculture also. Indeed, as it is, agriculture has not remained unaffected by the ongoing reform process in the country, as the indirect impact of liberalization of the economy in general on agriculture may turn out to be far more important than the possible impact of the liberalization measures directly affecting this sector (Schiff and Valdes 1992; Parikh *et al.* 1995). The overall liberalization of the economy would result in higher investment and growth in agriculture induced by favourable terms of trade (Parikh *et al.* 1995).

India, like several other East and South-east Asian countries, has a comparative advantage in agriculture, so that there is considerable scope for raising farm income and employment by stepping up agro-based exports without jeopardizing, and indeed by consolidating, the food security already achieved. Agriculture can thus serve as the biggest safety net in the process of structural adjustment in India. Indeed, in the successful reforming economies in East Asia where high growth has been associated with equitable sharing of benefits, agricultural reform and high agricultural growth preceded the overall economic reform process.

What should be the content of liberalization or market reforms for Indian agriculture at this stage? Should the reform package for non-agriculture be mechanically applied to agriculture? In other words, since there are no restrictions on capacity or scale of production in non-agriculture, should we do away with the ceiling on the ownership of agricultural land and also stop pre-empting institutional credit for agriculture? How should one mitigate the adverse effects of deregulation on employment and the environment? These are vital issues which need to be considered carefully, by taking into account the specific socio-economic features at the present stage of development, while devising a package of reforms and sequencing them not only for agriculture but for the economy as a whole.

Structural adjustment measures are designed essentially to improve allocation efficiency through the operation of incentives in a market economy. Emergence of surpluses and the incentives for greater investment and technological change are a corollary to improvements in the allocation efficiency. However, the institutional framework of Indian agriculture has been such that the inefficiencies in the allocation of resources have been fewer when compared with the command economies or even with non-agriculture in India. This is because of the persistence of individual farming within the framework of peasant proprietorship where millions of farmers compete in a free institutional setting. The beneficial effects of public intervention of a promotional nature such as the provision of infrastructure, investment in agricultural research and extension, and creation of appropriate price environment seem to have outweighed the negative impact of the restrictionist and distortionary measures such as restrictions on trade and the rise in input subsidies. Thus, whereas there are undoubted efficiency gains flowing from the liberalization of agricultural trade and reduction of input subsidies, such gains would be significantly less when compared to the gains in terms of increased investment in agriculture consequent to the liberalization of non-agriculture (Parikh *et al.* 1995).

It is now beyond controversy that agriculture in India has been 'disprotected', whereas industry has been heavily protected (Gulati and Pursell 1991). As a result, the terms of trade for agriculture have been unfavourable when compared to the situation that would have prevailed in the absence of such protection for industry. Therefore, liberalization of non-agriculture including trade and exchange rate liberalization would result, on balance, in higher returns to the farmers and hence in greater flow of investible resources into agriculture. At the moment, India seems to have comparative advantage in respect of certain foodgrains, particularly rice. This advantage could be eroded, at least in respect of some crops, when we enter the international market in a sizeable way. But, the agricultural product-mix can change in response to changing domestic and foreign demand. Apart from foodgrains, dairying, horticulture, floriculture, and agro-processing in general are likely to emerge as promising sectors. So long as we are surplus in foodgrains even after improving our policy for raising the effective domestic demand, there is no risk of compromising with food security. The export potential of foodgrains will further strengthen food security at home, because exports can be adjusted upto a point, to ensure adequate availability of foodgrains for the domestic market.

The prospects for such exports of foodgrains seem real, at least for a decade, if the growth rate in foodgrains output of around 3 per cent can be achieved, as the domestic demand for foodgrains is unlikely to exceed 2.6 per cent per annum, with even 7 per cent growth rate in gross domestic product (GDP), with the decline in the relative prices of foodgrains as in the 1980s, and after taking into account the rise in indirect demand for foodgrains as animal feed (Radhakrishna 1996; Rao and Gulati 1994; Kumar and Rosegrant 1995). It is true that in view of the experience of other countries, the indirect demand for foodgrains as animal feed can be expected to rise significantly when per capita income rises (Bhalla 1995). But considering the existing feeding practices for animals and the pattern of demand for meat in India, the country is unlikely to absorb domestically the whole of foodgrains output from a growth rate of around 3 per cent for quite sometime, unless drastic changes in income distribution can be effected. However, for the technological upgradation of agriculture and for stepping up investment, what is important is the opening up of the economy so as to benefit from the emerging opportunities for trade in agricultural commodities in general and not the prospect of 'surpluses' for exports in regard to any particular set of commodities like foodgrains.

Liberalization of domestic trade in agricultural commodities would imply limiting the role of public policy to guaranteeing minimum support prices for farmers and procuring, in addition, foodgrains at the ruling market prices, enough to maintain the required buffer stock and for meeting the commitments of the public distribution system (PDS) (Vyas 1994). At the moment, the distinction between minimum support and procurement prices has been obliterated resulting in vastly enlarged responsibility for public procurement and distribution with mounting subsidies and other inefficiencies associated with public handling of foodgrains on a large scale.

Whereas liberalization of trade, external as well as domestic, would improve the incentives for farmers, raise their resources position, and contribute to technological upgradation of agriculture, the available studies also show that there would be a significant rise in the domestic prices of foodgrains and other essential food items. Indeed, this would be so all over the world consequent to the implementation of Uruguay Round Agreement (ESCAP 1995). Therefore, the policy choice is between: (a) continuing the existing regime of controls with a view to keeping the food prices low for all classes of consumers even if it means slower growth of output and employment and (b) gradual opening up of trade by ensuring subsidized foodgrains to the low income groups. Since the food basket is getting diversified even for the low income groups, it may be difficult to ensure subsidized supplies of a large variety of food items through the PDS. Therefore, raising the purchasing power of the poor through employment and income generation has to be given a high priority in any policy package for liberalization.

Domestic Reforms Bearing on Subsidies

Subsidies on the technologically new inputs such as chemical fertilizers in the initial stages of the Green Revolution in India did induce the farmers to readily adopt the new technology. Over a period of time, however, these subsidies began to mount, even as the farmers became fully conscious of the profitability of the new technology. Moreover, the hidden subsidies arising from the inability to recover economic rates from the farmers for the use of irrigation water from surface sources and on power for pumping water, rose steeply. The amount of these subsidies—open as well as hidden—on fertilizers, irrigation, and power reached the level of total productive investment in agriculture by the government in the early 1990s (Rao and Gulati 1994) and were far in excess of such investment by 1999–2000 (Gulati and Narayanan 2003).

These subsidies have a most deleterious effect in terms of reduced public investment in agriculture on account of the erosion of investible resources, and wasteful use of scarce resources like water and power. Further, apart from causing unsustainable fiscal deficits, these subsidies, by encouraging the intensive use of inputs in limited pockets, have led to lowering the productivity of inputs, reducing employment elasticity of output through the substitution of capital for labour, and environmental degradation such as waterlogging and salinity, on the one hand, and lowering of water tables, on the other (Rao and Gulati 1994).

There is a case for subsidizing some of these inputs used by the small and marginal farmers, as they have little surplus to sell and so cannot benefit from the rising product prices. Already, the rise in the prices of fertilizers in the early 1990s following the reduction in subsidy seems to have lowered the incomes of small and marginal farmers by restricting the use of fertilizers, thus pushing many of them below the poverty line (Gupta 1996). However, if the savings from the removal of input subsidies are earmarked for investment in irrigation and for increasing outlays on poverty alleviation programmes, there would be a rise in growth as well as welfare (Parikh *et al.* 1995).

Institutional Framework: Farm Size and Tenure

With the population pressure on agricultural land persisting, and there not being, as yet, enough evidence of economies of scale in Indian agriculture, there is little justification for doing away with ceiling on the ownership of land at this stage, especially because farmers are able to augment their operational holdings in response to the changing technological and economic factors (Rao and Gulati 1994). Thus, if agriculture is to serve as a safety net for some time to come in the process of structural adjustment, there is no justification for relaxing restrictions on the ownership of agricultural land at this stage on the plea of liberalizing the agricultural sector on par with non-agriculture.

On the other hand, there is a case for extending long-term loans on liberal terms for the purchase of land to those below the poverty line who are willing to cultivate the land.

However, experience suggests that freeing the lease market for land may contribute to equity as well as efficiency by bringing into open the lease transactions (Appu 1995). The small and marginal farmers including the pure tenants will be able to augment their operational holdings where there is pressure on land. On the other hand, where population pressure on land is low and wages are high, the marginal farmers may gain by leasing out their area and taking up non-farm employment.

The rural credit system is now threatened by rising overdues and deficiencies in management. Improving the economic viability of credit institutions should, therefore, be high on the agenda for reform. The existing large differential between the concessional rates of interest charged by institutional sources and market rates is responsible for rent-seeking by the middlemen who re-lend credit, especially to the poorer households, at high rates of interest. Large farmers have been the major beneficiaries of long-term loans at a concessional rate of interest. The perpetuation of such concessional lending has undermined the viability of credit institutions. Also, it has led to high capital intensity and slow employment generation in agriculture. It would, therefore, be desirable to phase out these concessional rates of interest to the large farmers (Rao 1994). It is essential, however, to ensure adequate availability of institutional credit to the small and marginal farmers at affordable cost, by ensuring a stipulated share for agriculture and for small and marginal farmers. Otherwise, the well-known tendency of bankers to reduce unit costs by serving a small number of big borrowers, rather than a large number of small borrowers, would result in a credit squeeze for the needy borrowers. Together with these basic policy measures, management of credit institutions should be accorded greater autonomy by eliminating administrative and political interference in their day-to-day functioning.

Conclusion

To conclude, the prospects for agriculture in India are bright in the context of overall economic reform including liberalization of agricultural trade. However, these may result in raising the prices of essential food items. Moreover, immediate and premature deregulation of certain activities such as deep sea fishing would lead to the displacement and impoverishment of the poorer sections on a massive scale much before liberalization starts yielding positive results in terms of rise in employment and income for the poor. Further, the unregulated exploitation of natural resources, for example, large-scale shrimp farming in the coastal areas, is already proving to be harmful to environment. Therefore, the pace of liberalization of agriculture has to be complemented and supported by steps to strengthen supply side factors such as irrigation, watershed development, research and extension, and credit in order to augment agricultural production, as well as by the measures to protect the environment and widen the income earning opportunities for the weaker sections.

4

Trade Liberalization, WTO, and Viability of Indian Agriculture

Introduction: The Rationale Behind WTO

If transactions between parties could be spontaneous because they are mutually beneficial to the parties concerned, then where is the need for a multilateral institutional framework like the World Trade Organization (WTO) with mutually agreed and enforceable rules? The simple answer is that countries differ not only in regard to the comparative advantage in producing various goods and services but also in respect of the level playing field.

The principle of comparative advantage is built on the basis of the inter-country differences in costs and returns between different commodities, abstracting from taxes and subsidies influencing these costs and returns. In the chapter dealing with international trade in agricultural commodities in Ricardo's 'The Principles of Political Economy and Taxation', one does not find any mention of taxes or subsidies determining the relative costs of production or prices of commodities. In his examples, one finds only production factors like land, labour, and capital constituting the cost of production (Ricardo 1817). Now, if some rich countries because of their ability to subsidize agriculture can sell their produce at artificially lower prices and thus undercut the market for the genuinely efficient or low-cost producers, then the playing field is highly uneven as the principle of comparative advantage is not followed or is even thrown overboard. Similarly, if some countries are taxing or discriminating against agriculture by heavily protecting their industry and through overvalued exchange rates, as most developing countries have been doing till recently, then their competitiveness is eroded vis-á-vis countries which do not tax agriculture. In this case too, the principle of comparative advantage is denied a free play.

Moreover, despite increasing interdependence and integration among countries, the world is highly heterogenous with regard to the levels of development. There are countries which are at an advanced stage of development with regard to the levels of infrastructure and technology achieved over a period of a few centuries. On the other hand, there are several countries which have only recently emerged from long periods of colonial rule. They have a long way to go before they can achieve a level playing field vis-á-vis developed countries in regard to infrastructure, technology, and skills. Such countries may need protection for some time in certain specific areas before they can tap and realize their potential so as to be in a position to compete with the advanced countries as trading partners on an equal footing. This is akin to what is usually referred to in the literature approvingly as the 'infant industry' argument. Therefore, institutional arrangements such as the WTO are essential for ensuring a level playing field so that considerations of comparative advantage can have a free and fair play.

High Farm Support in Developed Countries

A major issue of contention during the Uruguay Round negotiations was the high domestic support being provided to agriculture in the developed countries, especially the European Union in the West and Japan in the East. Apart from restrictions on the imports of farm products through various tariff and non-tariff barriers, this support consisted of measures such as high support prices for farm produce and export subsidies, which are now shifted to direct measures for income support under the so-called Blue Box, such as deficiency payments in the USA, and compensations to farmers in the European Union via acreage and headage premiums which are exempt from reduction commitments. The developed countries did agree to a modest reduction in domestic support, but the experience in the last 6 years indicates that the implementation of such reduction commitments has been tardy, as evidenced by a significant rise in the share of advanced countries in global exports (Rakshit 2000; WTO 2001).

But why do the developed countries have a tendency to subsidize agriculture? The question assumes significance as this pattern has been in evidence with almost unfailing regularity in the process of development. It was the United States of America first in the 1950s and the 1960s, then came Japan and the European Union, and more recently, the Republic of Korea. It is indeed ironical that the European Union—the continent where David Ricardo was born and worked and propounded his theory of comparative advantage with extensive illustrations from agriculture—should now be at the top in the list in regard to the degree of farm support and thus in undermining the operation of the principle of comparative advantage in trade. This is a classic illustration of how domestic lobbies representing sectional interests can be at logger-heads with the universally acclaimed text-book propositions. The fears of Thomas Malthus—a contemporary of David Ricardo—with regard to population growth outpacing the growth in food output were first proved wrong in Europe on account of technological changes and the rise in agricultural productivity. It appears that the very processes which helped to overcome the Malthusian pessimism led to the growth of interest groups which are coming in the way of the operation of Ricardo's principle of comparative advantage.

The demand for farm products at higher levels of income responds little to changes in incomes and prices. This explains why a small increase in farm output results in a more than proportionate fall in its price. Thus farm incomes declined very often in developed countries like the USA despite, and indeed owing to, the rise in farm output. This was the genesis of support prices to the farmers. The problem was mitigated to some extent by finding markets for the export of foodgrains. However, the rising support prices perpetuated high-cost agriculture primarily because there was little incentive to shift resources away from agriculture, especially labour, whose opportunity cost rose on account of overall development and rise in wages. In the USA, for example, during the period 1992–7, agriculture accounted for a mere 2 per cent of gross domestic product (GDP), but employed 4 per cent of the total labour force. On the other hand, the services sector which accounted for 72 per cent of GDP, employed 63 per cent of labour force. The productivity of labour in agriculture is thus comparatively much lower. The position is similar in countries constituting the European Union. Over the corresponding period, agriculture contributed 2 per cent of GDP in France with 6 per cent share in labour force; in Germany, agriculture's contribution to GDP was 1 per cent with 3 per cent share in labour force; the corresponding figures for UK were 2 per cent and 3 per cent (World Bank, 2000). There is thus a deterioration in the relative productivity of labour in agriculture in USA and countries of EU on account of high farm support. The food surpluses of the farmers produced at high cost could not become competitive in the export market without heavy subsidies on exports.

One wonders how governments in countries where a mere 3–5 per cent of total labour force is employed in agriculture have to succumb to pressures from farm lobbies. Part of the explanation, of course, lies in the sheer ability of these rich countries to foot the bill. Another reason is that since agriculture in these countries is highly input-intensive, a large complex of agro-industries having backward linkage with agriculture as input suppliers constitute the highly organized and vocal sections of these farm lobbies. Moreover, these countries are, in any case, incurring huge expenditures on social security for the unemployed in the rest of the economy. The difference is that in the case of the farm sector, these payments take the form of compensation for lower farm prices, thus providing incentive for committing resources beyond what would otherwise have been allocated if farm prices were allowed to be determined by the market forces.

But the situation can change over time due to the pressures from the members of the WTO. Already, there is a marked shift away from support prices and export subsidies, which are considered highly trade distorting, towards direct payments in the form of deficiency payments and compensations related to acreage and livestock numbers, which are considered 'minimally trade distorting' and hence placed under the 'blue' and 'green' boxes which are exempt from reduction commitments (Zeeuw De Aart 1997). However, it would be a misnomer to call these payments as 'minimally trade distorting'. This is because, such payments, in so far as they are not fully delinked or decoupled from the use of inputs, do influence the allocation of resources, in the sense that in the absence of such payments, fewer resources would be committed to agriculture, leading to lower output, higher prices, and smaller export surpluses (WTO 2001).

However, there are indications that in EU agriculture, where the distortion in the allocation of resources appears to be highest, there is a significant scope for reducing unit costs through the wider application of known technologies. Already there are moves to retire farm labour over the age of 55 through payment of compensations which are fully decoupled. There is considerable scope for reducing labour costs by enlarging average farm size and thus reaping economies of scale. There is also a large potential for reducing unit costs through vertical integration of agro-processing industry—the growth of which has been surprisingly slow—with farming operations (Keyzer and Merbis

1999). The ongoing biotechnological revolution promises to work in the same direction. If some of these cost-reducing technologies have not already been adopted extensively, it is primarily because of heavy farm subsidies which dampen the incentives for cost reduction. It is very likely, therefore, that the observed trend of a secular decline in the real prices of farm products would be reinforced due to such reforms in the West, which has the requisite technological know-how, as well as the unilateral pursuit of reforms in certain developing countries towards trade liberalization by doing away with discrimination against agriculture (Valdes and Zietz 1995). A country like India needs, therefore, to prepare itself for competing with low-cost farm products rather than expecting a significant rise in their prices via reform-induced reduction in the export surpluses from the developed countries. Incidentally, this scenario should serve to dispel fears that those of the least developed countries which are net importers of food stand to lose heavily on account of the rise in the prices of food following the reduction of farm support in developed countries.

'Disprotection' of Agriculture in Developing Countries

While the advanced countries have been heavily protecting agriculture, leading to overproduction, rise in costs, and distortion in world trade, several developing countries have been 'disprotecting' agriculture by discriminating against it basically through the heavy protection of domestic industry and overvalued exchange rates (Bautista and Valdes 1989). This is a consequence of the pursuit of an inward-looking and import substituting development strategy which had an in-built bias against agriculture. The terms of trade were thus deliberately kept unfavourable to agriculture in keeping with the prevailing wisdom to 'extract' surpluses from this sector for promoting industrialization. Such discrimination has led to less than optimal allocation of resources to agriculture as well as denial of avenues for its technological upgradation in a liberalized trading environment, resulting in its slower growth (ESCAP 1996; Rao 1996).

This has proceeded independently of the protectionist policies pursued for agriculture in the developed countries. Already, the unshackling of agriculture through market reforms in developing countries like China and Vietnam have led to high agricultural growth and rise in their trade in agricultural commodities. A number of exercises on the post-Uruguay Round scenario have concluded that the expected rise in the prices of farm products on account of reduction commitments by the developed countries would be mitigated and even neutralized by the surge in output and trade due to market reforms and unilateral liberalization in certain developing countries (ESCAP 1995; Valdes and Zietz 1995). A major component of this growth in farm output is the expected rise in total factor productivity (TFP) in agriculture on account of technological changes induced by the liberalization of trade following the Uruguay Round commitments (ESCAP 1995). The recent price trends are consistent with the above prognoses.

It is clear from the above that liberalization of agriculture in developing economies has to proceed basically through macroeconomic reforms which do away with high protection accorded to industry and liberalize trade and exchange rate regime. Viability of Indian agriculture in the new international trade regime scenario has, therefore, to be seen not in isolation in terms of the prospects for each agricultural commodity under the provisions of the WTO, but in the wider context of the liberalization of the Indian economy. The fortunes of Indian agriculture, which now accounts for about 22–25 per cent of GDP, depend crucially on its relationship with the rest of the economy which contributes as much as 70 per cent to GDP. As such, the impact of macroeconomic reforms on the terms of trade for agriculture, private investment, and its ability to access modern technology and inputs deserve attention, in addition to the consequences of these reforms for public investment in agriculture.

Farm Support in India

The product-specific support for Indian agriculture in the year 1995–6—the year for which the latest official information from WTO is available—was negative to the extent of 38.5 per cent (Gulati 2001). However, because of the recent fall in the international prices of farm products and the steep rise in the minimum support or procurement prices for wheat and rice in the country, it is possible that the rate of 'disprotection' would now be much lower. Since the non-product specific support amounts to 7.5 per cent of the value of agricultural production, the aggregate measure of support (AMS) to Indian agriculture could still be well below the deminimis of 10 per cent in terms of the Uruguay Round stipulations. In its proposals on the Negotiations on WTO Agreements on Agriculture, India has suggested that the AMS, as the term suggests, be calculated as a sum of the product-specific and non-product specific support (WTO 2001). If the product-specific support is still negative in the case of India, then the aggregate measure of support would be below 7.5 per cent of the value of agricultural production. As it is, input subsidies to resource poor farmers which come under non-product specific support are exempt from reduction commitments under the WTO provisions. If India avails of this, the non-product specific support may come down to less than half of what is being shown today (Gulati 2001). In view of this, it may not be in India's interest to fight within the WTO for greater domestic support to agriculture, especially if it can blunt our opposition to slow reduction in farm support and inadequate access to markets in the advanced countries. For its further growth, Indian agriculture is in need of substantial public investments in irrigation, power, roads, and agricultural research and extension, rather than subsidies on inputs.

Besides, India's stand on agriculture in the WTO has to be an integral part of the overall position we take on trade liberalization, through the process of bargaining, which necessarily involves some trade-offs. For example, the consequences of the Uruguay Round agreements for the rural poor depend not merely on their possible impact on agricultural growth and employment but on wages and employment in the economy in general following complete Uruguay Round trade liberalization including the phasing out of the Multi-fibre Agreement (MFA). It has been estimated that the additional welfare gains for the countries of the Economic and Social Commission for Asia and the Pacific (ESCAP) region from complete liberalization of trade, including the phasing out of the MFA, could be two and a half times as high as the welfare gains arising from global agricultural liberalization only (ESCAP 1995).

As for protection through tariffs, India has already negotiated tariff bindings at the level of 100 per cent for raw commodities, 150 per cent for processed agro-commodities and 300 per cent for most edible oils. These may be considered sufficient to protect the relevant commodities against cheaper imports sustained by high domestic support in countries of their origin. For example, according to a study, the nominal rates of assistance to agriculture via trade policies in the post-Uruguay Round for agriculture and processed food amounts to 33 per cent in advanced industrial economies as well as newly industrialized economies (Hoekman and Anderson 1999). According to the estimates given by Ashok Gulati, the average producer support estimate (PSE) for 1997–9 was 61 per cent for Japan, 65 per cent for Korea, 66 per cent for Norway, 70 per cent for Switzerland, and 44 per cent for countries within the European Union (Gulati 2001). Producer support in several South and South-east Asian countries is either negligible or even negative. It is from these countries that India has been importing much of edible oils and to some extent other agro-commodities. It is clear, therefore, that tariff barriers in such cases, beyond a point, amount to blocking the import of efficiently produced or low cost-products. If prices of edible oils have fallen steeply in the country recently, despite high tariff bindings at 300 per cent, it is due to the failure of our market intelligence, lack of alertness, and inability to act promptly to raise import duties (Chand 2000; Gulati 2001).

The major challenge to the viability of agriculture of most developing countries, including India, is posed by the high domestic support, export subsidies, and denial of market access through various tariff and non-tariff barriers, in the developed countries. India has been fighting along with other developing countries in the WTO for the removal of such barriers. In the process of bargaining and in our own interest, the rate of protection to our industry which used to be among the highest in the world has been brought down to less than half of its earlier level. Our agriculture is a major beneficiary from this reduced protection to industry.

Trade Liberalization and Its Impact on Indian Agriculture

There is considerable potential for raising India's share in world exports of agricultural commodities. It is necessary to exploit this potential not only to earn foreign exchange but more importantly to widen the opportunities for raising farm income and employment by diversifying and modernizing agriculture. Dry land areas where wages are low and poverty is widespread may benefit significantly from trade, as they have a comparative advantage in horticulture and livestock products, the demand for which is less inelastic than for foodgrains. However, this would require large investments in agro-processing and other infrastructure.

Rice, cotton, and wheat seem to have emerged as good exportables up to a point, particularly after the recent adjustments in the exchange rate and the convertibility of the rupee on trade account, whereas the imports of edible oils, which have been heavily protected could be increased (Gulati and Sharma 1991). However, if input subsidies are brought down, there would be some diversion of resources from water- and fertilizer-intensive crops to semi-irrigated crops. This would narrow down the difference between the international and domestic price of cereals as well as oilseeds, unless farm subsidies are drastically reduced in the developed countries. Nevertheless, there may still be some gains through trade by specializing in crops like rice and cotton, particularly in the non-traditional areas like horticulture, and by importing edible oils up to a point.

However, world trade in grains is highly volatile and considering the possible impact of India's decision to export (import) grain on world prices, exports (imports) may cease to be profitable beyond a point. Further, the possibilities of inter-crop substitution with a view to stepping up the output of 'exportables' may not be as bright as would appear at first sight from the highly aggregated data on the relative profitabilities of 'competing' crops. Besides, in view of the uncertainties of world supplies, the country cannot run the risk of undermining its food security by running down the domestic stocks below a certain critical minimum considering the incidence of droughts and commitments of the public distribution system to meet the requirements of a large population still living below the poverty line. Also, care has to be taken to ensure that the prospects for technological change in respect of oilseeds are not jeopardized because of unremunerative prices resulting from heavy imports. It is important to recognize in this context that technological changes in the case of cereals such as wheat and rice after the mid-sixties were critical in altering the comparative advantage of different crops.

As expected, the liberalization of the Indian economy which had commenced from around the mid-1980s and accelerated with the launching of full-fledged macroeconomic reforms since the early 1990s has improved the incentive framework for agriculture. With the liberalization of exchange rate and opening up of the economy, the terms of trade for agriculture have shown a significant improvement. As a result, private investment in agriculture registered a steep rise in the post-reform period (Government of India 2000). The exports of agricultural commodities, particularly foodgrains, accelerated in this period. For example, for the first time since independence, India has been a net exporter of foodgrains consecutively for the last six years, net exports amounting, on an average, to around 1.8 million tonnes per annum (Government of India 2001).

In the light of this evidence, the fears being expressed in certain quarters that the import of foodgrains under the new liberalized trade regime is having a dampening effect on the foodgrain prices in the country is totally misplaced. It is true that, recently, the post-harvest prices of wheat and rice have been ruling below the minimum support prices in certain markets, but this is due to the inability of the Food Corporation of India (FCI) to lift the grain at the officially announced procurement prices and not due to the import of foodgrains. Indeed, we need to understand why there is a glut in the foodgrains market and mounting stocks with the FCI, despite the deceleration in the growth of foodgrains output in the last decade and the net export of foodgrains consecutively for the last six years. The present glut in the foodgrains market cannot be adequately explained by the import of wheat to the extent of 2.8 million tonnes during 1997–8 and 1998–9 when the government had imposed a ban on wheat exports and opened up imports at zero import duty.

A plausible explanation is that there has been a steep rise in procurement prices in the recent period, when there has in fact been a downward trend in international prices. This aspect is discussed in some detail in Chapter 10. The evidence presented does not lend credence to the view that trade liberalization would endanger India's food security. Achievement of effective food security when we can accumulate enough stocks of foodgrains, thanks to our comparative advantage in respect of major cereals, hinges basically on raising the purchasing power of the poor through the generation of employment opportunities. If the prices of foodgrains at the moment are out of the reach of the poor, it is not due to the rise in exports but to the steep rise in procurement and issue prices.

Policy Implications

As discussed in Chapter 5, the shortfalls in public investment and in the provision of agricultural services account for the failure of agricultural supplies to respond to the favourable incentive framework created by macroeconomic reforms, including trade liberalization, in the 1990s. The experience of the 1990s demonstrates that far from trade liberalization dampening the performance of agriculture, the failure of public investment and effort is responsible for our inability to benefit from trade liberalization by stepping up and diversifying agricultural output in a cost-effective way.

On the trade front, there is a need for extreme vigilance so as to be able to take timely measures, within the existing tariff bindings, to arrest heavy import of certain commodities. Also, since the philosophy behind trade liberalization is the maximization of global welfare through efficiency gains, mapping out comparative advantages across countries for different commodities in a dynamic setting is necessary as a basis for meaningful negotiations in the WTO. The developed countries are very well equipped with technical and legal expertise, even though these capabilities are used for advancing their case towards perpetuation of domestic support to agriculture and restriction of market access, that are quite untenable. On the other hand, the capabilities of developing countries, including India, are poor in this respect despite their approach and line of action on matters relating to agricultural trade being justifiable on theoretical as well as practical grounds. Therefore, there is a need to accord a high priority to the development of these skills in the country.

But our major effort on the domestic front for ensuring the viability of Indian agriculture has to be focused on raising productivity by stepping up public investment, by accelerating the evolution and adoption of cost-reducing technologies, and by removing restrictions on agricultural trade, marketing, and processing within the country. All this requires to be achieved through major reforms in governance and institutions, particularly at the state level. Such reforms hold the key for improving the viability of Indian agriculture in the wake of trade liberalization.

Section II

Agricultural Growth

5

Agricultural Growth

Post-reform Trends and Major Issues for Further Reform

Introduction

The recent or post-reform trends in the growth of Indian agriculture are discussed in this chapter. In doing so, it would be useful to keep in mind the changing economic environment in India, against which agriculture has to grow. The Indian economy is passing through the process of economic reforms, where macroeconomic policies are being adjusted and the industrial sector is undergoing structural reforms. On top of all this, there is a new dimension that has been added by the World Trade Organization (WTO), under which the member countries, including India, have to reduce support to agriculture and open it up to the world markets.

Agriculture seems to have slipped lower in the economic agenda of the country in the post-reform decade of the 1990s. This is the culmination of almost a decade of neglect, reflected in the declining real public investment in agriculture in the 1980s. After the humiliating experience with imports of foodgrains in the mid-1960s, there was a vigorous drive for achieving self-sufficiency in foodgrains by stepping up public investment in irrigation and by introducing new technology. The impressive achievements, particularly the accumulation of sizeable stocks of foodgrains by the government from the prosperous regions, seem to have induced complacency.

Fortunately, the agricultural sector in India was not subjected to the regulations in the same way as, for example, industry. Unlike in the former socialist countries, organization of Indian agriculture has been based on individual farming under the system of peasant proprietorship. So far as agriculture is concerned, the role of the government in India has been confined largely to investments in infrastructure including research and extension, and public procurement and distribution of foodgrains to the extent of about 10–15 per cent of output in a market setting where private traders also operate. Despite this, when agriculture is discussed in the context of economic reforms, the accent seems to be on deregulation and freeing markets. Apart from the prosperous farmers, many in the government and among the international financial institutions strongly believe that opening-up trade through deregulation and the consequent rise in farm prices will give a fillip to agricultural growth in this country through increased private investment.

It is argued in this chapter that deregulation, by itself, is unlikely to be effective in ensuring sustained agricultural growth. The policy agenda should emphasize, apart from removal of restrictions on trade in agricultural commodities, public and private capital formation in this sector, promotion of biotechnology, soil and moisture conservation, improvement of rural credit systems and better infrastructure management. Therefore, the question with which we are concerned relates to the nature of economic reforms and restructuring relevant to Indian agriculture. The critical question is whether these reforms are to be oriented to capacity augmentation through increased public investment and restructuring of institutions so as to induce greater private investment and effort, or to be oriented basically towards improved utilization of available capacities through deregulation and marketization as was the experience in China in the immediate post-reform period.

We shall first dwell upon the importance of initial conditions, especially the political economy, in India vis-á-vis some countries of East Asia, say, China and the Republic of Korea, which will determine the degree of response to these new challenges.

Political Economy of Development: India versus East Asia

There was considerable underutilization of capacity in agriculture in the former socialist economies both because of very high rate of capital accumulation for over four decades, achieved in part by using surplus labour for capital construction as in China, and because of the organization of agriculture under the system of collectives and communes leading to the suppression of markets and gross inefficiencies in the use of resources. Therefore, there was a big spurt in agricultural output in China in the 1980s when the communes were disbanded, inter-regional trade was opened, and terms of trade were shifted in favour of agriculture.

In India, on the other hand, the rate of capital formation in agriculture has been much lower and utilization of available capacities relatively more efficient. For example, the proportion of cultivated area irrigated in India is only about one-third, as against over 50 per cent in China. The level of human capital formation in terms of literacy, education, and health of rural population was also much higher in China when economic reforms were launched. Moreover, unlike in socialist countries including China, no attempts were made in India to deliberately shift the terms of trade against agriculture. Except for occasional restrictions on the interregional movement of foodgrains for purposes of public procurement, there has, by and large, been a free flow of commodities and resources between different regions in the country. The success of the green revolution would have been unthinkable in the absence of an integrated national market in India which has been conducive to regional specialization in the production of crops. Therefore, unlike in the socialist or command economies, there is little scope for stepping up agricultural output in India by merely improving the efficiency of resource-use at the farm level by restructuring the management of agriculture or by redefining the role of the state in relation to markets.

To bring the political economy factor into sharper focus, one could begin with the proposition that the initial or pre-reform conditions in East Asian countries such as China and the Republic of Korea were far more favourable than in India for rapid growth and speedy reduction in poverty. As mentioned in Chapter 2, even though China and the Republic of Korea are highly dissimilar in respect of their professed ideologies and socio-political systems, the socio-political systems in both the countries facilitated mobilization of requisite resources by the state for investment in physical infrastructure as well as human development. Further, the implementation of radical land reforms at the very start, human development and the resulting speedy demographic transition ensured that the trickle-down mechanisms were effective so that high growth resulted in the wider sharing of gains and speedy reduction in poverty. All this was possible because both countries displayed great political will and lent resolute state support in implementing their policies.

We shall discuss next the recent or post-reform performance of Indian agriculture and the major factors responsible for this, with a view to identifying the emerging challenges.

Agricultural Growth: Performance in the Recent (Post-reform) Period

Terms of Trade and Private Investment

As expected, measures for the liberalization of trade and industry that have already been introduced in India have had a beneficial impact on agriculture by turning the terms of trade in its favour which, in turn, have attracted greater private investments into this sector. The agriculture price index as per cent of manufacturing with 1993–4 as base (100) improved to 117.5 in 2001–02 (Government of India 2003, *Economic Survey* 2002–03). This improvement in terms of trade for agriculture was perhaps primarily due to bringing down the protection to industry and, to some extent, to the domestic policy of raising support prices for wheat and rice, especially during the second half of the 1990s (Gulati and Mullen 2003).

As a result of the improvement in terms of trade, private sector capital formation in agriculture rose by nearly 40 per cent betwen 1993–4 and 2000–01 raising its share to 76.5 per cent in total capital formation in agriculture. On the other hand, public sector capital formation in agriculture, which began showing a decline in the 1980s (Rao 1989; Shetty 1990), continued to drop in the post-reform period of 1990s, recording the lowest ever share (23.5 per cent) in total agriculture capital formation in 2000–01 (Government of India, *Economic Survey*, 2002–03). However, thanks to the significant rise in private sector capital formation in agriculture in the 1990s, the total gross capital formation in agriculture in the late 1990s recovered to the level of the late 1970s.

Decline in Public Investment: Causes and Consequences

A number of factors explain the decline in real public sector capital formation in agriculture. First, there has been a steep rise in the cost of construction since the mid-1970s. This is indicated by the fact that the implicit price index of gross capital formation in agriculture (GCFA) has been rising at more than twice the rate at which the implicit index of prices for computing gross domestic product (GDP) in agriculture has been rising (Rath 1989). But, the decline in public investment is basically attributable to the erosion of the resource base of states on account of the steep rise in farm subsidies.

The decline of public investment in agriculture in the 1980s essentially resulted in reducing the potential benefits in the 1990s and later. The observed steadiness in the growth of agricultural output in the eighties and the early 1990s despite the decline in capital formation can be explained basically in terms of better utilization of the existing infrastructure by stepping up the use of current inputs like fertilizers and, by extending the green revolution to the crops and regions hitherto lagging behind. This is corroborated by the increase in the consumption of fertilizers during the 1980s at a faster rate in the eastern and western regions than in the northern and southern regions. What is more, unlike in the 1970s, fertilizers consumed in kharif season increased at a much faster rate than in rabi season, particularly in the eastern region, indicating the spread of new technology to the rainfed and unfavourable areas (Rao 1994). Clearly, the importance of fertilizers, relative to irrigation, as a source of growth has increased considerably in the recent period.

We have seen that the use of high yielding varieties of seeds and fertilizers in rain-fed areas in kharif season has became an important source of agricultural growth during the 1980s. Besides, unlike in the early years of planning, the area irrigated itself has, of late, become increasingly sensitive to monsoons (Ray 1992). These factors may explain why the sensitivity of foodgrains output to variations in rainfall has increased in the post-green revolution period, despite the rise in the proportion of area irrigated. However, thanks to the succession of a series of good harvests there seems to be some reduction in fluctuations in foodgrains output in the 1990s. But considering the spread of new technology to rainfed areas, the country should be prepared for severe shortfall in foodgrains output in the event of failure of monsoons.

This has in fact happened in 2002–03, when the monsoons were below normal. However, our capacity to cope with the consequences of drought has considerably improved mainly because of the rise in the stocks of foodgrains which the government procured from the prosperous and assured irrigated areas. This enhanced ability to withstand droughts is often mistaken in the official circles for the success in drought-proofing of agriculture which, in reality, has not made much headway. These weather-shocks are being absorbed mainly by the rural poor, particularly in the dry regions and in the remote tribal areas, where they continue to experience severe fluctuations in employment and income with inadequate access to foodgrains.

Complementarity Between Public and Private Investment

A more favourable price environment, by itself, may not be sufficient to evoke an adequate supply response by attracting the desired level of private investment. This is because there is a high complementarity between public and private investment in agriculture (Krishnamurty 1985; Bhattacharya and Rao 1986), so that the decline in public investment would have dampened the incentives for private investment in agriculture. In other words, stepping up public investment in infrastructure and human resource development in the less developed areas would have attracted even greater private investment in these areas, thus ensuring a broad-based and employment-oriented growth.

Apart from public investment and terms of trade, private investment is also influenced by technological change and institutional arrangements like land tenures, consolidation of holdings and availability of credit. Some of these factors assume significance for understanding the recent recovery in private investment despite the continued decline in public investment.

One of the most widely debated issues in Indian agriculture in recent years is the phenomenon of declining real public investment and the related issue of complementarity between public and private investment. Since, of late, private investment has been rising despite the continued decline in public investment, it has been contended that 'complementarity' between public and private investment, in the sense of the former inducing the latter, is no longer valid (Mishra and Ramesh Chand 1995; Misra and Hazell 1996). An important policy implication of this finding, if true, is that private investment has acquired an autonomy of its own so that it can continue to grow without the stimulus of public investment and that, therefore, declining public investment should not cause an undue worry. This proposition has been contested by bringing in other variables influencing private investment such as terms of trade and agricultural income and by using the micro-level data on private investment in canal irrigated areas (Dhawan 1996).

This controversy would not have arisen in the first place if the limitations of the data on public investment in agriculture, as given in the National Accounts Statistics (NAS), were widely known. 96–98 per cent of the reported investments under this head relate to investments by the state governments in major and medium irrigation projects. Public investments in rural electrification and in power supplied to agriculture are not included under this head but are subsumed under the power sector. Similarly, the investments in rural roads are not included under this head as they are part of the investments in the overall roads sector. Investments in agricultural research are also not reflected under this head. Therefore, investments reported are a severe underestimate of public investment in agriculture and this bias has been increasing over time. For example, over the 1980s and the 1990s, 75–80 per cent of increments in irrigated area are accounted by minor irrigation sources which are mainly dependent on electricity for pumping water. Thus the proportion of electricity consumed in agriculture to total electricity rose steadily from around 14 per cent in the mid-1970s to 30 per cent by the mid-1990s (Government of India 1996).

If public investments made in agriculture are properly accounted for, and other variables influencing private investment are brought in, the so-called 'complementarity' between public and private investment comes out prominently. Although, as noted above, the terms of trade for agriculture have shown a significant improvement in the post-reform period of 1990s, it appears that economic reforms undertaken so far have yet to find their full reflection in the improvement in terms of trade for agriculture.

Ashok Gulati and Seema Bathla constructed, in addition to the existing official series on public GCFA, two alternative series: one, by extending the coverage of public sector capital formation to include a part of investment in power sector that goes to agriculture, and another, by adding further the investments in agriculture and allied sectors as defined in the government budgets of the Centre and the states. The comprehensive statistical testing done by them on the basis of such estimates proves that 'public investment in agriculture, represented by canal irrigation and power supplies (in cumulative forms), has a positive influence (inducement effect) on private sector investment in agriculture. Favourable terms of trade to agriculture and easy access to institutional credit are the other two variables that strongly affect private sector investments in agriculture' (Gulati and Bathla 2002).

Therefore, there is no basis for complacency on the role of public investment in agriculture which is going to be extremely important for inducing private investment further and indeed for deriving full benefit from the opportunities opened up by economic reforms, until the private sector comes in, in a big way for investing in infrastructure which has, hitherto, been provided by the public sector.

Irrigation

Corresponding to the decline in public gross capital formation in agriculture in the 1990s, there has been a decline in the growth of quality irrigation, fertilizer consumption, and institutional credit. While public investment in irrigation has declined, the area under irrigation, according to the official land-use statistics, is reported to have grown at about the same rate in the 1990s as in the 1980s. Some growth in irrigated area can be expected from the investments made in the earlier period, because of long gestation lags between the investment made and the potential realized. However, there is overwhelming evidence of a severe deterioration in the existing irrigation systems. This would have led to both the slower growth or even decline in the quantity of water delivered from the system, even when the area under irrigation has increased, and to the deterioration in the quality in terms of the timeliness of supplies. Further, in large parts of the country, the groundwater table has gone down steeply resulting in reduced supplies from such sources owing to the depletion of aquifers as well as high cost of pumping water (Government of India, Planning Commission, 2000, *Mid-term Appraisal of the Ninth Five Year Plan*). Thus, the area under high yielding varieties of seeds, which has been growing in tandem with irrigation on account of reduction in yield risk, and which recorded a trend growth rate of 8.1 per cent per annum during the 1980s, decelerated to 4.4 per cent per annum in the 1990s (RBI 2003a). The major issues confronting this sector are discussed in Chapter 7.

Fertilizers

Whereas the consumption of all fertilizers (NPK) more than doubled during the 1980s from 5.5 million tonnes in 1980–1 to 12.5 million tonnes in 1990–1, their consumption stood at 16.7 million tonnes in 2000–01, representing a rise of only about 33 per cent over the 1990s (Government of India, *Economic Survey*, 2002–03). What is worse, subsidy on urea has resulted in an unbalanced use of nitrogen, phosphorus, and potassium fertilizers which was in the ratio of 8.5:3.1:1 in 1998–9 as against the desirable ratio of 4: 2: 1 (RBI 2003a). This has led to a decline in the productivity of fertilizers apart from depleting soil nutrients. These issues are discussed in some detail in the chapter on Agricultural Research and Technology.

Institutional Credit

Although there is marginal improvement in the growth rate of direct institutional credit to agriculture and allied activities in the 1990s, the growth of credit to the small and marginal farmers and for investment slowed down considerably in this period. According to the Reserve Bank of India (RBI) *Report on Currency and Finance*, 2001–02, '...there is a deceleration in the scheduled commercial banks' disbursements of direct finance to small farmers from 15.1 per cent in the 1980s to 11.0 per cent in the 1990s. Similarly, the annual compound growth rate of direct finance (disbursements) to marginal farmers, decelerated to 13.0 per cent from 18.1 per cent during the same period. The annual compound growth rates of medium/long term loans disbursed to agriculture and allied activities (direct advances), which are important for private sector capital formation in agriculture, have shown deceleration to 9.7 per cent in the 1990s from 11.5 per cent in the preceding decade' (RBI 2003, *Report on Currency and Finance*). The issues in rural credit reform are discussed in Chapter 8.

Growth Rate of Agriculture and Allied Activities

The decline in public investment in agriculture and slowdown in the growth of farm inputs has resulted in a decline in the growth rate of agricultural output in the 1990s, despite the fact that India has been blessed with normal monsoons without interruption in the 1990s. The trend growth rate of total crop production declined from 3.2 per cent per annum in the 1980s (1980–1 to 1989–90) to 2.3 per cent per annum in the 1990s (1990–1 to 1999–2000). The growth rate of average yield per hectare from crops halved from 2.6 per cent to 1.3 per cent over the same period (RBI 2003a). However, owing to the increasing diversification of agriculture away from crop production to dairying, meat, poultry, vegetables and fruits, in response to the rise in their demand on account of the rise in per capita income and the consequent changes in the tastes and preferences of consumers, the growth rate of GDP from agriculture and allied activities showed a smaller decline over this period.

The RBI computed such growth rates by excluding the crisis year of 1991–2 when the growth of agriculture and allied activities registered a decline of 1.5 per cent and the overall GDP rose only by 1.3 per cent (RBI 2003a). The trend growth rate of real gross domestic product from agriculture and allied activities, according to the RBI, declined from 3.1 per cent in the decade preceding reforms (1981–2 to 1990–1) to 2.5 per cent in the period of reforms (1992–3 to 2002–03). However, with respect to the monsoon, the year 2002–03 was quite below normal. But even when we exclude this year, the growth rate is lower at 2.76 per cent for this period. The deceleration in the growth rate of GDP from agriculture and allied activities between the first half of 1990s and the later period is glaring, as shown below.

Table 5.1: Growth Rate of GDP from Agriculture and Allied Activities

Period	Growth Rate
1992–3 to 1996–7	3.85*
1997–8 to 2002–03	1.64*
1997–8 to 2001–02	2.31
1992–3 to 2001–02	2.76

* *Source*: Gulati and Mullen (2003).

While comparing the decadal growth rates, it should be borne in mind that such growth rates are quite sensitive to the inclusion or exclusion of even a single year at the beginning or the end of a period. This is clear from the estimates by Gulati and Mullen (2003). However, even abstracting from the decadal (pre- and post-reform) growth rates, it should be clear that in view of the continued decline in public investment in agriculture in the post-reform period and because there is complementarity between public and private investment, agriculture in India could not derive full benefit from macroeconomic reforms of the 1990s by way of higher growth rate which would have been possible if the fiscal reforms were put in place to raise public investment in agriculture.

Productivity

An encouraging feature of agricultural growth in India during the 1980s was the spread of the green revolution to the central and eastern parts of India where productivity is low but the potential for increase in productivity is high and where poverty is widespread. This trend seems to have been maintained in the early 1990s but tapered off very soon with the onset of economic reforms and the consequent fiscal squeeze adversely affecting public expenditure on agriculture.

It appears that the deceleration in foodgrains output in the 1990s is explained not only by the slow growth of inputs such as irrigation and fertilizers but also by the declining contribution of total factor productivity (TFP). According to a recent study, the contribution of TFP to the growth rate in output, which had risen substantially to a little over 40 per cent in the post-green revolution period of the 1960s and the 1970s, had already declined to around 30 per cent in the late 1980s (Desai and Namboodiri 1997). This declining trend in TFP has continued in the 1990s basically on account of the stagnation in the expenditure on agricultural research and extension as a proportion to GDP from agriculture (Kumar 2002).

Government expenditure on agricultural research and education being the most important determinant of TFP, its level in relation to the value of agricultural output and its distribution over different commodities and regions would hold the key to the growth of output, efficiency in resource allocation, and the distribution of gains from the growth in productivity. This aspect is discussed in some detail in Chapter 6.

Farm Subsidies versus Investment

It would be instructive to know the increase in the magnitude of subsidies for agriculture incurred by the Centre and states together in relation to the plan expenditure for the development of this sector. For irrigation we are considering only the subsidy incurred on account of the non-recovery of operation and maintenance charges leaving out the cost of capital deployed. Further, based on the world prices of fertilizers, we are assuming that only about half the actual subsidy on fertilizers benefits the farmers and the consumers (Gulati 1990).

The input subsidies, so calculated, on fertilizers, irrigation, electricity, and credit combined constituted around one-third of total plan expenditure on agriculture, irrigation (including flood control), and Special Area Programmes incurred by the Centre as well as the state governments in 1980–1, and rose steeply to as high as 90 per cent of such plan expenditure in 1989–90. If annualized cost of capital in irrigation is also accounted for at historical cost, which is quite modest when compared to the replacement cost, the subsidy on surface irrigation during the Seventh Plan Period (Rs 11,800 crores) exceeded the Seventh Plan expenditure (Rs 11,000) on major and medium irrigation. The subsidy on rural electricity during the Seventh Plan period amounted to 11,700 crores which is about three times the 8th Plan outlay of 4000 crores provided in the state plans for rural electrification in the power sector (Government of India, *Eighth Five Year Plan*, p. 197).

The amount of these input subsidies increased further in the subsequent period. Ironically, the level of input subsidies in the post-reform period of 1990s was much higher than in the 1980s. Whereas in 1989–90, the total of farm subsidies on power, fertilizer, and irrigation at 1981–2 prices rose to Rs 53 billion, they nearly doubled reaching Rs 104 billion in 1999–2000. At 1993–4 prices, they crossed Rs 250 billion in the same year (Gulati and Narayanan 2003). As against this, public sector GCFA at 1993–4 prices stood at less than Rs 50 billion in 1999–2000 (Gulati and Narayanan 2003). It is clear from this that even a modest reduction of subsidies, say, to the extent of 20 per cent could enable the government to double its investment in agriculture.

It is imperative to reduce these subsidies for stepping up public investment in agriculture. However, there is considerable political resistance and, in a democratic polity like India, the process of change towards rational pricing of inputs is bound to be slow. In these days of globalization and easy flow of information, it is becoming difficult to convince the Indian farmers about the need to reduce such subsidies when their counterparts in the 'market economies' like the United States, European Community, and Japan enjoy much higher levels of subsidies. It is not easy to convince the farmers in India that our resources are scarcer and their alternative uses in agriculture are more productive.

In this context, the Union government could have given better signals to the state governments and the farmers at large through the post-reform budgets by earmarking a good part of the savings on fertilizer subsidy for the development of infrastructure like irrigation rather than using it entirely to reduce budgetary deficits. Despite some reduction in fertilizer subsidy, the plan investment in agriculture has been declining because of the negligible rise in the central assistance to state plans on account of the drive to reduce fiscal deficit. Also, the states' resources have been eroded by the slow rise in revenues from shareable taxes like income tax and union excise duties consequent to the reduction in tax rates.

It would be instructive to recall, in this context, the observations of Dharm Narain and Raj Krishna, both of whom have done pioneering work on the supply response of Indian agriculture. According to Narain (1976), 'An oversimplistic and, therefore, excessive preoccupation with price can do more harm than good by distracting attention from the harder but more important tasks which belong in the non-price world of achieving technological breakthroughs and releasing such real constraints as stand in the way of their becoming a reality on the farmers' fields'. In a survey of agricultural supply response in several developing countries, Krishna (1982) found that the elasticity of output with respect to major technological shifters such as irrigation was 1.5 to 5.5 times the price elasticity. Maintaining that these elasticities 'would in all probability remain higher even if price elasticity were measured to include the effect of price-induced innovations', he concluded that 'National Policy makers and international development bankers will therefore do well to devote at least as much attention and effort to the development of technology, infrastructure, and human capital as to the price environment'.

Conclusion

The deceleration in the GDP from agriculture, especially crop output, during the 1990s is explained by economic reform related factors—insufficient reforms in the management of rural infrastructure or improper sequencing of reforms bearing on supply side factors such as irrigation and fertilizers; reforms in the management of irrigation systems for recovering user-charges will take time to yield results; as such, resources need to be raised in the intervening period to protect capital and maintenance expenditures. However, the emphasis so far has been on containing fiscal deficit by reducing these essential expenditures which has led to a slow down in the expansion of irrigated area.

Subsidies on these inputs need to be cut down in order to raise public sector investments in agricultural research and extension, canal irrigation, and rural electrification. The reduction in subsidies would also have a favourable impact on the efficiency of input use, equity, and environment. This requires major reforms in pricing and institutions for the management of these inputs (Rao and Gulati 1997). These issues, sector-wise, are discussed in the subsequent three chapters.

6

Agricultural Research and Technology

New Perspectives

Major Objectives

Achieving food security through self-sufficiency in foodgrains has so far been the overriding goal of agricultural policy in India. As such, the inputs and technology tended to be concentrated in irrigated areas where the results were quick, substantial, and assured. One can now discern the beginnings of a significant shift in the perspective for agriculture in India. Consolidating the food security already achieved and moving much further to avail of the opportunities opened up by trade is emerging as the guiding principle of agricultural policy in the period ahead.

The growth of foodgrains output has so far been limited by domestic demand. Population growth and the rise in per capita income will no doubt necessitate a significant rise in the output of foodgrains. However, it is necessary to note the significant downward shift taking place in the demand for foodgrains. This is on account of the change in the consumer tastes with the availability of a wide variety of goods and services even in rural areas (Chapter 9). If agricultural growth is not to be constrained by the domestic demand but should indeed contribute to raising the overall economic growth, then agricultural output needs to be stepped up for exports by diversifying into areas such as dairying and other animal products, horticulture, and floriculture, the demand for which is more favourable than for foodgrains. Trade in these areas will contribute to modernizing these sectors in the sphere of production as well as processing and marketing. The rain-fed or dry land areas in the country have a comparative advantage in animal husbandry, horticulture, and floriculture. The development of new technologies for these activities can thus benefit the agriculturally backward areas where poverty is widespread.

These new activities, which have a favourable domestic as well as export demand are also employment-intensive. But the experience shows that the substitution of capital for labour in high-wage areas has been basically responsible for the decline in the employment per unit of output. This experience suggests that new technologies suited to low-wage areas such as rain-fed or dry land areas offer better prospects for labour absorption, and underline the need for location-specific research and extension, for maximizing the employment opportunities.

Raising the productivity of resources used in agriculture through their better allocation between different crops and regions and by adopting improved technologies is a major objective of liberalization. Export-orientation will provide incentives for the regional specialization in crops according to their comparative advantage as well as for the adoption of new technologies in production, processing, and marketing. However, the productivity of resources can be enhanced further by extending infrastructure to the less developed areas and by introducing new technologies there. Removal of input subsidies where they have outlived their utility would also promote the efficient allocation of such inputs as well as give impetus to the evolution of cost-reducing innovations.

In the early years of the green revolution, when the attainment of food security was the overriding objective, ecological concerns were not in the forefront of agricultural policy. In course of time, however, population growth as well as the growing demand from the affluent sections has been exerting pressure on the environment. Further, the unregulated exploitation of natural resources caused, among other things, by the under-pricing of inputs such as irrigation water and electricity for pumping groundwater have contributed to the degradation of environment. Although, as yet, chemicalization of agriculture as such is not a serious problem, the evolution of new biotechnologies to save on chemical inputs has to be accorded a high priority in agricultural research. Besides, the efforts for conservation of soil and water resources in dry land areas need to be stepped up with a view to creating the necessary conditions for profitable application of yield-increasing technology.

Contribution of Productivity

The area under foodgrains had declined somewhat during the 1980s. The entire increase in foodgrains output during this period was, therefore, the result of the rise in productivity per acre on account of the increase in yield-raising inputs. However, the efficiency of resource-use consequent to the application of new technology is measured by the total factor productivity (TFP) or the productivity of all the inputs combined. The contribution of TFP growth to the growth of crop production in India is estimated to account for about half the growth of crop production in India between 1956 and 1987 (Evenson *et al.* 1999). The contribution of TFP to growth of crop production slowed down significantly in the post-reform period of the 1990s, owing to the sluggish growth of public expenditure on agricultural research and extension (Rosegrant and Hazell 2000; Kalirajan and Shand 1997).

Public research and extension and private research have been the major sources of increase in TFP, the former accounting for over two-thirds of this increase after 1975. During the mature green revolution (1977–87) when new technology was more widely adopted geographically, the marginal impact of research on TFP was 50 per cent higher than before the green revolution and 17 per cent higher than in its early years. This high impact of TFP is explained by the high rate of return on investment in public research—greater than 50 per cent (Evenson *et al.* 1999). Further, 'The rates of return to extension, domestic private research and development, and to improved modern varieties generated by the International Agricultural Research Centres (IARCs) were also high. The sustained high rates of return to research and extension suggest that investment in these productivity-enhancing activities should be increased' (Evenson *et al.* 1999).

These high rates of return on investment in research and extension indicate that there is considerable scope for improving productivity through the extensive application of known technology as well as by evolving new technologies. The studies conducted by the International Food Policy Research Institute in collaboration with the Indian Council of Agricultural Research show that the potential for productivity increase by extending the known technology to new regions and crops by redeploying the existing resources is significant. These potential gains are attributable mainly to two sources. First, by bridging the gap between the actual and the potential productivity from the use of fertilizers in respect of crops and regions where the level of fertilizer-use is far below the optimum levels. Such a potential is found to be quite high in Uttar Pradesh, and eastern and central regions. The second major source is the balanced application of nitrogenous, phosphatic, and potassic fertilizers in all the regions (Rao and Gulati 1994).

Fertilizer Use

The level of fertilizer-use in the country has become very uneven over a period of time. For example, as much as 50 per cent of total fertilizers consumed in the country were accounted by the top 20 per cent of the districts. Owing to the diminishing returns to fertilizer-use at higher levels, the aggregate response of output from the use of fertilizers has declined. If the decline in productivity due to the unbalanced use is also accounted for, the output response has gone down from 1:10 to 1:6. It has been estimated in a joint study by the International Food Policy Research Institute (IFPRI) and the Indian Council of Agricultural Research (ICAR) that, for wheat, an optimal distribution of fertilizers as between different regions would increase output by 1.6 million tonnes. A change towards balanced use of NPK, by raising both P and K per unit of N, would raise output by 2 million tonnes. Both the adjustments together, that is, optimal regional distribution as well as best NPK mix would increase wheat output by 12 per cent with a marginal increase of half a million tonnes in fertilizer consumption (Rao 1994a; Rao and Gulati 1994).

Similarly, in the case of rice, a change in NPK mix results in an increase in output to the extent of 1.2 million tonnes. Diversion of fertilizers away from the northern to eastern regions would yield 9 million tonnes with 1.5 million tonnes of additional fertilizers. Thus optimal levels of fertilizer distribution with the best NPK mix (2: 1: 1) leads to about 20 per cent increase with 1.5 million tonnes of additional consumption of fertilizers (Rao 1994a; Rao and Gulati 1994).

There was little increase in the farm gate prices of fertilizers throughout the 1980s despite a steady rise in the cost of inputs and a significant rise in the prices of crops. However, there was a sudden rise of 30 per cent in the prices of nitrogenous fertilizers and a doubling of the prices of phosphatic and potassic fertilizers following their decontrol in the early 1990s. This led to a sharp decline in the growth rate of fertilizer consumption from around 8 per cent per annum during the 1980s to only about 2 per cent per annum in the first half of the 1990s. What is more ominous, is that there has been an absolute decline in the consumption of phosphatic and potassic fertilizers in this period resulting in an adverse NPK ratio which may have reduced the productivity of fertilizers, apart from causing damage to the soils.

A distinction should be made for policy purposes between subsidies on surface irrigation and power on the one hand, and the subsidies on fertilizers, on the other. The rise in water and power rates, which at present are in the nature of fixed charges per hectare or per horse power, may not result in a decline in the use of these inputs, as the cost of inputs is not related to the volume of their use. On the other hand, cost of fertilizer being proportional to its volume, its consumption is sensitive to its price relative to the prices of crops. Over a period of time, the price elasticity of demand for fertilizers has increased on account of the decline in its productivity at the margin (Rao 1994b). This diminishing marginal productivity may be due to its intensive use following the rise in subsidy as well as to a slow increase in complementary inputs such as irrigation.

Fertilizer being a land-augmenting input, despite credit constraint, small and marginal farmers who have surplus labour are found to apply it as much per hectare as large farmers. The cut- back in its use by them in the event of a decline in subsidy could be greater as they have little surplus produce to sell. These facts suggest that the reduction in fertilizer subsidy or the rise in its price bears some meaningful relationship to the opening up of agriculture as well as to the rise in complementary inputs like irrigation and to improvements in the fertilizer-saving technology, all of which would raise the profitability of its application.

Further, in so far as import of fertilizers is cheaper, it has been argued that doing away with the existing system of administered prices for fertilizers and allowing an increase in their imports, up to a point, would contribute to improving the competitiveness of the domestic fertilizer industry, apart from cutting down the subsidy bill even without raising the prices for farmers (Government of India 1998).

Development and Diffusion of New Technology

Adequate funding for public research, appropriate economic signals for setting right priorities in research, whether public or private, and a favourable institutional framework and the resulting incentives for the absorption of new technology are the three basic prerequisites for the proper development and diffusion of new technology. These are best ensured when the demarcation of the relative roles of the state and markets or the public and private sectors in agriculture is rational. A number of studies have shown that a favourable macroeconomic environment including openness in trade has been conducive to the development and diffusion of new cost-reducing technologies in agriculture. This has happened due to favourable terms of trade for agriculture, inducement to improve quality and reduce costs for becoming internationally competitive—prices truly reflecting the scarcities of resources so that research is directed to saving the scarce factors—and the adequate allocation of resources, public as well as private, for research and extension.

Economic analysis, following the contributions of John Hicks (1932), has been focusing on the significance of relative prices of factors of production in inducing cost-reducing innovations directed towards saving the scarce factors through the greater use of the abundant factors. For example, heavy subsidies on inputs like fertilizers, surface irrigation, electricity for pumping water, and farm credit discourage research in biotechnology which saves on chemical inputs and is environment-friendly; and in general encourage capital-intensive techniques. Private research and extension is becoming increasingly important on account of scientific breakthroughs such as the emergence of biotechnology with low investment requirements in applied research and the greater responsiveness of private research to the user-requirements which vary considerably across agro-climatic regions. In a situation like this, adequate intellectual property protection becomes necessary to provide incentives for private investment and effort in research.

Apart from the incentive framework conducive to technological change mentioned above, the development of certain forms of infrastructure including human capital is essential to raise the profitability of investment in research. Development of irrigation, roads and processing and marketing network would facilitate the widespread adoption of new technology by raising the yields, reducing their variability and by ensuring remunerative and assured prices for the products. Improvements in the literacy levels of the farmers and in the dissemination of information through the increasing use of modern information technology (IT) is essential, particularly when the new practices are sophisticated and the rate of technological advance is rapid. The importance of infrastructure development for Indian agriculture is underlined by the fact that both in respect of irrigation and literacy, only a little over 50 per cent of the potential has been effectively realized so far.

Even after the full potential for irrigation is achieved, nearly half the cultivated area will still be dependent on rainfall. The rain-fed or dry land areas in the country are being degraded due to the depletion of soil fertility and moisture. Experience has shown that a critical minimum of soil fertility and moisture levels are essential for the profitable adoption of new technology (Jain 1993). Research in the evolution of new seeds and improved practices, by itself, has proved to be insufficient for such areas (Jodha 1989). The existing programmes for soil and moisture conservation have failed to make an impact on account of inadequate planning of works on watershed basis, failure to involve the beneficiaries in the planning and implementation of works and a lack of coordination among departments concerned with these programmes. A high priority has, therefore, to be given to the soil and moisture conservation in the dry land areas to create the necessary conditions for the adoption of improved agricultural practices. The guidelines under the new strategy as recommended by the Technical Committee on the Drought Prone Area Programme and Desert Development Programme, have been under implementation since 1995 (Government of India, Ministry of Rural Development 1994).

The annual growth rate in real public expenditure on agricultural research and education having accelerated in the post-green revolution period of the 1970s slowed down since the mid-1980s and hovered round 0.5 per cent of agricultural gross domestic product (GDP) in the 1990s (Pal, Jha, and Singh 1997), as against the requirements of the Ninth Plan at 1 per cent projected by the ICAR. A recent exercise on research priorities in Indian agriculture shows that the level of research expenditure is sub-optimal or significantly lower than desired in the central and eastern states for example, Bihar, Orissa, Madhya Pradesh, Uttar Pradesh, and West Bengal where productivity is low and poverty is widespread. Further, crops like rice, certain coarse cereals, pulses, and oilseeds show sub-optimal expenditures on research. The research expenditures are also not in tune with the diversification of agriculture and are not quite environment friendly in so far as livestock, horticulture, agro-forestry, and dry land areas receive less than the desired expenditures (Pal, Jha, and Singh 1997).

Biotechnology

The achievements of the Indian agricultural research system so far in respect of raising yields in the unirrigated and unfavourable agro-climatic regions are not comparable with those realized for the irrigated areas in the early years of green revolution. Even in irrigated areas, the yields under seed–fertilizer technology have been hovering around their peak for some time. The tools of emerging biotechnology like genetic engineering, tissue culture, and so on offer significant possibilities for breaking these barriers. The most important feature of biotechnology distinguishing it from the seed–fertilizer technology is the possible saving on chemical inputs like pesticides and fertilizers (Peacock 1991, Rao 1991).

The pro-poor bias of biotechnology arises from this saving on chemical inputs, from its scale-neutrality at the farm level, relative stability in yields and improved prospects for crops grown in agro-climatically unfavourable areas (Rao 1991). Biotechnology may also contribute to the protection and regeneration of the environment by reducing the dependence on chemical inputs. If farm subsidies are reduced significantly in the developed countries, in pursuance of the Uruguay Round Agreements, chemical fertilizers may increasingly be replaced by the renewable source like biologically fixed nitrogen (Jain 1993). More significantly, biotechnologies may contribute to eco-protection by raising yields and thus releasing marginal lands from cultivation. They also facilitate large-scale afforestation through tissue culture techniques.

However, being knowledge-intensive and skill-intensive, they necessitate greater investment in research as well as in improving the capabilities of farmers. Although some advanced centres for research in biotechnology have been established in the country, it is not clear how such priorities find their place in the existing agricultural research system in India. It is necessary to have a fresh look at the priorities of the Indian agricultural research system in the light of these emerging prospects and for adequately taking into account the socio-economic factors relevant in the evolution of new technologies.

As mentioned above, India is currently investing only about 0.5 per cent of its agricultural GDP in agricultural research, as against 0.7 per cent in the developing countries, and as much as 2–3 per cent in the developed countries (Jain 1993). Therefore, so far as India is concerned, there is considerable scope for diverting incremental outlays for the priority areas in research. Strengthening indigenous capabilities in biotechnology by involving the private sector in research as well as in the multiplication and distribution of seeds provides an effective safeguard, in the long-run, against the patenting of seeds and other restrictive practices by the multinational corporations.

Research Management

While there is need for a significant step-up in real public expenditure on agricultural research and extension as well as its optimal distribution over different regions and commodities, major reforms in the management of public agricultural research and extension are overdue to improve the overall productivity of the system. These reforms need to be directed essentially towards de-bureaucratizing and decentralizing management with a view to ensuring autonomy in decision making as well as accountability at various levels. Such conditions alone can ensure right priorities in research, professional excellence, and cost-effectiveness (Pal and Saxena 2003).

7

Irrigation Reforms

Major Issues

Profile of Expansion

In the course of 50 years of planning from the First to the Ninth Five Year Plan, the Government of India invested huge amounts for the creation of irrigation facilities through major, medium, and minor irrigation projects, in addition to the public investment for rural electrification, which has been largely deployed for pumping water for irrigation. As a result of these efforts, India has exploited nearly 60 per cent of its available irrigation potential of 58.5 million hectares from the major and medium irrigation projects. When the ongoing projects are completed, bulk of the available irrigation potential will have been exploited.

Due to the easy availability of power in large parts of the country for pumping water for irrigation, as much as 78 per cent of the available potential of 81.4 million hectares from minor irrigation sources, consisting predominantly of groundwater resources, has already been exploited. Further progress towards the exploitation of the remaining potential hinges on the availability of power for pumping water in the eastern states where as much as 75 per cent of their groundwater potential still remains to be exploited (Government of India, *Ninth Five Year Plan*). The share of agriculture in the electricity consumed increased significantly in the post-green revolution period. From about 4 per cent of total electricity consumed in 1950–1, the share of agriculture rose to 26 per cent in 1990–1 (Government of India, *Economic Survey 1992–3*) and to 30 per cent by mid-1990s (Chapter 5). Agriculture in Haryana accounted for over 40 per cent of the total electricity consumed in the state, followed by the Punjab, Uttar Pradesh, and West Bengal. The share of agriculture was much below the national average in some of the central and eastern states, for example, Bihar, Madhya Pradesh, and Orissa.

Performance

Productivity

In view of the very high complementarity between irrigation and bio-chemical technology, it would be meaningful from the policy point of view to assess the contribution of irrigation to the growth of output as the combined effect of irrigation and the use of complementary inputs like high-yielding varieties of seeds and fertilizers. In the late 1980s the per hectare yields of foodgrains under irrigated conditions were two to six times higher than the yields under rain-fed conditions (Rao 1994). Further, contrary to some perceptions (Vaidyanathan 1991), yields of foodgrains under irrigation grew at the annual rate of 1.6 per cent to 2.6 per cent per annum in certain states, whereas the annual yield growth rate of foodgrains under rain-fed conditions was either negligible or barely 1 per cent (Rao 1994). The significant rise in the contribution of irrigation to the total foodgrains output in the post-green-revolution period is understandable in view of: (a) expansion of area under cultivation becoming insignificant as a source of growth in the post-green revolution period; and (b) technological change becoming favourable to irrigated crops like wheat and rice resulting in high-yield growth.

Stability

Irrigation reduces weather-induced fluctuations in output by reducing instability both in area under the crops and in their yields. The instability in yields as well as output for irrigated crops, as indicated by the coefficient of variation in yields, is less than half of that for unirrigated crops (Dhawan 1993). One should, therefore, expect the fluctuations in employment and income of agricultural labour to be much less in irrigated areas compared to rain-fed areas.

However, despite the rise in the percentage of cultivated area under irrigation, the instability in foodgrains output tended to increase in the post-green revolution period, except in the case of crops like wheat which are predominantly irrigated (Rao, Ray, and Subbarao 1988). The persistence in instability is attributable to the increasing vulnerability of rain-fed agriculture to weather on account of the expansion of cultivation to marginal and sub-marginal lands and also because of the increasing application of seed–fertilizer technology under rain-fed conditions. Since irrigation as such reduces yield instability, a significant rise in irrigation from dependable sources may contribute to bringing down the overall instability in agricultural output.

Poverty and Inequality

The impact of irrigation on reducing poverty is striking, although its potential for reducing poverty further and also for reducing regional and size-class disparities in income can be harnessed only through appropriate policies for the exploitation of the remaining irrigation potential. Because of the rise in the demand for labour, the wage rates in irrigated areas are significantly higher than those in the unirrigated areas, despite the large-scale in-migration of labour to the irrigated areas. Moreover, since the elasticity of substitution between capital and labour in Indian agriculture is found to be generally less than unity (Rao 1975), the wage income of farm labour, as a group, would rise despite the displacement of some labour due to mechanization. Because of the rise in employment and wages on account of irrigation and also because of the relative stability in employment and income, the proportion of rural population below the poverty line is significantly lower in regions where the percentage of gross cropped area irrigated is above 50 per cent. Among different regions, the proportion of people below the poverty line increases as the level of irrigation declines, the poverty level being very high in regions where the irrigation ratio is less than 10 per cent (Rao 1994).

On account of the scarcity of land and adequate availability of family labour per unit of land, small and marginal farmers are particularly responsive to land-augmenting technological changes like irrigation. The percentage of gross cropped area irrigated and cropping intensity are significantly higher among the small and marginal farmers. This has been brought out by a number of studies and surveys including those by the National Sample Survey (NSS) in the pre- as well as the post-green revolution period (Government of India, Department of Agriculture, *All India Report on Input Survey 1981–2*). Small and marginal farmers have an advantage in respect of traditional labour-intensive methods of lifting water, especially where the water table is high.

Irrigation from public canals and tubewells can be expected to benefit all classes of farmers in the command area in proportion to the area held by them. The farmers located at head-reaches of public canals manage to derive greater benefit than those at the tail-ends, but there is no reason to believe that this would result in discrimination against small and marginal farmers. In the case of private tubewells, however, small farmers are at a disadvantage because of their low investible capacity as well as non-viability of holdings. The available evidence suggests that in the post-green revolution period, medium and large farmers have taken a lead in the exploitation of groundwater and have driven down the water table. Small and marginal farmers, being late-comers, face receded water table, so they have to incur heavier costs for pumping water. Also, they are becoming increasingly dependent on the more resourceful farmers for buying water, the market for which has been expanding.

Sustainability

Water being a renewable resource with immense capacity for augmentation of biomass, can contribute to ecological conservation and sustainability. At the present stage of agricultural development in India, the degradation of environment is caused not so much by the intensive cultivation through the greater use of chemical inputs as by the extension of cultivation to marginal and sub-marginal lands. Land-saving technological change represented by irrigation contributes to easing pressures for extending cultivation to ecologically vulnerable areas. Besides, by augmenting the supply of biomass, in general, and raising the incomes of the poor, in particular, irrigation reduces pressures for deforestation.

On the negative side, irrigation development has, on occasions, led to the submergence of valuable forests and water-logging and salinity. Indiscriminate exploitation of groundwater has, among other things, led to the shortage of drinking water and increased the severity of droughts. However, these adverse consequences are essentially the result of defective planning and designing of projects, in so far as they have inadequately taken into account ecological concerns; faulty systems of water releases and management; and defective pricing of electricity for pumping water. In the designing of irrigation projects now, ecological concerns are being accommodated, as a rule, and there is insistence on compensatory afforestation as a necessary element in the completion of ongoing irrigation projects (Government of India, Planning Commission 1992).

However, rehabilitation of persons displaced by irrigation projects deserves greater concern and attention than hitherto. In most cases, the costs of rehabilitation are not prohibitive and would be amply justified by the benefits to the society accruing from the development of irrigation.

Siltation of reservoirs on account of deforestation in the catchment areas is another problem affecting the useful life and operational efficiency of some of the irrigation systems. This, again, is not a consequence of irrigation as such but rather a result of the overall process of denudation. The loss of forests due to irrigation constitutes a small fraction of the annual denudation of forests on account of the overall socio-economic processes.

Clearly, the favourable impact of irrigation on environment far outweighs the negative effects, most of which are avoidable through better planning of projects and efficient management of the systems in operation. There is evidence to show that, in the post-green revolution period, the pressure for the extension of cultivation to new areas has been greater where the percentage of cultivated area irrigated is smaller. In the states where the percentage of net sown area irrigated is significantly higher, there has actually been a decline in the net sown area in the post-green revolution period (Rao 1994). There has been a significant rise in the area under fallows in the country in the 1980s, signifying declining pressure for cultivation on marginal and sub-marginal lands. This rise in fallows is explained basically by the increase in the percentage of cultivated area irrigated, particularly through tapping the groundwater potential by the farmers (Ray 1992). The same relationship has been found in a disaggregated analysis for Andhra Pradesh (Reddy 1991).

There has been a significant decline in area under forests. According to Khoshoo (1986), as much as half of this decline is accounted for by the encroachments for the purpose of expanding the area under the crops. The decline in forest area has been substantial precisely in those states where the percentage of cultivated area under irrigation is low, agricultural wages are low and the incidence of rural poverty is higher (Rao 1994). These facts suggest that the development of irrigation led to reduced pressures on forest land for bringing it under plough. The rise in agricultural wages and reduction in rural poverty have also reduced deforestation both because of high labour cost for felling and transporting trees and also because of reduced pressures from the poor for augmenting their incomes from forest resources.

Major Areas of Concern

Decline in Real Investment

In the wake of the food crisis of the mid-1960s, public investment in agriculture, especially in irrigation, was stepped up. Because of high complementarity between public and private investment in agriculture and high profitability of high yielding variety (HYV) technology then introduced, private investment in irrigation also increased substantially during the 1970s. During the 1980s, however, real gross capital formation in agriculture, including irrigation, by the public and private sectors combined showed a decline (Rao 1989; Shetty 1990). As pointed out in Chapter 5, the declining trend in public investment in agriculture, comprising mainly irrigation, continued in the 1990s.

The declining real investment in irrigation during the 1980s and the 1990s is undoubtedly the most disquieting feature of the recent experience. Even the comparatively well-off states like Gujarat and Maharashtra, where irrigation from major and medium sources still to be exploited is substantial, have shown a significant decline in real gross capital formation in irrigation in the public sector. On the other hand, it is worth noting that in many of the less developed states where the irrigation potential remaining to be exploited is significant, the rate of decline in real gross capital formation is lower than the national average, despite their weaker resource position (Rao 1994).

Thin Spread of Investment

As aptly summed up by the Eighth Plan document, 'the biggest single malady in the major and medium irrigation sector right from the First Plan has been the continued tendency to start more and more new projects resulting in wanton proliferation of projects, thin spreading of resources and consequent time and cost overruns' (Government of India, *Eighth Five Year Plan* 1992, p. 58).

According to the Ninth Five Year Plan, as many as 400 major and medium irrigation projects were still at various stages of implementation (Government of India, *Ninth Five Year Plan*, 1997–2002). Many of the less developed states like Bihar, Madhya Pradesh, Orissa, and Uttar Pradesh have to incur in future a substantial proportion of the estimated total cost of these projects. The benefits yet to be realized are also quite large for these states.

The tendency to start a number of new projects even when the ongoing ones are under-funded is inherent in a democratic system where, because of the large benefits from irrigation, there would be a popular demand and pressure for new projects. The populism centred around irrigation is also reflected in protracted inter-state disputes resulting from 'claims' to water from certain states by starting projects, which have to be kept pending or whose construction is delayed. These result in serious inefficiency in resource-use, as realization of benefits from investment already made is postponed. These time overruns, among other factors, account for the steep rise in the average cost per hectare of potential created from around Rs 1060 during the First Plan to over Rs 42,700 in the Seventh Plan (ibid, p. 57), and to Rs 98,495 in the Eighth Plan (Kumar 2001).

Low Recovery of Costs

Apart from the pressures to start new projects, the unwillingness and resistance of the farmers to pay for the benefits received is inherent in the system. This has led to the shortage of resources with the government for further investment, accentuating, in turn, the problem of time and cost overruns.

The subsidy on irrigation on account of the non-recovery of operation and maintenance charges represents a lower bound, constituting a small fraction of the subsidy on irrigation, when annualized (amortized) cost of capital deployed on major and medium irrigation schemes, besides working expenses, is also taken into account. For example, in 1989–90, irrigation subsidy according to the first definition, amounted to Rs 342 crore as against Rs 2602 crore, if annualized cost of capital is accounted for at historical cost, and as high as Rs 25,107 crore if it is accounted for at replacement cost (Gulati and Katula 1992).

Electricity subsidy consists of the difference between the average cost of supplying electricity and the average revenue realized per unit of electricity sold to the agricultural sector. The total subsidy on electricity for agriculture exceeded the subsidy on surface irrigation, according to the first definition, throughout the 1980s; and since 1987–8 it has exceeded the subsidy on surface irrigation even according to the second definition (Rao and Gulati 1994).

These facts suggest that even a modest reduction in subsidy on irrigation, say by 20 per cent, could have helped raise the Seventh Plan expenditure on major and medium irrigation by 20 per cent. Putting it differently, a subsidy reduction of even 5 per cent, say in 1986–7, would have helped at least double the expenditure on operation and maintenance of Rs 493 crore incurred in that year (Vaidyanathan 1993). This would have, of course, entailed over three-fold rise in the collection of gross revenue from the farmers in that year (Rs 167 crore: Vaidyanathan 1993).

Decline in Water Table

There has been a steady decline in water table in the recent period in several parts of the country, especially in the western dry region, on account of overexploitation of groundwater and insufficient recharge from rain-water. Deforestation and loss of vegetative cover, in general, have led to the speedy run-off and insufficient percolation of rain-water. Consequently, not only irrigation has suffered but even drinking water is becoming scarce. Thus droughts are becoming increasingly severe, notwithstanding the improvement in our capacity to cope with the consequences of drought by making available foodgrains accumulated in years of good harvests.

The programmes of dry farming and for drought-proofing through soil and moisture conservation and water harvesting on a watershed basis have been in operation for over two decades, but they have failed so far to neutralize the adverse impact of the overall processes of ecological degradation and receding water table.

Wastages and Inefficiences in Water Use

The absence of financial accountability on the part of the project authorities and the low rates charged for canal water which are unrelated to the quantity of water used are responsible for large wastages of water both before and after it reaches the fields as well as for the excessive use of water for crops grown (Rao and Gulati 1994).

Water use efficiency under the existing irrigation projects in India is estimated to be only about 40 per cent (Navalawala 1994). According to a study, experiments carried out on the actual losses in upper Ganges canal revealed that out of the water entering canal, as much as 44 per cent was lost in canal, in distributaries and in village water courses. Of the remaining 56 per cent actually entering the fields, the farmer wasted another 27 per cent in excessive irrigation, that actually used by crops being only 29 per cent (Veeraiah and Madankumar 1994).

As against this, in the advanced systems of the West, as much as 60–70 per cent of the water diverted in large surface system is available for plant use (Repetto 1986).

This enormous wastage of water during conveyance and on the field arises basically on account of the absence of incentives to conserve water. In the absence of financial accountability and operational autonomy, project authorities do not have any incentive to conserve water through measures for lining of canals or for supplying water on a volumetric basis. Similarly, since water rates are low and unrelated to the quantity of water used, the farmers have no incentive to save water. On the other hand, the prevailing pricing system provides an inducement to substitute cheap and 'abundant' water for measures like levelling the fields and for weeding. In cases of improper levelling of fields, farmers are found to apply excess amount of water to ensure that enough water reaches plants situated on high grounds. Farmers also resort to the submergence of rice fields to check weed growth and thus increase yields (Veeraiah and Madankumar 1994).

Not only is water use excessive in the command areas of surface irrigation systems, but crop yields are only about half those achieved under private irrigation from tubewells (Dhawan 1985). This is basically attributable to the uncontrolled nature of water supplies in the surface irrigation systems, which could be remedied to a large extent if there are incentives at the project level for modernizing the systems and spreading water to larger areas. Controlled irrigation would not only raise yields but would facilitate extension of water thus saved to new areas. Apart from avoiding water-logging and salinity, modernization of systems and incentives to economize water on the fields would appear to result in at least doubling output from the available water resources by raising yields as well as expanding area under irrigation.

A disquieting consequence of underpricing of surface water is the persistent pressure exerted by the farmers at the head-reaches to water their fields intensively, leaving the tail-enders with sparse supplies. This tendency is responsible, in a significant way, for the departure from the original concept of protective systems of irrigation. The intensive systems of water-use which have come to be established, particularly at the head-reaches, are responsible, to a significant extent, for the effective command areas of the systems becoming smaller than those originally envisaged. This excessive use of water at the head-reaches has not only resulted in serious inequity as between such farmers and those at the tail-end, but also considerably lowered the productivity per unit of water used.

Non-involvement of Users

Inadequacy of public investment in irrigation and the inefficient management of the systems in operation may be attributed, on the one hand, to the prevailing modes of management that are at once excessively technocratic and bureaucratic, and to the politicization of the cost-recovery processes by the political elite, on the other. These problems are basically traceable to the non-involvement of the farmers using irrigation services in the decision making as well as the implementation processes.

The irrigation establishments have an overwhelming bias towards designing and construction of projects without the commensurate concerns and expertise on the utilization of the potential created and the operation and maintenance of the projects completed (Vaidyanathan 1999). Even in the designing and construction of projects, the approach is almost wholly technocratic, there being very little say for the concerns and perceptions of the users of irrigation water. The management, including the operation and maintenance of the systems, is the responsibility of the top–down bureaucratic structures with hardly any participation by the farmers and their groups in the command areas concerned.

This divorce between the 'operation and maintenance' and user interests has virtually alienated the farmers in the irrigation command areas from the authorities managing the systems. Even the payment of water rates is seldom perceived by the farmers as a service charge; it is seen rather as a tax, particularly when it is collected for augmenting the general revenues by the revenue authorities, who have little to do with the improvement and maintenance of the irrigation systems.

The absence of a link between the payment of service charges and the prospect of improvement in the services provided by the system in response to the user-requirements has provided a fertile ground for the politicization of the cost-recovery processes. The members of the political elite, irrespective of their affiliation, have tended to become populist rather than development-oriented with a sense of commitment for sharing the costs of development out of the benefits realized.

Potential and Prospects

Over the 1980s and the 1990s, the average annual increase in the area irrigated from the major and medium irrigation sources has been much smaller at 0.5 million hectares as against 1.6 million hectares from the minor sources. If exploitation proceeds at this rate, it may take another 40 years to fully exploit the remaining known potential from the major and medium sources. Even if no new project is undertaken, the potential to be realized from the ongoing projects may take 20 years, if there is no step-up in the current effort on this front. In the case of minor irrigation, on the other hand, the remaining known potential may be exhausted very soon at the current rate of exploitation.

As much as 80 per cent of the known potential, as of now, from minor sources has been exploited as against about 60 per cent of the potential from major and medium sources. Considering the rate of recharge of groundwater, it is possible that the rate of extraction has been higher than the permissible optimum.

About two-thirds of the minor irrigation potential yet to be exploited is located in the central and eastern states. The southern states account for the bulk of the rest. In the case of major and medium sources too, most of the central and eastern states account for a large share (40 per cent) of the remaining potential followed by the northern states (28 per cent).

As mentioned earlier, the cost per hectare of irrigation has increased steeply. Apart from the secular rise in the cost of construction, this increase is attributable to qualitative improvements in projects and more adequate provision for the costs of compensatory afforestation as well as rehabilitation of the persons displaced. In a significant measure, these high costs also arise from the fact that the new projects are located in the more inaccessible and difficult terrain.

As between different states, the utilization of the potential from minor sources, consisting largely of groundwater, bears a clear relationship with the extent of rural electrification and the proportion of pumpsets energized. In the states where the proportion of villages electrified is lower than the national average, the proportion of pumpsets energized is also lower than the national average (Rao 1994). The higher rate of exploitation of groundwater in Uttar Pradesh despite lower level of rural electrification is explained by the rapid growth of diesel pumpsets. However, the expansion in tubewell irrigation in eastern India, whether through electric or diesel pumpsets, largely replaced the irrigation from open wells, the area under the latter showing a net decline of 75 per cent during the Plan period (Prasad and Sharma 1991).

The availability of groundwater resources had not been a major determinant of the rate of exploitation until the 1970s. The rate of exploitation was quite high even in the western hard-rock region, where the groundwater resources are low and the cost of extraction is high. On the other hand, the rate of exploitation was low in the eastern region despite the abundance of groundwater resources. However, with the spread of the green revolution to the eastern states, the pattern of exploitation seems to be changing in the subsequent period.

The profitability of groundwater exploitation (demand) seems to be influenced by the level of rainfall and the availability of electricity, which is much cheaper for the farmer than diesel. In the western region and in parts of the south, the low level of rainfall as well as the higher level of rural electrification seem to have contributed to a greater exploitation of groundwater. On the other hand, in the eastern region—except in West Bengal where the exploitation of groundwater has been significant—high rainfall, low level of rural electrification, slow progress in respect of technologies appropriate to agro-climatic conditions of the region, and fragmentation of land holdings may account for the slow rate of exploitation of groundwater, the favourable water table notwithstanding.

As between different states, irrigation potential from minor irrigation sources, consisting largely of groundwater, is more unequally distributed than the potential from major and medium sources. Moreover, the potential exploited from minor sources so far shows much greater inter-state variation than the variation in the ultimate potential from these sources (Rao 1994). It appears that irrigation policy, on the whole, has failed to ensure a regionally equitable exploitation of water resources. This is attributable to the slow pace of rural electrification, low investible capacity as well as the non-viability of small holdings in areas where groundwater resources are plentiful. It may be noted that when the irrigation potential from all the sources is fully exploited, inter-state disparities in irrigation would be lower than at present, as the coefficient of (inter-state) variation in the ultimate potential is lower than that in the potential exploited so far (Rao 1994).

Major Areas of Reform

Expansion in Irrigated Area

Despite various inefficiencies in the operation of the existing irrigation systems, the expansion of area under irrigation has contributed to the bulk of the increase in foodgrains output in the post-green revolution period. Increase in irrigated area has thus been the single most important factor in achieving food security. While improvement in the efficiency of the existing irrigation systems is extremely important, it would be wrong, at this stage, to pose the issue in terms of expansion versus efficiency. This is because there is ample need as well as scope for both expansion and improvement in efficiency. Emphasizing one, to the neglect of the other, may have adverse consequences for growth and equity.

The fact that irrigated yields in India are much below those in other countries and are below the realizable potential within the country need not lead to the pessimistic conclusion that 'far more attention is being given to the area under irrigation than is justified. What should be a matter of greater concern is the apparently limited effectiveness of irrigation in raising the productivity of land' (Vaidyanathan 1991). Slow down in the expansion of area under irrigation in the medium term carries the risk of jeopardizing food security and of undermining seriously the export potential from agriculture. Likewise, neglecting the efficiency of the existing systems would perpetuate the wastages in resource allocation and sub-optimal use of water resources. It would also erode further the resource base of the government, affecting adversely proper maintenance of the systems as well as expansion in irrigated area.

Needless to say that, in course of time, as the remaining irrigation potential becomes smaller, gains from improvement in efficiency would assume much greater importance than expansion. It is, however, important to recognize that in a developing economy with competing claims between different interest groups inherent in a democratic polity, improvement in efficiency is bound to be a time-consuming process and it would be risky to place exclusive reliance on efficiency gains by neglecting expansion.

For the country as a whole, the targeted output growth of foodgrains may have to be matched by equivalent growth in area irrigated, as the elasticity of foodgrains output with respect to irrigation, from the mid-sixties to the mid-eighties, turned out to be around unity (Dhawan 1993). It would be unwise to overlook this experience in the short and medium run. However, if yield growth rates of irrigated corps accelerate or yield growth rates of unirrigated crops pick up significantly, the targets for foodgrains output can be achieved with less than proportionate increase in irrigated area.

National Water Planning

Speedy exploitation of the remaining irrigation potential from major and medium sources holds the key to the overall expansion of area under irrigation because of the existence of the significant unexploited potential from these sources. There are, however, several impediments such as heavy investment requirements, preparation and clearance of appropriate project proposals, and resolution of inter-country and inter-state disputes. Although irrigation is a state subject, the initiative from the Central government is extremely important for assistance in the preparation of river-basin plans, preparing plans for inter-basin transfer of water through interlinking of rivers, working for settlement of disputes with other countries, and bringing together the affected states for speedy resolution of disputes. Also, some of the big irrigation projects undertaken by the resource-poor states may have to be taken over, or alternatively heavily funded, by the Centre.

Stepping up Public Investment in Irrigation

The declining trend in public investment in irrigation since the 1980s would essentially affect the addition to irrigated area from these sources in the current and the next decade. This trend of declining public investment must now be reversed. Although over 95 per cent of the outlay on irrigation is incurred by the states, the Centre does have the necessary mechanisms to induce adequate outlays by the states for this sector at the time of plan formulation and for protecting such outlays subsequently.

The system of matching grants by the Centre through the centrally sponsored schemes has played an important role in ensuring adequate outlays for certain sectors such as poverty alleviation programmes. Under the Gadgil Formula for central assistance to the state plans, as originally adopted in 1968, 10 per cent of assistance was earmarked for major irrigation and power projects, although there was no fixed criterion for inter se distribution of this amount among states. This criterion was done away with in 1980, when the Gadgil Formula was modified.

There is a strong case now for reviving this formula by earmarking at least 10 per cent of the central assistance under the modified Gadgil Formula as matching assistance to the states for the ongoing major and medium irrigation projects, which are at the advanced stage of completion. The *inter se* distribution of this assistance among states can be made according to the population or, preferably, in an inverse proportion to their per capita income adjusted with population.

A substantial part of the amount saved by the Centre on account of the reduction in fertilizer subsidy may be earmarked as grants to the states specifically for the development of irrigation. Since irrigation is the most important determinant of fertilizer consumption, the use of fertilizers may increase despite the rise in their prices. Also, there will be an increase in the productivity per unit of fertilizers used. Besides, such a measure may weaken the resistance to the reduction in fertilizer subsidy on the part of the farmers and state governments.

Prioritizing Public Investment

It is now an accepted policy that no new major and medium irrigation projects would be undertaken before the ongoing ones are completed, except that, in rare cases, medium irrigation projects could be undertaken in drought-prone and tribal areas. Thus in the investment allocations, priority would be given to projects, which are at an advanced stage of completion, for renovation and modernization of the old projects and for the essential maintenance of the existing systems (GOI, Planning Commission 1992, *Eighth Five Year Plan*, Vol. II). It would also be necessary to give high priority to investments in the longer canal distribution systems with a view to ensuring wider distribution of water and thus raising the productivity per unit of water used. The return on investment in these priority sectors would be much greater than when the same investment is spread over a large number of projects by starting new ones.

Raising Profitability of Groundwater Exploitation and Augmenting Groundwater Resources

Raising the profitability of investment in the exploitation of groundwater in areas, where there is an abundance of these resources, such as eastern India, is going to be critical for further expansion of area under minor irrigation. Experience shows that the consolidation of small fragmented holdings in eastern Uttar Pradesh has induced widespread installation of pumpsets by raising substantially the profitability of investment (Singh 1985). Expansion of rural electrification, evolution of technological packages suited to the highly variable agro-climatic conditions in this region, improving the viability of credit institutions and development of roads and regulated market centres to ensure remunerative prices to farmers are going to be extremely important for raising the profitability of private investment in irrigation in the eastern region.

Thus, as in the case of major and medium irrigation, stepping up public investment in rural infrastructure, physical as well as institutional, is essential for expanding area under minor irrigation by inducing greater private investment and effort. Since the unexploited potential from major and medium irrigation sources is also significant in eastern India, there are immense prospects for conjunctive use of different sources in this region. This region requires, therefore, significant public investment and effort for exploitation of the available potential.

Whereas raising profitability of investment in the exploitation of groundwater is a major issue in the eastern Gangetic plains and in certain high-rainfall areas, augmenting the groundwater resources is a major problem in several parts of the country, especially in the western dry region, where rainfall is low and highly uncertain. Experience with the Drought Prone Area Programme (DPAP) and the National Watershed Development Programme for Rain-fed Areas (NWDPRA) shows that the prospects for groundwater recharge and water harvesting are quite good if the run-off could be arrested even in areas with low rainfall. Three major tasks continue to confront the implementing agencies in this field in the period ahead. These are: comprehensive planning of works for soil and moisture conservation on a watershed basis; effective coordination between different departments such as agriculture, minor irrigation, forestry, and rural development, and ensuring the full participation of the people in planning as well as execution of projects as required under the new guidelines (Government of India 1994).

Rational Pricing of Irrigation Water and Electricity for Pumping Water

While cost-recovery subject to the paying capacity of farmers is the ultimate objective of pricing irrigation water and electricity for pumping water, three immediate concerns of pricing, which have assumed importance, are: conserving scarce water and energy resources; efficient allocation of water to raise productivity per unit of water; and protection of environment by avoiding water-logging and salinity, on the one hand, and moderating the rigours of drought caused by the excess drawing of groundwater, on the other. The pursuit of these immediate concerns in no way conflicts with the larger objective, as these would necessitate raising the prices of water and electricity. Farmers' capacity to pay for irrigation services has improved significantly over a period of time on account of the rise in the profitability of irrigated agriculture. Recovery of a good part of the costs has become imperative for the proper maintenance of services and further investment towards the expansion of these services.

In a large majority of states, incidence of irrigation charges per se relative to productivity of irrigated land ranged between 1–2.5 per cent (Government of India, *The Report of the Committee on Pricing of Irrigation Water* 1994). Since the output attributable to irrigation can be assumed on an average, to be about half the output on irrigated area, the incidence of irrigation rates can be expected to range between 2–5 per cent of such output. The Committee of State Irrigation Ministers reviewing the problem way back in the mid-1960s suggested that the water rates should be fixed at 25–40 per cent of the additional net benefits from irrigation (Rao and Gulati 1994).

The objectives set out above would be best served, when irrigation water provided by surface systems as well as electricity for pumping water are priced on a volumetric basis. According to a technical committee recently appointed by the Planning Commission, introduction of volumetric basis for pricing surface water would require considerable improvement in the existing delivery systems at the outlets to make them technically amenable to such pricing and delegation of the tasks for distribution and pricing of water to the user-groups, as it would not be possible for the project authorities to extend the volumetric system to the individual farm level (Vaidyanathan 1993). The immediate objective, therefore, should be to rationalize the existing area-based uniform water rates according to seasons and agro-climatic regions and to raise them so as to cover the actual working expenses on the irrigation systems and a small part of the interest, say, 1 per cent. Even this would require a five-fold increase in water charges actually collected per hectare of irrigated area, though these enhanced charges may not exceed 6 per cent of value of gross crop output (Vaidyanathan 1993).

Even a modest beginning in the above direction would call for a strong political will and ingenuity to de-politicize the measure by means of a consensus among political parties. Securing the consent of the user-farmers by involving them in the management of delivery systems is a prerequisite for even a moderate rise in water rates.

Though equally difficult politically, raising electricity rates for pumping water by making them volumetric rather than fixed, on the basis of horse power of the electric motor, as at present, is technically feasible. Under the existing method in most states, the marginal cost of electricity has become zero so that there is incentive for overdrawing groundwater even in water-scarce regions. This has lowered productivity per unit of water on account of its intensive use and has adversely affected the employment of labour as well as the environment. Since profitability of groundwater irrigation is high on account of the control that the farmer can exercise over its use and since it is technically feasible to introduce volumetric pricing of electricity, it may be less difficult to bring about political consensus in this case in favour of increase in rates than in the case of surface irrigation, especially if it is combined with a subsidy for small and marginal farmers.

The experiencc in this regard, however, has not shown this to be any more feasible politically than in the case of surface irrigation. It is often asserted that metering the consumption of electricity in millions of farms is unmanageable and that it would be impossible to police metering to prevent thefts or destruction of the equipment installed. This is, however, true only to the extent that under the present arrangements, the issue of cost-recovery has been politicized. Therefore, as in the case of surface irrigation, there is no alternative to de-politicizing and de-bureaucratizing the cost-recovery processes in the case of electricity too.

The steep fall in the revenue of electricity boards on account of unduly low tariff is acting as a deterrent to major investments in this area by the private sector. The upward revision of rates by making them volumetric cannot be postponed, if investment in this area is to be made attractive to the private sector. An immediate reform towards this end would be to privatize the distribution of electricity. To begin with, the minimum tariff rate charged from the agricultural sector should be raised to 50 paise per unit and this should be revised every year. Otherwise, private investment will not be forthcoming, regardless of the concessions offered. Collections could be improved by selling electricity to user groups, cooperatives of farmers, and private individuals and having them collect the dues (Gulati and Pursell 1993; Sharma 1994).

This is not to suggest, that the existing maintenance expenditures of the irrigation departments and electricity boards, particularly the salaries, are entirely justified and the farmers should, therefore, be called upon to bear their burden. The case for charging economic rates from the farmers rests basically on the profitability of the use of irrigation water and the revenues so collected should be ploughed back into investment by containing expenditure on salaries and perquisites.

Involvement of User-farmers in the Management of Irrigation Systems

The twin objectives of de-bureaucratization and de-politicization discussed above can be achieved best through the participation of the users or user-groups in the management of the systems at different levels so that the link between the rise in water rates and the improvement in the efficiency of services provided is clearly established.

Farmers may not be willing to take on responsibilities merely at the lower end of the system involving basically the tasks of maintenance 'unless they can in return assume greater control over key management decisions, especially decisions about the amount and timing of water delivered to the head of their section of the system' (Bottrall 1991). Their involvement in the decision-making processes concerning the designing as well as management of irrigation systems represents a radical departure from the existing arrangements. Vaidyanathan (1991) suggests that 'a beginning could be made by making the management of each system an autonomous entity, building up a cadre of professionals with a broad concept of water management and preferably employed permanently by each system organization, and using the proceeds of water fees from the command area of each system for maintenance and administration'. It may become necessary to explore even more modest arrangements, to begin with, for associating the farmers' representatives with decision making at different levels with a view to making the system more responsive to the user-requirements, preventing wastages in water-use, and inducing the users to pay for the costs of maintenance of the improved systems.

The experience in several countries which aimed at achieving financial accountability through decentralization of management with the involvement of water users' associations (WUAs) has been quite encouraging in the recent period, enabling them to increase water rates from 4 to 8 times and to improve water use efficiency substantially (Ruth *et al.* 1994; Repetto 1986).

Since there is considerable slack in the existing surface irrigation systems, a strategy which can augment water resources for the farmers from the existing systems and raise the productivity from the available water resources through better management of deliveries can result in a significant increase in output, so that the farmers should be willing to pay a higher share from the increments in output (Ruth *et al.* 1994). On the basis of the facts discussed earlier, if it is assumed that the net incomes of the farmers can be increased by at least 50 per cent by reducing wastages of water and raising the productivity per unit of water supplied, and if farmers can be induced to pay 30 per cent of the increments in income by way of increased water charges, the increase in revenue would constitute 15 per cent of the existing level of gross output, representing over seven-fold increase in rates, as the existing rates, on an average, constitute only about 2 per cent of gross output. In reality, as pointed out earlier, the scope for increasing farm output from the efficient management of the existing irrigation projects is much higher than implied in the above illustration.

The experience with different types of water users associations in certain states in India has been quite encouraging. For example, WUAs formed for irrigation management under Baldeva Medium Irrigation Project and Pigut Medium Irrigation Project located in Gujarat which have been entrusted with water management, fixation of water rates and their collection has revealed encouraging results within a short period: in the case of the former, the revenue collection was 100 per cent in 1992–3, which increased by 57 per cent in just one year. In the latter case, the recovery increased from 89 per cent in the first year, that is, 1989, to almost 100 per cent in 1992–3. Also, water used per unit of cultivated area declined by about 40 per cent over the corresponding period, indicating improved water-use efficiency (Navalawala 1994). Another example is the Mohini Pilot Project in Gujarat, where wholesaling of water volumetrically from the irrigation agency to the WUA was undertaken, which then collected charges from its members. The results have been promising (Ruth *et al.* 1994).

These promising results notwithstanding, a survey of the performance of these institutions in Andhra Pradesh, Bihar, Gujarat, and Maharashtra shows that the primary focus of these institutions was on better management of existing irrigation systems through farmers' participation and cost recovery was never the central issue, although farmers' participation indirectly reduced the costs of operation and maintenance. Further, the organizations or groups which initially perform well under the supervision of the government agencies, fail to continue working effectively once this support has been withdrawn.

Therefore, to sustain their interest on a long-term basis, they should be made co-owners of the systems, by issuing them certain equity shares which would allow them to be involved in management at the designing and construction phases (Gulati *et al.* 1994).

A number of evaluation studies on the working of WUAs in India show that the major factors influencing the future of WUAs in India are comprehensive changes in laws and policies, autonomy in the working of WUAs, accountability of irrigation departments towards WUAs and the attitudinal changes in bureaucracy (Navalawala 1994). The revitalization of village level elected (Panchayati Raj) institutions following the recent (73rd) Amendment Act of the Constitution passed by Indian Parliament holds out the promise for decentralizing the management of irrigation systems, if the states can muster enough political will to transfer the management of these systems to local-level institutions. The agricultural breakthrough achieved in West Bengal recently points to the efficacy of decentralized management of infrastructure like irrigation (Sen 1993).

In addition to the involvement of the WUAs, the ownership of canal networks (starting with the distributaries) through 'water bonds' should be placed high on the agenda for reforming the irrigation sector (Gulati *et al.* 1994). Another complementary policy reform often advocated is the establishment of tradeable water rights (Rosegrant and Binswanger 1994; Saleth 1996). Markets in tradeable rights, it is argued, would induce water users to consider the opportunity cost of water and thus improve the efficiency of water use. It is true that improvement in irrigation technology for conveyance, diversion and metering; institutional improvement in the management of irrigation systems and development of community organizations to manage water allocation will facilitate the effective development of markets in tradeable water rights (Rosegrant and Binswanger 1994). These major institutional reforms need to be accomplished before privatization of irrigation becomes a workable alternative (Vaidyanathan 1999; see also Chapter 18).

Making Groundwater Markets Equitable

In the case of groundwater resources, the area irrigated in some areas is apparently turning out to be larger than the estimated potential, despite the intensive use of water per unit of land. This may be attributable, in no small measure, to the prevailing system of pricing electricity, which has induced overdrawing of water. As in the case of surface water, both equity and productivity have suffered in respect of groundwater exploitation.

The recent proliferation of groundwater markets has no doubt made water accessible to the small farmers in certain situations. For example, in certain areas of eastern UP, water sold accounted for the bulk of the area irrigated from tubewells (58 per cent), marginal farmers being the main purchasers of water (57 per cent of the total water purchased) and medium farmers, the largest sellers (Shankar 1992). The existing system of pricing electricity has made the extraction of water cheaper and thus the market rates for the sale of water may be lower than what they would have been, if the pricing of electricity were volumetric (Shah 1993). Even so, the prevailing rates in most cases in eastern India are found to be much higher than warranted by the costs of extraction, especially when water is sold by the big farmers to the economically and socially disadvantaged ones (Pant 1991).

Even though public tubewells cannot be targeted strictly to small and marginal farmers, they still hold a promise in areas where investment in pumping water is beyond the means of most of the individual farmers. However, owing to various inefficiencies in management, the utilization of capacity for public tubewells has been very low and operating costs very high, resulting in much higher costs per hectare than from private tubewells, electric or diesel (Prasad and Sharma 1991).

The solution lies basically in making exploitation of groundwater attractive for small farmers through consolidation of holdings and liberal provision of credit and technical services for drilling, etc. to such resource-poor farmers on a preferential basis. A two-stage consolidation of holdings, whereby not only the fragments of individual holdings are brought together but several small holdings, so consolidated, are also brought together to form viable blocks of land, can induce small farmers to form water cooperatives. Such cooperatives are already working in quite a few places, including on blocks of land allotted to the socially and economically weaker sections. Such measures will reduce the dependence of small and marginal farmers on groundwater markets and, in the process, make these markets less inequitable.

8

Rural Credit Reforms

Major Issues of Concern

There is a general consensus in the literature on the major policy issues, especially on those bearing on the viability of the rural credit institutions. Restoration of their health and improving their economic viability has to be an overriding goal. Equitable access to credit continues to be a major concern, which must be addressed vigorously, particularly because there is no inherent conflict between the objectives of viability and equity. Further, the need to enhance the developmental role of rural banking institutions cannot be overemphasized, if they have to cope with the emerging challenges effectively. Finally, it would be necessary to initiate processes for ensuring the effective participation of farmers in the pursuit of the above objectives through innovative methods such as group-lending, on the pattern of self-help groups (SHGs), with a view to reducing transaction costs, ensuring credit-worthiness through 'joint liability', and improving repayment performance. Only then will a healthy and dynamic rural credit system flourish.

Expansion of Institutional Credit

The most distinguishing feature of rural credit since independence has been its phenomenal expansion from the institutional sources. Four phases can easily be marked in this regard. In the first period lasting for nearly two decades from the early 1950s to the late 1960s, the major policy objective was replacement of the informal sources of credit which had been exploitative in respect of terms and conditions, including the interest rates charged, even though the informal sources are considered to be convenient in certain respects even to this day by the farmers. The second phase started with the nationalization of leading commercial banks in the immediate post-green revolution period in the late 1960s and continued up to the early 1980s. During this phase there was a massive expansion in the branches of commercial banks in rural areas; agriculture was regarded as a priority sector for commercial bank lending; and a number of schemes for mandatory lending on concessional terms were launched. This phase took a decisive turn in the early 1980s with the beginning of the Sixth Five Year Plan, when a nation-wide poverty alleviation programme, namely, Integrated Rural Development Programme (IRDP), was launched with a sizeable subsidy on asset-endowment for the rural poor. This phase, especially, in the late 1980s, was characterized by growing overdues in respect of loan repayment, loan-waivers, and write-offs, resulting in the unviability and sickness of the formal rural credit institutions. In the post-reform phase starting from the early 1990s, the major concern has ostensibly been the viability of credit institutions, but in practice this has been side-stepped and there has been a retrogression in credit policy leading to the neglect of agricultural lending, notably in the backward regions and for the small and marginal farmers (Mujumdar 2001; Shetty 2003).

During the period of nearly five decades since the early 1950s, a good part of the increase in institutional credit merely substituted the credit from the informal sources. This is probably why the impact of expansion of institutional credit on the growth in agricultural output is found to be modest (Binswanger and Khandker 1992), even though the bulk of this credit was used for financing current inputs as well as investment in minor irrigation, farm implements, etc. However, part of the credit was used to finance inputs like tractors, which merely replaced bullocks and human labour without resulting in an increase in output (Binswanger and Khandker 1992). This inference is strengthened by the fact that the bulk of the term credit from the commercial banks was availed of by big farmers. The availability of cheap credit for big farmers has expectedly led to the increasing substitution of capital for labour in agriculture.

The share of institutional sources in the total rural credit rose from around 12 per cent in 1951–2 to over 63 per cent in the 1980s (Desai 1988). According to the All India Debt and Investment Survey, 1991, the institutional agencies accounted for two-thirds of total borrowings (NABARD 2001a). But, the impact of this development on the informal rural credit market is not known. However, one should expect this to have made the terms and conditions less stringent in the informal credit market, with a softening impact on the rates of interest charged. These aspects need to be investigated.

The expansion of commercial banks in rural areas has been instrumental in mopping up rural savings significantly, the credit–deposit ratio being significantly less than unity. The disparity in the rural–urban saving rates came down during this period, even though the potential for mobilizing rural savings has not yet been fully exploited.

Access to Institutional Credit

Regional Disparities

Pre-reform Period

The avowed objective of nationalization of major commercial banks was to make credit easily accessible to the regions and classes of farmers, who had been inadequately served earlier. Ironically, the proliferation of branches of commercial banks and the expansion of credit seem to have occurred basically around the areas, where banking infrastructure had already been well developed. Under these circumstances, the emergence of commercial banks as the dominant suppliers of agricultural credit led to a skewness in the distribution of credit as between different regions. This being mainly a supply-led phenomenon, there does not seem to have been adequate adjustment to the emerging demand for rural credit from different regions in the country. For example, in the mid-1980s, the southern region alone with only 19 per cent of the cultivated area in the country accounted for 28 per cent of the rural branches of commercial banks, 23 per cent of the deposits, and one-third of the credit in the country with a very high credit–deposit ratio of 95 per cent (Rao 1994). The per capita advances were the lowest in the eastern region and were more than twice as high in the western and southern regions.

The slow growth of short-term credit over the 1980s seems to have caused an imbalance between the demand for and supply of such credit, especially in the less developed regions, where the banking infrastructure is not well developed. Whereas in the mid-1970s the total crop loans from all financial institutions to agriculture could cover nearly 47 per cent of the cost on five inputs (chemical fertilizers, irrigation charges, electricity, pesticides and insecticides, and diesel oil), these loans could hardly cover more than 37 per cent of the cost on such inputs in the mid-1980s (Rath 1989).

As noted earlier, over the 1980s, the consumption of fertilizers increased at a faster rate in the eastern and western regions than the national average. The output of foodgrains also increased at a faster rate in the eastern region than the national average (Rao 1994). Despite this, the share of the western as well as the eastern states in the short-term institutional credit declined (Rath 1989). It appears that the share of short-term loans relative to the share of fertilizers came down significantly in the eastern and the western states.

Whereas in the relatively developed states like Gujarat and Maharashtra, part of the gap between the demand for and supply of short-term credit may have been met from the farmers' own surpluses, in the less developed states such an imbalance could have led to a greater recourse to informal sources for meeting the needs for production credit. As it is, the dependence of many of the poorer states on non-institutional sources for cash loans was much higher than the national average (Haque and Verma 1988).

Regional disparities in the access to credit from commercial banks come out sharply when we consider the distribution of outstanding direct finance from these institutions. The southern region alone accounted for 73 per cent of short-term loans outstanding and 52 per cent of total loans outstanding in the country in the mid-1980s. The eastern and central states with nearly 42 per cent of the cropped area of the country accounted for only about 24 per cent of the total loans outstanding (Dadibhavi 1988).

Post-reform Period

There was a retrogression in the supply of commercial bank credit in the post-reform period of the 1990s. Shetty (2003) brings out the skewness in the distribution of commercial bank credit in the post-reform period of 1990s. The number of rural branches of commercial banks in the country declined from over 35,000 in the early 1990s to 32,423 by March 2002 through mergers and swapping of rural branches. Correspondingly, the share of agriculture in total bank credit (both direct and indirect) declined sharply from a peak of 15.9 per cent in March 1990 to 9.6 per cent by March 2001. The credit–deposit ratio of rural branches declined steeply from over 97 per cent in the early 1990s to around 49 per cent in March 2002. The failure of scheduled commercial banks to expand their credit base for agriculture is reflected in a significant reduction in the number of agricultural loan accounts from the peak of 24.5 million in March 1996 to 19.8 million by March 2001.

The decline in the credit–deposit ratios has been much steeper in the backward states and regions: In the eastern region, the credit–deposit ratio dropped from 54 per cent in March 1981 to 37 per cent in March 2001; in the central region (Madhya Pradesh and Uttar Pradesh), it dropped from 50 per cent in March 1991 to 33 per cent by March 2001; and in the north-eastern region from 50–28 per cent over the same period (Shetty 2003).

The share of agriculture in bank credit which, as noted above, had slipped to below 10 per cent in March 2001, has recovered somewhat in the subsequent period but is still well below the prescribed share of 18 per cent. The Rural Infrastructure Development Fund (RIDF) was launched in the mid-1990s to utilise part of such shortfall in commercial bank credit to agriculture for financing infrastructure development projects with matching contributions from the states. But the progress of the scheme has been very slow despite this becoming an easier alternative to direct lending for agriculture. Thus, even after accounting for RIDF allocations, public investment in agriculture has slackened (Reddy 2001). Since 1995 National Bank for Agriculture and Rural Development (NABARD) has accumulated Rs 18,000 crores under RIDF, but its utilization is hardly 30 per cent of the total (Mujumdar 2001).

Size-wise Disparities

Pre-reform Period

Whereas regional disparities in the access to institutional credit for agriculture seem to have increased following the nationalization of major commercial banks, the disparities between different size-groups of farms show a mixed picture during this period. Institutional credit advanced to small and marginal farmers (below two hectares), both from the primary agricultural societies and scheduled commercial banks, increased at a faster rate than that advanced to farmers holding above two hectares during the 1970s and the 1980s (Haque and Verma 1988). As a result, small and marginal farmers operating 26.3 per cent of the total operated area in the country accounted for as much as 42.6 per cent of the total supply of institutional credit. It is significant that the share of credit for large farmers was also high relative to their share in the operated area, whereas the share for medium farmers was significantly lower than their share in the operated area (Desai 1988).

A note of caution: these data at the aggregate level conceal a number of features which are special and even disquieting. In the first place, the 'high share' of small and marginal farmers is apparently explained, in a large measure, by the IRDP loans. Second, as noted earlier, certain states, especially the southern ones, have accounted for a disproportionately large share in the institutional credit and the average size of farm in some of these states is much lower than the national average, which may result in a large share for small farms at the national level. For example, the average farm size in Kerala is 0.43 hectares and in Tamil Nadu, 1.07 hectares, as against the All India average of 1.82 hectares (Directorate of Economics and Statistics 1987). As noted before, these two states together accounted for as much as 22.3 per cent of the total short-term credit (Rath 1989). The available data also show that small and marginal farmers in these two states accounted for over three-fourths of short-term credit advanced by commercial banks.

Third, only a small proportion of small landholders are members of the cooperatives and this proportion increases steeply with the increase in the size of holding. Only about 30 per cent of the landholders below one hectare were members of the primary cooperative societies in 1981, whereas in the case of farmers above four hectares almost all of them were members. Further, the proportion of members borrowing is also small among those holding below one hectare. As a result, only about 10.7 per cent of landholders below one hectare borrowed from cooperatives as against 41.3 per cent in the case of big farmers (Rath 1989). In many of the eastern states, the proportion of landholders borrowing from cooperatives was lower than the national average.

Finally, because of the mandatory and concessional lending to small and marginal farmers, several middle and even large farmers manage to get sizeable loans in the name of small farmers, thus inflating the amount of credit extended to 'small and marginal farmers'. This has resulted, inter alia, in a high level of advances per hectare for them which declines steeply as the size of holding increases (Rath 1989).

Since most smallholders are not covered by cooperatives, they depend on non-institutional sources for their credit needs. For example, in 1981, those with assets below Rs 10,000 depended on non-institutional sources to the extent of 67.5–92 per cent of their total borrowings, whereas those with assets above Rs 1 lakh depended on such sources only to the extent of 5–24 per cent of their total borrowings (Haque and Verma 1988). Although those with smaller assets borrow significantly from friends and relatives, yet their dependence on landlords, moneylenders, and traders, whose terms and conditions are onerous, is much greater. A significant aspect of inequity is that a large proportion of loans is cornered by big farmers, particularly term credit at lower rates of interest, which they re-lend at higher rates of interest in the informal market. The large overdues among these farmers may indeed reflect their recycling of credit in the informal market.

Post-reform Period

The experience in this regard in the post-reform period is most distressing. The share of farmers below 2.5 acres in the number of accounts (in terms of loans issued) declined rapidly from 48 per cent in 1990–1 to 40 per cent in the 1990s. Correspondingly, the percentage share in terms of the amount involved declined rather steeply in the 1990s (Shetty 2003). According to the Expert Committee on Rural Credit, while there was an overall increase in the credit outstanding by 29.2 per cent for the period 1997–9, the outstanding amount for small loanees increased by a mere 5.2 per cent (NABARD 2001a).

The number of small bank accounts, that is, those with credit limits of Rs 25,000 and less declined by 253 lakhs between March 1992 and March 2001, while the borrowal accounts with higher credit limits of above Rs 25,000 have shown an increase of 118 lakhs during the same period. As a result, the advances for weaker sections have steadily declined from 9.7 per cent of net bank credit in March 1991 to 7.3 per cent in March 2001, as against the prescribed share of 10 per cent. Similarly, the number of borrowers under the Differential Interest Rate (DRI) Scheme declined from 35 lakhs in March 1991 to a very low of 11 lakhs by March 1999, and their share in total outstanding advances fell from 0.7–0.2 per cent (Shetty 2003).

Viability

In the initial stages of development, when there is a rapid expansion of services from banks and other credit institutions in rural areas, there is bound to be a rise in the unit cost of services provided, because the overhead costs are high when these institutions have to deal with a large number of small depositors and borrowers and are unable to provide services of reasonable quality by attracting personnel of requisite ability and experience. The deficiencies are particularly glaring in the case of cooperative banks, which are essentially rural-based. For example, according to the Agricultural Credit Review Committee (RBI 1989), even though the Primary Agricultural Cooperatives (PACs) had the highest income per Rs 100 of loans outstanding during the mid-1980s, they showed the highest losses basically on account of high financial and transaction costs.

The high costs of rural banking can be justified, up to a point, when one takes a long-term view with due regard for the developmental role of these institutions, as the benefits in the long-run from rural banking can be quite high. Also, the objective of assisting the economically and socially weaker sections may entail some costs to the society for a certain period. In the short run, such costs could be met through cross-subsidization and, to some extent, through an outright subsidy by the Government in the expectation that these institutions will become self-sustaining as economic growth in rural areas picks up and that the subsidies to the weaker sections would be phased out.

The experience since the major commercial banks were nationalized and agriculture was treated as a priority sector for lending demonstrates that the costs of development and assistance to the weaker sections are now surpassed by the costs arising from mismanagement and wilful default on the part of those who have the capacity to repay the loans. The rural credit system is now threatened by these avoidable costs in the form of rising overdues, unduly low lending rates for bigger loans and deficiencies in internal management, within a policy environment-cum-political culture that encourages lending for not-so-productive activities at subsidized rates, discourages professional approach and follow-up in lending, and promotes wilful default.

In the period following the green revolution, there has been a sustained, though modest, increase in agricultural output per head; the proportion of gross domestic product (GDP) from agriculture has come down significantly; and there is diversification of income-earning opportunities in rural areas, signifying the emergence of new avenues for profitable absorption of rural credit as well as the enhanced ability to repay loans taken for agricultural and other purposes. Further, thanks to the overall development achieved, the technical and managerial capabilities that the system can now offer are much better than those in the 1960s. The non-viability of rural credit institutions is, therefore, explained basically in terms of the prevailing policy environment-cum-political culture that prevents the harnessing of techno-economic opportunities opened up for viable banking in rural areas.

The credit-deposit ratios of the public sector banks in rural and semi-urban areas were significantly lower than the average in the 1970s but rose significantly in the 1980s, the credit-deposit ratio for the rural areas approaching the average ratio (RBI 1989). Thus, so far as the volume of business in rural areas is concerned, the situation has, of late, been favourable for reducing unit costs by realizing the economies of scale, albeit within the limits imposed by the number of branches in relation to population.

Contrary to the general belief, there had been a steady improvement in the recovery performance of the commercial banks over a greater part of the 1980s. Recovery of loans as percentage of demand (current plus accumulated) had been significantly higher for short-term loans than for term-loans contracted essentially by big farmers. However, the rate of recovery improved in both the cases by about 5 percentage points between 1981 and 1987 (RBI 1989). The position was reversed by the end of the 1980s when the loan-waiver scheme was introduced. However, according to a recent NABARD study (Gulati and Bathla 2002), bad debts as a percentage of total loans outstanding across rural financial institutions in the country improved towards the mid-1990s to the level obtaining in the mid-1980s, but slipped again in 1996 and 1997.

Corresponding to the improvement in the recovery performance, there was a simultaneous decline in the percentage of overdues to demand in the case of commercial banks. However, there had been a significant rise in overdues in the case of regional rural banks (RRBs), which showed the highest level of overdues (51 per cent) among all the agencies. Even though PACs and Land Development Bank (LDBs) showed some decline in overdues in the 1980s, the overdues in the mid-1980s were still very high when compared to their position in the mid-1970s. These overdues for various agencies, ranging from 40 per cent to 50 per cent in the mid-1980s, were, according to the Agricultural Credit Review Committee, unduly high by any standards. The Committee had, therefore, stipulated that credit institutions and all their branches should raise their recovery performance under current demand to at least 80 per cent by June 1992 (RBI 1989).

The overdues position was particularly bad in the north-eastern and eastern regions of the country, where the overdues for various agencies ranged from 57 to over 80 per cent. Southern and northern regions can be regarded as comparatively better performing areas, whereas the central and western regions fell in between. Thus there was a broad correspondence between the infrastructural, institutional, and technological development of the regions, on the one hand, and the level of overdues, on the other. North-eastern and eastern states were poorly placed in respect of infrastructural development, land tenure systems, and the level of new technology used in agriculture. On the other hand, northern and southern states were much better placed with regard to the level of irrigation and rural electrification, land tenure systems, development of credit and marketing institutions, and the extent of use of new technology in agriculture.

The Report of the Agricultural Credit Review Committee pointed out that the lowest level of overdues (34 per cent), in the mid-1980s, related to the highly irrigated/ assured rainfall areas, whereas the highest level (60.8 per cent) was found in the hilly and tribal areas. The level of overdues for the moderately irrigated areas was found to be 50.7 per cent and for the less monetized and unirrigated areas, quite high (57.7 per cent). The above regional pattern with regard to recovery performance and overdues remained broadly the same in the late 1990s (NABARD 2001b).

The study conducted by the Agricultural Credit Review Committee reveals that in the case of large farmers borrowing from commercial banks, the incidence of overdues is higher than the average and, in the case of the marginal farmers it was the lowest. A reverse position held in the case of the PACs, where the incidence of overdues was the lowest in the case of large farmers and the highest for marginal farmers.

The factors bearing on the viability of credit institutions in rural areas can be traced broadly to three sources. The factors which are internal to the management of credit institutions can be grouped into one category. These range from the preparation of viable credit plans in the context of area development plans to the technical examination of the specific loan proposals from the point of view of their bankability, decisions as to the quantum of loan to be advanced that is reasonable or economically viable, follow-up measures to ensure proper utilization of loan amount, realistic repayment schedules, and others.

The second group of factors are those which are external to the credit institutions and which determine the profitability of investment. These range from the agro-climatic conditions to land tenures, infrastructural development, technological practices, price levels, etc. Even though these factors are beyond the control of credit institutions, the latter can nevertheless adjust, in principle, their lending practices to these varying circumstances.

The third group of factors are those which are also external to, and beyond the control of, the credit system but, unlike the second group of factors, work as constraints on the credit system. These relate to the policies on mandatory or directed credit, subsidies and lending rates, remissions on recoveries and loan-waivers. Political and administrative interference with the day-to-day functioning of credit institutions also belongs to this last category.

As analysed earlier, the economic environment has become conducive, over a period of time, to viable banking in rural areas on account of infrastructural development, institutional changes, and extension of new technologies. The factors 'internal' to the credit system are no doubt conditioned, to a large extent, by the structure of credit institutions such as lack of competition among banks, the rules governing the conditions of service of employees, the degree of managerial autonomy enjoyed by the institutions, etc. But, basically, it is the lending policies prescribed from above and the administrative and political interference that account for the growing unviability of rural credit institutions in recent years. In the short run, at any rate, these issues should be addressed with the highest priority.

Prospects

The prospects in agriculture in the post-green revolution period so far have been marked by the rising profitability of crop production involving greater use of current inputs like fertilizers and private investment in tubewells for irrigation. The production- as well as term-credit advanced has been conditioned largely by such requirements. The agricultural output-mix is likely to undergo drastic changes in future in response to the rising per capita income in the country as well as the emerging export prospects consequent upon the liberalization of foreign trade. In general, the farm products, the demand for which is highly income-elastic, whether at home or abroad, will attract greater resources from the farmers. These are: dairying and other livestock products, horticulture, farm forestry, and agro-processing.

The new activities will, in general, be land-saving but capital-intensive and skill-intensive. The investment requirements will, therefore, be much higher than before. Altogether, the scenario facing the credit system is that of more remunerative agriculture expanding at a faster rate than to date. It is also likely to be, on the whole, less risky in so far as livestock enterprises, and even horticulture practised under controlled irrigation, would be less vulnerable to weather-shocks than crop production. Equally important from the point of view of reducing risks for the farmers as well as credit institutions is that these enterprises are more amenable to insurance against yield and price risks than crop production. However, these products being perishable, require the development of infrastructure for example, roads, maketing, storage, and processing for minimizing post-harvest losses to farmers.

The tendency of a decline in the average size of farm observed in the past is likely to persist for some time because of the ceiling on land holdings and the sub-division of land holdings owing to the continued dependence of a large proportion of population on agriculture. Small and medium but more productive and remunerative farms may become a dominant feature for quite some time in large parts of the country. Owing to the land-saving character of many of the new activities, the income-earning prospects for small farmers may improve if the requisite technical and credit support is made available. Even though there will be a significant diversification of agriculture, crop production with greater weight for non-foodgrains will continue to occupy an important place. However, there may be significant locational shifts in the growth rates of crop output, the regions where the potential still to be exploited is significant, such as the eastern Gangetic plains, experiencing a higher growth than the national average.

The implications of the emerging agricultural scenario for the functioning of rural credit institutions are obvious. The amount of loans advanced to agriculture, both short-term and long-term, may have to expand faster than in the recent past with a focus on small and medium farms and the less developed regions, where there is a large untapped potential and which are now heavily dependent on informal sources. Thanks to the rising incomes of farmers, the scope for mobilization of deposits in rural areas would be greater, apart from enhanced credit-worthiness and improved ability to repay loans. The credit institutions will have to prepare themselves for responding to the demands from the wide range of enterprises. The technical expertise needed for appraisal of schemes and follow-up is going to be far more specialized and sophisticated than before. From financing mainly production activities, the tasks will have to be diversified encompassing support for training in skills for the farmers, agro-processing, and marketing of output as well as inputs.

Policy Implications

Expansion versus Consolidation

The existing weaknesses of rural credit institutions in India are sometimes attributed to the rapid expansion of institutional credit in the post-independence period (Dandekar and Wadia 1989). However, the policies regarding mandatory lending to certain specified sectors, rates of interest charged and loan write-offs, as also political interference, are largely neutral to the rate of expansion of rural credit. Many of the observed weaknesses would have persisted even if the growth of credit were to be significantly low. On the other hand, a more rational policy framework and political will to protect the health of credit institutions can greatly strengthen the capacity of these institutions to expand credit at a faster rate to meet the growing demand.

Besides, a distinction should be made between the expansion of credit and the increase in the number of branches and staff of rural banks. Except in certain underbanked rural areas, like the eastern and north-eastern states, there is no case, at this stage, for a significant expansion in the number of branches and employees. What is needed in most cases is the upgradation of services provided through better management and training of personnel. Therefore, with regard to the volume of business (deposits as well as advances), the goal should be greater expansion; with regard to the infrastructure of these institutions, it should be consolidation.

A number of reasons dictate why agricultural credit must expand at a faster rate than before. In the first place, as rightly pointed out by Dandekar and Wadia (1989) and many others, despite the rapid expansion of credit, the dependence of small and marginal farmers and of less developed regions on the informal sources for credit is still quite high. Therefore, a good part of the increase in credit may have to be directed for quite some time merely to substitute for credit from the informal sources.

Second, the realized growth rates of agricultural output have so far been lower than the targeted rates. If the export objective is taken into account, the targeted growth rates of agricultural output have to be significantly higher than before.

Third, the expected changes in the agricultural product-mix favouring larger investment requirements would generate greater demand for credit to purchase current inputs as well as to finance long-term investments.

Finally, the declining trend in real public investment in agriculture has to be reversed if the production potential in the future is not to be adversely affected. As public investment picks up and profitability of private investment rises, so will the demand for term-credit for financing investment increase.

Ensuring Equitable Access to Institutional Credit

In view of the scarcity of credit and the exorbitant rates of interest charged in the informal rural credit markets, the small and marginal farmers would stand to benefit more from the easy and timely availability of credit from the institutional sources than from the low interest rates charged (Rao 1975). Since the interest rates charged in the informal rural credit markets are exorbitantly high, ranging from 60–100 per cent in certain parts of the country (Bandyopadhyay 1984), concessional interest rates charged by the institutional sources, even for the large farmers, introduce an unduly large differential between the market and the official rates; thereby providing incentives for the rent-seeking middlemen to corner institutional credit at concessional rates and re-lend it to the weaker sections at market rates.

Past experience has shown that the major benefits from concessional lending by the institutional sources have accrued to the large farmers (Nickel and Khan 1993). Since large farmers can meet their investment requirements from their own surpluses as well as from institutional and other sources at the going rates of interest, there is no justification in giving them loans at concessional rates of interest. The perpetuation of concessional lending for them would violate the norms of equity as well as viability of credit institutions. As pointed out earlier, this would also have adverse allocational effects—resulting in high capital-intensity and slow employment generation in agriculture. It would, therefore, be desirable to do away with the concessional rates of interest for large farmers. Such a step would also contribute to improving the viability of rural banking, through a rise in interest income and an improvement in the repayment performance, as the cost of delayed repayment would rise.

It would, however, be essential to ensure the availability of institutional credit to the small, marginal, and medium farmers through appropriate rationing of credit, for example, by stipulating that the institutional credit advanced to them should rise at a rate necessary to meet their growing production and investment requirements by reducing significantly their dependence on the informal sources. In the absence of such a direction, the natural tendency on the part of the banks would be to try to reduce their unit costs by concentrating on a small number of big borrowers through the diversion of resources from a large number of small borrowers.

The Narasimham Committee (1991) recommended that the directed credit 'should cover a redefined priority sector, consisting of the small and marginal farmers, tiny sector of industry, small business and transport operators, village and cottage industries, rural artisans and other weaker sections' and that 'the credit target for this redefined priority sector henceforth be fixed at 10 per cent of aggregate bank credit, which, the Committee has observed, would be broadly in line with the credit flows to these sectors at present'. This recommendation for pegging vaguely the share of the redefined priority sector around its existing share in total credit does not take into account the need to replace rapidly the informal sources, on which these sectors are at present heavily dependent. By clubbing the small and marginal farmers with a number of other categories, one cannot be certain that even the existing share of these farmers would be protected, let alone increasing it to meet their growing demand. However, this particular recommendation of the Committee was not accepted by the Reserve Bank of India.

The demand for credit from the weaker sections, being related mostly to the immediate and unavoidable commitments, is inelastic, so major procedural reforms would be needed to enable the institutional sources to meet such requirements in time and in a flexible manner. Also, non-credit interventions by the government, such as provision of minimum health care facilities and extension of the public distribution system to the weaker sections, would be necessary to reduce their abject dependence on the informal sources, so that they can borrow from the institutional sources on reasonable terms (Sarap 1991).

We have noted earlier the emerging imbalances between the demand for and supply of institutional credit in the less developed areas like the eastern region, where agricultural growth has been picking up. In view of the expected agricultural breakthrough in such areas, their share of institutional credit should be stepped up by strengthening banking infrastructure in rural areas, where necessary.

Improving the Viability of Credit Institutions

We have seen that the growing non-viability of the formal rural credit institutions has been associated with inequity and is indeed a consequence of subsidized credit and large overdues, the benefits of which have accrued mostly to prosperous and influential farmers. Cheap credit is at once a cause of non-viability and inefficiency in resource allocation. A major casualty of overdues and indiscriminate loan write-offs is the recycling of credit, the losers being present as well as prospective borrowers. Therefore, improving viability of credit institutions should be foremost on the policy agenda in the interest of growth, equity, and efficiency.

As discussed in the previous section, the emerging agricultural scenario in India is favourable for viable banking because of the prospects of a rise in the profitability of investment and the consequent improvement in the farmers' capacity to repay loans. However, the policy framework has to be made favourable for viable banking in rural areas. With 43 per cent of their branches in rural areas, commercial banks could mobilize only 12.5 per cent of their total deposits from rural areas in the late 1980s (RBI, 1989). Deposit mobilization has suffered in the recent period, particularly in the case of PACs, partly on account of an erosion in the confidence of the depositors in these institutions, and partly because of the growing attractiveness of alternative channels of investment. Reducing overdues and losses would, by itself, restore the confidence of the depositors. The average return on rural lending by commercial banks will have to be improved as it had been only about 11.5 per cent as against 14 per cent for non-rural lending in 1986 (RBI, 1989).

The managements of credit institutions have to be accorded greater autonomy by doing away with administrative and political interference in their day-to-day functioning. The managerial cadre and the other staff have to be professionalized through new recruitment and appropriate training. Loan advances should be based on a professional appraisal of projects, not on the targets for disbursement of credit, as is often the practice now. Loan sanctions should be accompanied by professional follow-up to ensure profitability of investment by reducing mortality and sickness rates in these ventures.

While directed credit for self-employment programmes, in keeping with the targets for poverty reduction, should continue, a number of changes are urgently called for in the selection of beneficiaries, manner of preparing project proposals, and methods for follow-up. There should be a direct relationship between the clients and the banks.

These reforms would presuppose considerable flexibility in the allocation of resources between self-employment and wage-employment activities in different regions, keeping in view the levels of infrastructural development. This would also require formulation of schemes as part of area planning by the elected local institutions with the involvement of non-governmental organizations (NGOs). The viability of poverty alleviation programmes will improve, if there is effective communication about alternative income-earning opportunities available and procedures for availing of loans. Encouragement of lending for group-oriented schemes would also be a step in the right direction.

A right policy framework is only a necessary precondition. Its effectiveness depends on the political will that can be brought to bear on its implementation. Public financial institutions in rural areas can still be made to function efficiently with a social purpose, if sufficient autonomy is given to them through de-bureaucratization and de-politicization. This model is worth a trial, because perpetuation of the existing inefficiencies would be fatal to growth as well as social justice. This is the only course left, if privatization of public financial institutions in rural areas is to be avoided at this stage.

Enhancing the Developmental Role of Rural Banking

The task of mobilizing deposits from the resourceful farmers receives the highest priority from a typical banker in rural areas. Extending loans to the 'credit-worthy' and 'progressive' farmers, who are generally the large farmers, gets the next priority. In either case, the focus is on the relatively well-to-do sections, their poor repayment performance notwithstanding. Thus, the bankers' preoccupation is basically with the current commercial transactions at the counter. Planning for future and concern for weaker sections are usually not high on their agenda (Dasgupta 1993).

A forward-looking approach is essential for any imaginative banking. This is all the more important for public financial institutions, whose avowed objective is to assist in the development of backward regions and weaker sections. The preparation of district credit plans by the lead banks and the service area approach, whereby each village in the country had been assigned to a single bank for coordinating all the banking activities, did have some elements of planning but has not proved effective.

At least four major areas of long-term planning for rural banking can be delineated. These are:

a. Identification of potentially bankable activities in the light of the resource potential of each region;

b. Collaboration with scientific and technical institutions for the generation and dissemination of new technologies by building upon the local people's own innovations;

c. Strategies to reduce risks (for example, by supporting projects for water-harvesting, watershed management, and soil conservation in ecologically fragile areas) and to cope with risks through venture capital and insurance promotion, where viable; and

d. Planning and supporting activities for training in skills for farmers as well as for centres providing various services (Gupta, Anil 1991).

As noted earlier, only about 10 per cent of small and marginal farmers borrow from cooperatives. Rural banks have to play a much greater role than at present not only in providing production and investment credit directly to the poor farmers but also in supporting pilot projects for identifying productive enterprises for the resource-poor farmers. They should provide extension services and carry out evaluations, so that the experience gained is used for selecting projects capable of being replicated. Thanks to their resources, skills, and organizational capabilities, rural banks could become active agents in the fulfilment of the national objective of lifting up the disadvantaged sections of farmers.

Long-term planning on the above lines, with a focus on the backward regions and weaker sections by committing the needed resources, has to become a major component of the policy framework and guidelines for the public financial institutions, so that it becomes an important criterion for their performance evaluation. For example, in the performance evaluation of the banks and the individual functionaries, greater weightage should be given to areas where the performance has so far been poor, for example, in mobilization of deposits from the weaker sections and recovery of loans from the affluent farmers (Dasgupta 1993).

Enlisting Participation of Client-farmers

Feedback regarding the local resource-potential and the ongoing innovations at the grass roots level, and vigilance to ensure the proper utilization of funds are possible only by enlisting the participation of client-farmers. The proliferation of various schemes has given rise to the emergence of 'enterprising' middlemen, who have access to the necessary information and possess the skills for getting over the procedural hurdles in the way of sanctions for schemes. However, their methods are predatory and exploitative, so the targeted farmers receive a very small portion of the benefits intended for them. It would be necessary to formalize such services for consultancy, delivery of inputs, and even sub-contracting of the task for loan recovery (Gupta, Anil 1991; Dasgupta 1993). To a large extent, group-oriented activities, including group-loaning schemes, may serve this purpose. Involvement of people's committees by the banks may be desirable for activities ranging from the preparation of long-term plans to loan-recovery drives. Participation of NGOs, women activists, thrift societies etc., especially in the backward regions, would contribute to reducing transaction costs to the banks as well as clients and would ensure better repayment performance (Gupta, Anil 1991; Mujumdar 2001).

All this calls for a reorientation of the outlook of banks, posting of competent personnel in rural areas, and a system of incentives and rewards related to the performance of the specific tasks having a bearing on long-term development and social justice (Dasgupta 1993).

Emergence of Self-help Groups

The recent emergence of SHGs linked with banks holds considerable promise, as they have been encouraging savings from members, promoting viable enterprises for self-employment and showing an exceptionally good repayment performance. Since over 90 per cent of such micro credit institutions are being run by women, they have also become vehicles of social change (Shetty 2003).

However, the amount of credit disbursed to them through linkage so far is miniscule (Mujumdar 2001). Also, the distribution of such institutions is highly skewed now, southern states accounting for 78 per cent, with Andhra Pradesh alone accounting for more than one-half of the total number of SHGs in the country (Shetty 2003). Even so, the experience with SHGs in the country so far does offer valuable insights and lessons for experimenting with innovative institutions so as to link mainstream financial institutions with small farmers and other weaker sections for promoting thrift, viable farm as well as non-farm enterprises, and satisfactory repayment performance (Puhazhendhi and Satyasai 2000).

However, care has to be taken to see that the SHGs, especially those to be sponsored under the newly launched self-employment programme for example, Swarnjayanti Gram Swarozgar Yojana (SGSY), do not promote subsidy culture like the earlier poverty alleviation programmes (NABARD 2001a). In any case, the success of the SHGs on a wider scale would depend crucially on the strategy for raising agricultural productivity through the creation of appropriate infrastructure for irrigation, agro-processing, and the rural non-farm sector which will raise demand for credit for productive purposes (Jayaraman 2001).

Section III

Food Security

development—development accompanied by social justice—will enhance the ability of the poorer population to withstand the rigours of life. It will improve their staying power, thereby reducing pressure on the environment, for example, on land, water, and forests.

This definition of sustainable development does not centre around the so-called 'trade off' between present and future consumption. It does not rigidly say that the concern for meeting present needs will necessarily undermine the capacity of future generations to meet their needs. It only says that methods for meeting the present needs should not be at the cost of the future generation's ability to meet its needs. To give a simple example, in drought-prone areas, the management of resources is such that even the present needs are not met. People, in fact, migrate to other regions to meet their immediate needs.

Yet we have seen models—Ralegan Siddhi, Adgaon or Sukhomajri—places which lie in the very same dry belt, where, due to proper management of resources, not only has the capacity to meet basic needs of the present generation improved, but they have also been able to preserve the stock of natural capital or even enhance it for future generations. This complementary relationship between the present and the future arising from the methods of management of resources is extremely important and is not precluded in this definition. But at the same time, it should be noted that it is only places like Sukhomajri, Adgaon, or Ralegan Siddhi, which have been lucky to have motivated and committed leaders, who have been able to organize the people to manage their resources in a sustainable way. Otherwise, the overall situation is depressing.

This definition does not also look at the capabilities of future generations merely in terms of the capabilities of the present generation. It allows for the improvement of knowledge. Technologies which may not be known or available at present, may become available only to future generations. Therefore, it talks about the ability of future generations to meet their requirements. We have to allow for the possibility that with technological improvements, more choices will be open for the future generations. The abilities of the future generations are, therefore, not to be looked at purely from a static angle, that is, in the light of present knowledge and present stock of resources.

Operationally, there are three major indicators of sustainability in agriculture in the drought-prone areas. The first is the groundwater table. In all the drought-prone areas evaluated recently, the water table

9

Declining Per Capita Demand for Foodgrains in Rural India

Causes and Implications

Introduction

While some of the projections in regard to the demand for foodgrains in India in the next 20 years have been mind-boggling (for a comment on some such projections, see, Murty 1998), scholars like R. Radhakrishna and C. Ravi (1992), Praduman Kumar, and V.C. Mathur (1996), and K.N. Murty (1999), in the recent period have come out with a sobering—though startling—finding, based on the National Sample Survey (NSS) data, that the per capita household demand for foodgrains has been declining. Since per capita income has been rising, this would have led to some rise in per capita demand for foodgrains. Moreover, the prices of foodgrains relative to the index of non-foodgrains prices have declined over a greater part of the last two decades, which would have also resulted in some rise in the demand for foodgrains. If, despite these factors favouring increased demand, the actual per capita demand for foodgrains has been declining, there must be powerful forces operating in our economic system which are dampening the demand for foodgrains.

Radhakrishna and Ravi (1992) and Murty (1999) in their studies mentioned earlier have attributed this dampening demand to the changes in tastes and preferences of consumers away from foodgrains. There can, no doubt, be such changes in tastes and preferences. But have we exhausted all the identifiable economic factors in explaining the observed decline in per capita demand for foodgrains? It is proposed to probe into some such factors—other than changes in tastes and preferences—in this chapter. Needless to say, an understanding of the factors at work contributing to the decline in demand for foodgrains would have important implications not only for foodgrains demand projections but also for development policies. In particular, the unearthing of some of these factors could have implications for the development of marketing infrastructure in rural areas.

Trends in Per Capita Cereal Consumption

Let us, at the outset, look at the broad trends with regard to the per capita demand for foodgrains in the rural and urban areas and the associated factors like changes in expenditure and prices, as revealed by the NSS data. For the sake of convenience, the present analysis is restricted to cereals only, as it is well-known that per capita consumption of pulses has also been declining. Over a period of two decades, that is, between 1972–3 and 1993–4, the per capita consumption of cereals has shown a steeper decline (by around 12 per cent) in rural areas than in urban areas (around 5 per cent). There is a further decline in per capita consumption in 1999–2000 (Table 9.2), despite a possible overestimation of consumption in that year. It is also significant to note that the per capita consumption of cereals in all the three periods was higher in rural when compared to urban areas. However, this rural–urban differential has come down, even though rural per capita consumption was still higher by nearly 22 per cent in 1999–2000 (Table 9.4).

There are significant regional variations in these trends. For example, states like Kerala and West Bengal where per capita consumption of cereals both in rural and urban areas was way below the national average in 1972–3, have shown a significant increase in 1993–4. On the other hand, some of the states showing a steeper decline in per capita rural consumption such as Haryana and Punjab are those where per capita consumption was higher than the national average in 1972–3, and which experienced a high rate of mechanization of agriculture (Table 9.1).

Another notable feature is that the poorest or the bottom 30 per cent of population experienced a slight increase in per capita consumption of cereals when compared to 1972–3, while the middle 40 per cent and the top 30 per cent of population have shown a decline in their per capita consumption, the decline being sharper for the top 30 per cent in both rural and urban areas. The rural–urban difference in the per capita consumption of cereals for the top 30 per cent was as high as 64 per cent in 1972–3. This remained quite high

Table 9.1: Per Capita Cereal Consumption: States

(Kg per month)

State	Rural			Urban		
	1972–3	1993–4	1999–2000	1972–3	1993–4	1999–2000
Andhra Pradesh	15.25	13.27	12.66	12.68	11.30	10.94
Assam	14.81	13.17	12.63	12.55	12.05	12.26
Bihar	15.58	14.31	13.76	13.49	12.82	12.70
Gujarat	13.32	10.66	10.19	10.77	8.96	8.49
Haryana	17.57	12.92	11.38	11.86	10.46	9.36
Karnataka	15.63	13.15	11.53	11.32	10.87	10.21
Kerala	7.97	10.11	9.89	8.17	9.46	9.25
Madhya Pradesh	17.28	14.20	12.93	12.88	11.32	11.09
Maharashtra	12.60	11.39	11.32	8.95	9.37	9.35
Orissa	15.22	15.93	15.09	13.77	13.36	14.51
Punjab	15.38	10.78	10.58	10.71	9.01	9.21
Rajasthan	18.17	14.85	14.19	13.21	11.52	11.56
Tamil Nadu	14.53	11.72	10.66	11.12	10.05	9.65
Uttar Pradesh	16.83	13.91	13.66	12.24	11.08	10.79
West Bengal	13.64	14.96	13.59	10.53	11.64	11.17
All India	15.26	13.40	12.72	11.24	10.63	10.42

Source: Government of India (GOI), National Sample Survey Organization (NSSO), 25th, 50th and 55th Rounds.

Table 9.2: Percentage Change in Cereal Consumption

State	Rural		Urban	
	1972–3 to 1993–4	1993–4 to 1999–2000	1972–3 to 1993–4	1993–4 to 1999–2000
Andhra Pradesh	–12.98	–4.63	–10.88	–3.19
Assam	–11.07	–4.09	–3.98	1.74
Bihar	–8.15	–3.83	–4.97	–0.94
Gujarat	–19.97	–4.44	–16.81	–5.25
Haryana	–26.47	–11.91	–11.80	–10.52
Karnataka	–15.87	–12.34	–3.98	–6.07
Kerala	26.85	–2.20	15.79	–2.22
Madhya Pradesh	–17.82	–8.93	–12.11	–2.03
Maharashtra	–9.60	–0.66	4.69	–0.21
Orissa	4.66	–5.27	–2.98	8.61
Punjab	–29.91	–1.89	–15.87	2.22
Rajasthan	–18.27	–4.43	–12.79	0.35
Tamil Nadu	–19.34	–9.07	–9.62	–3.98
Uttar Pradesh	–17.35	–1.80	–9.48	–2.62
West Bengal	9.68	–9.14	10.54	–4.04
All India	–12.19	–5.07	–5.43	–1.98

Source: Same as Table 9.1.

in 1993–4 at around 40 per cent and around 33 per cent in 1999–2000 (Table 9.4). These facts underscore the point that, to identify the factors accounting for the observed decline in per capita consumption of cereals in the country, one should look closely at the consumption behaviour in rural areas and among upper expenditure groups in certain states.

Table 9.3: Per Capita Cereal Consumption by Decile Group: All India

(*Kg per month*)

Decile Group	1972–3	1993–4	1999–2000
		Rural	
Lowest 30 per cent	11.36	11.76	11.44
Middle 40 per cent	15.32	13.61	12.95
Top 30 per cent	19.08	14.77	13.69
All	15.26	13.40	12.72
		Urban	
Lowest 30 per cent	10.12	10.29	10.20
Middle 40 per cent	11.78	10.94	10.69
Top 30 per cent	11.64	10.56	10.32
All	11.24	10.63	10.43

Source: Same as Table 9.1.

Table 9.4: Rural–Urban Differential in Cereal Consumption

Decile Group	Rural–Urban Differential (Per cent)		
	1972–3	1993–4	1999–2000
Lowest 30 per cent	12.25	14.29	112.18
Middle 40 per cent	30.05	24.41	121.15
Top 30 per cent	63.92	39.87	132.70
All	35.77	26.06	121.95

Source: Same as Table 9.1.

The rural–urban disparity in per capita total expenditure has widened over the last three decades. The per capita total expenditure in rural areas in 1972–3 was around 30 per cent lower than that in urban areas, but this disparity had risen to 39 per cent by 1993–4 and to 43 per cent by 1999–2000 (Table 9.6). The fact that despite the lower per capita total expenditure in rural areas when compared to urban areas in both the periods, the per capita consumption of cereals was significantly higher in rural areas points to the importance of factors other than income working in the opposite direction.

Table 9.5: Per Capita Total Expenditure (Rs) by Decile Group: All India

Decile Group	1972–3	1993–4	1999–2000
		Rural	
Lowest 30 per cent	22.04	149.70	271.18
Middle 40 per cent	37.69	240.32	424.42
Top 30 per cent	74.94	467.87	783.20
All	44.17	281.40	486.08
		Urban	
Lowest 30 per cent	29.26	207.03	379.57
Middle 40 per cent	50.47	363.91	679.21
Top 30 per cent	114.54	834.55	1563.98
All	63.33	458.04	854.75

Source: Same as Table 9.1.

Table 9.6: Rural–Urban Differential in Total Per Capita Expenditure

Decile Group	Rural–Urban Differential (Per cent of Urban)		
	1972–3	1993–4	1999–2000
Lowest 30 per cent	75.32	72.31	71.44
Middle 40 per cent	74.68	66.04	62.49
Top 30 per cent	65.43	56.06	50.08
All	69.75	61.44	56.87

Source: Same as Table 9.1.

The prices of cereals were about 11 per cent lower in rural areas when compared to urban areas in 1972–3. This rural–urban difference in cereal prices had risen to 16 per cent in 1993–4 and 1999–2000 (Table 9.8). It is significant that the rural–urban difference in the per capita consumption of cereals has narrowed down somewhat despite the rising price difference. This again underscores the importance of factors other than income and prices in explaining the rural–urban difference in cereal consumption. In all the three periods, the rural–urban disparity in cereal prices was smaller for the lower expenditure groups when compared to that for the top 30 per cent. This is understandable as the rural poor have to buy a good part of their cereal requirements from the market whereas the rural rich meet their requirements from their own produce. This is consistent with the fact noted earlier that the rural–urban difference in the per capita consumption of cereals is sharper in the case of the top expenditure group.

Table 9.7: Average Cereal Price: All India

(*Rs/Kg*)

Decile Group	1972–3	1993–4	1999–2000
		Rural	
Lowest 30 per cent	1.09	4.73	7.92
Middle 40 per cent	1.17	5.15	8.42
Top 30 per cent	1.22	5.28	8.98
All	1.17	5.08	8.47
		Urban	
Lowest 30 per cent	1.21	5.35	8.77
Middle 40 per cent	1.32	5.97	9.89
Top 30 per cent	1.40	6.82	11.77
All	1.31	6.05	10.12

Source: Same as Table 9.1.

Table 9.8: Rural–Urban Differential in Average Cereal Price: All India

Decile Group	Rural–Urban Differential (Per cent of Urban)		
	1972–3	1993–4	1999–2000
Lowest 30 per cent	90.43	88.47	90.35
Middle 40 per cent	88.91	86.24	85.19
Top 30 per cent	87.34	77.44	76.31
All	89.64	84.04	83.70

Source: Same as Table 9.1.

Factors Behind Higher Cereal Consumption in Rural Areas

To explain the higher per capita consumption of cereals in rural areas, one can think of at least four factors other than income and foodgrain prices: (a) higher prices of non-foodgrain and non-food items; (b) higher energy requirements of the rural poor due to heavy manual labour; (c) payment of wages in kind by the large farmers in the form of cooked food; and (d) the poor state of health and environment resulting in low efficiency of conversion of food into energy. While discussing the first two factors, which are quantifiable to some extent, the ideas are borrowed from a paper written in 1969 and the debate that followed (Rao 1969a; Srinivasan and Bardhan 1969; Rao 1969b).

Higher Prices of Non-foodgrains and Non-food Items

To start with the first factor, namely, the prices of goods and services—other than foodgrains—in rural areas, these goods and services range from food items such as milk, eggs, meat, and fish to a host of urban goods and services such as textiles, modern furniture, cosmetics, medicines, radio and television sets, and access to cinema houses and entertainment, to mention only a few. We do not have data readily available on rural prices of several of these urban goods of consumption. But at least in the case of some of the essential urban goods of consumption which are traditionally marketed in rural areas such as coarse cloth, edible oil, sugar, and kerosene, it would be reasonable to assume that their prices would be higher in rural areas when compared to their urban prices, at least to the same extent as the foodgrain prices in urban areas are over their rural prices. This is because transport costs and traders' margins are involved in both the cases.

For several other urban goods of consumption, rural marketing is not as well developed as the traditional foodgrain marketing in urban centres, although the position would have improved somewhat over the last few decades. As such, the rural–urban price differential in their case can be expected to be greater than for those having an established market in rural areas. Moreover, even the food basket effectively open to the rural population is restricted when compared to the one open to the urban population. The latter contains protective foods, for example, meat, eggs, milk, vegetables, fruits, etc. in a larger measure. This part of the basket is available to the urban population in a greater measure owing to the existence of a large market for these commodities. For a single village, the availability of some of these goods is restricted—even excluded in quite a few cases—because of the restricted market and the resulting diseconomies of (small) scale in marketing.

The basket of non-agricultural goods available for urban population is far more diversified because of the existence of the large market as well as the availability of necessary infrastructure leading to economies of scale in marketing. For individual villages, in a large number of cases, the availability of many of these urban goods and services is ruled out owing to the non-availability of supporting infrastructure such as electricity and roads and the resulting extreme diseconomies of (small) scale in marketing. The position has, of course, improved somewhat over a period of time with some of these urban goods and services becoming available in rural areas. However, to the extent that some such goods and services—food as well as non-food—can be obtained by the rural consumers only by visiting urban markets, they add to the cost of purchase or prices of these goods and services for rural consumers. Indeed, it can be shown that certain higher expenditure groups in rural areas, whose budget consists predominantly of expenditure on urban goods and services, may be experiencing lower real incomes as compared to their urban counterparts because of higher prices and high cost for getting access to such goods and services (Rao 1969a; Srinivasan and Bardhan 1969).

Because of large cultural diversity and consequent differences in food histories across different regions in the country, there can be some differences in tastes and preferences of consumers across the regions (Minhas 1991). However, within any region, the rural–urban differences in tastes and preferences of people are unlikely to be a major factor in accounting for the rural–urban difference in per capita consumption of foodgrains. Indeed, in the course of the debate on this theme in 1969 mentioned before, on the basis of the NSS data on per capita consumption of foodgrains for the year 1959–60, Srinivasan and Bardhan concluded that 'the assumption that the preference structures of rural and urban consumers for same expenditure class are identical is not contradicted' (Srinivasan and Bardhan 1969).

Therefore, in view of high prices or high cost of obtaining urban goods and services in rural areas, high per capita consumption of foodgrains in rural areas can be explained in terms of the familiar demand theory—that is, apart from income and prices of foodgrains, the cross elasticity of demand for foodgrains in rural areas with respect to the prices or the actual cost of obtaining the basket of non-foodgrain items in rural areas would be a relevant factor (see Appendix A9). It should be clear from the above discussion, that the prices of foodgrains relative to the overall index of non-foodgrains prices may not fully reflect the true cost of obtaining access to urban goods and services in rural areas.

Higher Energy Requirement in Rural Areas

Owing to the heavy manual or physical labour involved in agriculture arising from the labour-intensity of operations as well as harder physical environment in rural areas, the requirements of foodgrains for calories can be expected to be higher than those in urban areas. This part of the requirement may be lower now than a few decades ago but may persist, though at a diminishing rate, until most of the agricultural operations and rural transportation are mechanized.

Wage Payment in Kind

The third factor is the payment of wages in kind in the form of cooked meals for agricultural labour as well as for domestic services. According to Minhas, 'The NSS records all "cooked" meals in the budgets of the serving households. Meals provided to employees, guests visiting the household or invited to ceremonies, cleaning ladies, religious functionaries, etc., whether prepared in the household kitchen, in the field or at some ceremonial location, get included in the domestic consumption account of the household. Also the food served to household pets is booked in the domestic consumption account of the household' (Minhas 1991). With increasing monetization of agricultural and rural wages over a period of time, the average per capita consumption of foodgrains can be expected to come down, as quantity of foodgrains purchased by wage earners at market price could be lower than when it is received in the form of cooked meals. However, one can only point to the relevance of this issue now, as it would be difficult at this stage to empirically test the possible impact of monetization of such wages on the rural per capita consumption of foodgrains. This is because of the 'practical difficulty of estimating the quantities and values of individual items used in preparing the meals served to employees and others' (Minhas, 1991), and the non-availability of other relevant data.

Poor State of Environment

The pioneering contribution of P.V. Sukhatme to nutrition theory, particularly with respect to the interaction between genetic and environmental factors, is well-known. He explained how efficiency of conversion of food intake into energy would depend on the access to primary health care, primary education, and environmental factors bearing on health. Since the position in this regard has been improving over a period of time, especially in rural areas, one should expect a slow—almost invisible—decline in the quantity of foodgrains consumed per head without any adverse effect on the efficiency of work. Again, one can only flag this issue without venturing into any empirical examination, as that would be intractable at the moment.

The effects of per capita income or expenditure and prices of foodgrains on their per capita consumption have been studied extensively in the existing literature. The overall conclusion from these studies is that both the income and price variables do influence the per capita consumption of foodgrains in the expected direction, but their impact is more pronounced among the lower expenditure groups and their overall impact is wearing out over a period of time. This conclusion is generally borne out by the findings from the exercises undertaken for this chapter.

Impact of Rural Infrastructure and Farm Mechanization on Food Consumption

The main concern in this chapter is to explore the possible impact of rural infrastructure—bearing on the marketing of non-foodgrain items of consumption—and mechanization of agriculture, on the rural per capita consumption of cereals. Given the dearth of data on rural infrastructure or urbanization of rural areas, one cannot think of a better proxy than the road length (km) per '000 sq. km of geographical area. To measure mechanization of agriculture, the combined units of horse power from tractors, electric motors, and oil engines per '000 hectares of net sown area have been used (Table 9.9). Road length, in so far as it facilitates mechanized transportation, reflects, to some extent, the declining need for physical labour.

Between states, the rural per capita consumption of cereals is negatively correlated with road length both in 1973–4 and 1993–4, implying that better availability of urban goods and services consequent to the urbanization of rural areas may lead to a decline in per capita consumption of cereals in rural areas. Mechanization of agriculture also bears a similar negative relationship with the per capita consumption of cereals, particularly in 1993–4 when the rate of mechanization was quite high in certain states. The negative correlation with road length looks stronger than with mechanization (Table 9.10). These correlations are in line with the argument by Kumar and Mathur (1996) that 'the demand for food is not only influenced by income changes, but also by differences in the urban and rural lifestyles, the development of more advanced marketing systems, occupational changes that are closely linked with increasing per capita income'.

An attempt is made to explain the inter-state variation in the rural per capita consumption of cereals in terms of road length and mechanization of agriculture, apart from per capita total expenditure

Table 9.9: Road Length and Horse Power from Tractors and Pump Sets

State	Road Length (km/'000 sq. km)		HP from Tractors and Pump Sets	
	1975–6*	1991–2**	1972*	1987**
Andhra Pradesh	379.0	556.0	133.4	551.4
Assam	689.0	878.0	9.5	18.4
Bihar	536.0	504.0	83.5	313.5
Gujarat	248.0	472.0	258.9	530.7
Haryana	583.0	673.0	343.1	1572.2
Karnataka	525.0	711.0	121.8	354.2
Kerala	2248.0	3534.0	87.5	519.5
Madhya Pradesh	211.0	309.0	40.0	248.8
Maharashtra	368.0	799.0	116.3	204.7
Orissa	310.0	428.0	17.0	43.1
Punjab	797.0	1116.0	763.5	1666.2
Rajasthan	164.0	358.0	51.6	400.3
Tamil Nadu	847.0	1434.0	731.0	1143.3
Uttar Pradesh	653.0	756.0	146.2	960.3
West Bengal	610.0	665.0	10.4	723.4
All India	380.0	628.0	153.7	761.8

Notes: 1. Pump sets include both electric and diesel pump sets,
2. * Data used for 1972–3,
** Data used for 1993–4,
3. In case of Orissa, the total road length in 1991–2 is arrived at by assuming the growth rate of surface road length.
Sources: 1. For road length: Centre for Monitoring Indian Economy (1996), *Infrastructure in India*, CMIE, November, 1996.
2. For horse power (HP): *Statistical Abstract of India*, 1997, Vol. I, CSO, Ministry of Planning and Programme Implementation, GOI.

and prices of cereals. These four variables together explain nearly 80 per cent of the variation in per capita consumption of cereals in 1973–4 and 65 per cent in 1993–4. Roads show a negative relationship in 1973–4, which seems to have been blurred in 1993–4, except perhaps for the bottom 30 per cent of population. The index of agricultural mechanization, on the other hand, shows a negative relationship in both the periods, the relationship being significant in 1993–4 (Table 9.11).

Before discussing some of the implications of this analysis, one must add a note of caution. Inter-state comparison is necessarily at a high level of aggregation. A state is generally a highly heterogenous

Table 9.10: Correlation Ratio Between Rural Cereal Consumption and Related Variables

	Rural Per Capita Cereal Consumption							
	1972–3				1993–4			
	Per cent				Per cent			
	Bottom 30	Middle 40	Top 30	All	Bottom 30	Middle 40	Top 30	All
Total Expenditure	0.4647	0.2601	0.1521	0.2688	–0.4492	–0.6417	–0.6114	–0.6301
	(1.8922)	(0.9712)	(0.5549)	(1.0062)	(–1.8128)	(–3.0167)	(–2.7858)	(–2.9257)
Price	–0.8792	–0.8382	–0.7420	–0.8531	0.0032	0.0179	–0.0939	–0.0244
	(–6.6533)	(–5.5416)	(–3.9906)	(–5.8954)	(0.0115)	(0.0645)	(–0.3401)	(–0.088)
Road length	–0.5901	–0.7983	–0.7420	–0.7449	–0.6545	–0.5918	–0.5930	–0.6142
	(–2.6354)	(–4.7792)	(–3.9906)	(–4.0256)	(–3.1212)	(–2.6471)	(–2.6553)	(–2.8062)
Tractors and pumpsets	0.1368	0.0475	–0.0385	0.0481	–0.3091	–0.3709	–0.3684	–0.3592
(HP)	(0.4979)	(0.1715)	(–0.1389)	(0.1736)	(–1.1719)	(–1.44)	(–1.4288)	(–1.3877)

Note: Figures in parentheses are t-ratios.
Source: Authors' calculations.

Table 9.11: Results of Regression Analysis (Dependent Variable: Rural Per Capita Consumption; Equation: Log-log)

	1972–3				1993–4			
	Per cent				Per cent			
	Bottom 30	Middle 40	Top 30	All	Bottom 30	Middle 40	Top 30	All
Total Expenditure	0.3908	0.1062	–0.0363	0.0490	–0.1332	–0.3720	–0.3210	–0.3388
	(2.704)	(0.636)	(–0.219)	(0.303)	(–0.74)	(–2.032)	(–1.72)	(–1.792)
Price	–1.3351	–1.0163	–0.6704	–0.9908	–0.0309	–0.2873	–0.3415	–0.3019
	(–6.191)	(–3.458)	(–2.814)	(–4.012)	(–0.152)	(–1.359)	(–1.727)	(–1.417)
Road length	–0.1117	–0.1013	–0.0834	–0.0817	–0.0735	0.0094	0.0152	0.0070
	(–2.379)	(–1.734)	(–1.469)	(–1.531)	(–1.164)	(0.151)	(0.238)	(0.109)
Tractor and pumpsets	–0.0487	–0.0358	–0.0178	–0.0315	–0.0492	–0.0609	–0.0539	–0.0571
(H.P)	(–2.005)	(–1.26)	(–0.601)	(–1.155)	(–1.775)	(–2.355)	(–2.025)	(–2.211)
Constant	2.2157	3.2675	3.8308	3.3334	3.7991	5.3015	5.3867	5.1834
	(4.65)	(5.326)	(5.133)	(5.287)	(4.327)	(5.409)	(4.947)	(5.043)
R-Square	0.8946	0.7879	0.6758	0.7933	0.5773	0.6658	0.6415	0.6551

Notes: All the variables are taken in log form;
Figures in the parentheses are t-ratios.
Source: Authors' calculations.

unit both in regard to infrastructure development like roads and the degree of mechanization of agriculture. This is more so in the case of larger states. It would, therefore, be rewarding if an exercise like this is undertaken at the disaggregated level of NSS regions which, incidentally, would give a much larger number of observations. In the absence of such an exercise at a sufficiently disaggregated level, the results from the present exercise should, at best, be regarded as suggestive in the nature of hypotheses (for a note of scepticism on the present results, see Saha 2000).

Implications

One obvious question that arises from the declining trend in per capita consumption of cereals is with regard to the nutritional status of the poor. In fact, the per capita consumption of cereals by the bottom 30 per cent of the population had declined marginally over the three decades under study even as there has been a significant shift from the relatively cheap 'coarse cereals' to the more expensive rice and wheat. This is puzzling because cereals, especially coarse cereals, are a cheaper source of energy. The available information does not help us to explain this aspect of consumer behaviour. An opinion survey of consumer behaviour where such questions are directly addressed to the interviewees may help to unravel some of the underlying attitudinal factors.

Other factors constraining consumption of foodgrains among the poor could be the need for increased expenditure on fuel and lights, and on miscellaneous goods and services including on conveyance and medical services, which have together recorded a sharp jump for the bottom four expenditure classes of rural population between 1970–1 and 1993–4, that is, between the 25th and 49th NSS rounds (Saha 2000). However, since expenditure and price elasticities of demand for cereals are higher for the poor, if there had been a significant increase in their employment, income, and wages and if the cereal prices faced by them relative to those faced by their urban counterparts were lower as in the case of the top 30 per cent of population, the per capita consumption of cereals among them would have been substantially higher. To this extent the decline in the average per capita consumption of cereals in the country would have been lower.

Nevertheless, it appears that the saturation point with respect to the consumption of cereals would soon be reached even among the poor.

This is evident from the significant decline in per capita consumption of cereals among the middle 40 per cent of population. The evidence presented also shows the strong negative impact of roads and mechanization on cereal consumption among the poor. Even so, cereals being a low cost source of energy, the nutritional status of the poor can be improved substantially through the subsidized sale of foodgrains from the public distribution system (PDS). However, the non-poor are found to be purchasing from the PDS almost as much quantity of foodgrains per head as the poor (Radhakrishna *et al.* 1997). Therefore, if the PDS is effectively targeted to the poor, it has the potential of trebling the availability of foodgrains for the poor without increasing the total commitment from the PDS.

Another major implication of this analysis is that the demand projections for foodgrains need to take into account the possibility of a further fall in per capita demand on account of the development of rural infrastructure and mechanization. The average road length per sq. km of geographical area in the country in 1991–2 was only about half of that in states like Punjab and Tamil Nadu—not to speak of Kerala where one can see a rural–urban continuum. Similarly, the average rate of agricultural mechanization in the country in 1987 was less than half of that in Punjab and Haryana (Table 9.9). There is thus a considerable potential for modernization of rural areas on these counts.

Further, since the rural–urban differential in per capita consumption of foodgrains is quite high even now, one should expect a significant decline in average per capita consumption of foodgrains in the country with increasing urbanization. On account of all these factors, it would not be unreasonable to expect a further decline in per capita consumption of foodgrains, say, by 2020 AD, at the same rate as witnessed over the two decades covered by our analysis, that is, by about 10 per cent. Given the expected population growth by 2020, this declining trend in per capita consumption on account of the development of rural infrastructure, mechanization, urbanization, and other factors including changes in tastes and preferences, is likely to make a difference of about 20 million tonnes to the household demand for foodgrains in 2020. However, this may be neutralized by the increasing demand for cereals as animal feed to the extent of about 10 million tonnes (Radhakrishna and Ravi 1992). Despite this fall in per capita demand, the total demand for foodgrains will increase on account of population growth.

The actual outcome would, of course, depend upon the pace of development of rural areas. It will depend crucially on the development of market infrastructure in rural areas for the sale of non-foodgrain items of food and other urban goods and services. In particular, innovative marketing methods and strategies for minimizing the diseconomies of small scale in marketing of such goods and services in rural areas have a great potential for reducing their cost to the consumers, and thus inducing them to exchange part of the foodgrains for non-foodgrain items of food and other urban goods and services.

Finally, it is clear that the decline in per capita consumption of foodgrains on account of the factors enumerated above would be associated with improvement in the welfare of the rural consumers in general. The decline in the cost of obtaining access to non-foodgrain items would raise the real income for large sections of rural consumers; the decline in consumption on account of reduced physical labour would be associated with freedom from drudgery; higher nutritional efficiency would be associated with improved health and environment; and even the reduced dependence of rural workers on cooked meals from the rural rich should be welcome, as it would enhance human dignity. It is thus interesting—though it may appear paradoxical—that, up to a point, a reduction in the intake of foodgrains on certain counts should in fact be associated with improvement in human welfare.

10

Foodgrains Surpluses

Causes and Policy Implications

Introduction

From the chronic shortage of foodgrains and virtually 'ship-to-mouth' existence in the mid-1960s, India has made considerable strides towards achieving food security. Thanks to the green revolution, the country has not only achieved self-sufficiency in foodgrains, but has become a net exporter. For the first time in the history of independent India, the country has been a net exporter of foodgrains consecutively for the last seven years. What is more, the Food Corporation of India (FCI) had, by 2002, accumulated over 60 million tonnes of foodgrains—nearly three times the normal requirement for buffer stocks and the public distribution system (PDS). There has been a significant decline in the incidence of poverty since the mid-1960s. Even then, according to the latest official estimates, at least 26 per cent of the population or 260 million people were still below the poverty line in the year 1999–2000. This implies that despite the availability of foodgrains for meeting the requirements of the entire population, we are still far from generating the necessary purchasing power or effective demand from the poor to satisfy their needs. Since effective food security implies achievement of both physical and economic access to food, a large section of our population can still be considered to be suffering from food insecurity despite the bulging stocks of foodgrains with the FCI.

In terms of its performance, the food economy of India reveals three distinct phases. The first phase from the beginning of the plan period to the mid-1960s was characterized by severe imbalances between the demand for food and its domestic supply. Over the post-green revolution period from about the mid-1960s to the close of the 1980s, the country achieved near self-sufficiency in the availability of food and experienced an improvement in effective food security in so far as there was a significant reduction in the incidence of poverty, especially in the 1980s. As such, this second phase itself warrants sub-grouping into the 1970s characterized by the emergence of inter-regional and inter-crop imbalances in agricultural growth and the 1980s when crops such as rice, oilseeds, and pulses registered high growth, especially in the eastern and central regions where poverty is widespread and which were largely bypassed in the early phase of the green revolution. The third phase is represented by the post-economic reform period of the 1990s when a series of measures for macroeconomic stabilization and structural adjustment were launched. The immediate or short-run consequences of these reforms for the food economy were negative.

Foodgrains production in the pre-green revolution period barely kept pace with population growth, the annual growth rate in per capita output being negative in the 1960s (Rao and Radhakrishna 1997). Growth in foodgrains output in this period was achieved mainly through the increase in area under cultivation by using traditional technology. The imports of foodgrains increased reaching a level of 14 per cent of domestic availability in 1966. The droughts of 1965 and 1966 and the rising prices of food highlighted the imbalance in India's food economy: sluggish growth in productivity with slow rise in the use of inputs like irrigation, fertilizers, and high yielding seeds in the face of growing demand for food on account of rapid growth of population and rise in per capita income.

This crisis prompted the government to accord an overriding priority to the goal of achieving self-sufficiency in foodgrains by launching the green revolution. Public investment in irrigation and agricultural research was stepped up. As a result of this and the rise in total factor productivity, the per head growth rate in the output of foodgrains was close to 1 per cent in the first decade of the green revolution and accelerated further to slightly over 1.5 per cent during the 1980s (Rao and Radhakrishna, 1997). Consequently, the dependence on imports declined in the post-Green Revolution period. Net imports of foodgrains were either negative or less than 1 per cent of domestic availability over much of this period. The relative prices of foodgrains showed a decline after the mid-1970s and there was a rise in real wages of farm labour.

In the post-reform period of the 1990s, however, the growth rate in foodgrains output at around 1.7 per cent has been lagging behind the population growth rate of 1.9 per cent. The rate of inflation was high, at 10 per cent or more, consecutively for four years in the first half of the 1990s, the rise in the prices of foodgrains being even higher. As such, there was a rise in poverty and inequality in the immediate post-reform period (Gupta 1995), and slower reduction in poverty thereafter.

Public intervention in the foodgrains market assumed greater significance in the post-green revolution period both for ensuring remunerative prices for the farmers and for stabilizing consumption. Procurement of foodgrains by the government increased steadily from well below 5 per cent of output over much of the pre-green revolution period to well above 10 per cent and 15 per cent of output in the 1980s and the 1990s. Correspondingly, the volume of public distribution of foodgrains increased significantly—exceeding 10 per cent of domestic availability in the post-green revolution period. As a result of procurement operations, the terms of trade for agriculture improved (Radhakrishna and Rao 1995), the annual fluctuations in the per capita availability of foodgrains declined during the 1980s and the 1990s when compared to the previous period (Rao and Radhakrishna 1997), and there was a decline in the seasonal as well as regional variation in the prices of foodgrains (Bhalla 1995).

The foregoing overview suggests that the most important problem concerning food management in India is to overcome chronic or long-term food insecurity by ensuring adequate nutrition to the whole population on a sustainable basis (Radhakrishna 1996). This would require augmentation of food supplies to meet the expanding food basket which, as discussed in the previous chapter, is getting increasingly diversified on account of changing tastes and preferences. The experience of the green revolution demonstrates that with necessary investments in agricultural infrastructure and research and an appropriate policy environment, it should be possible to achieve the desired growth in the availability of food.

However, the real challenge is to ensure adequate purchasing power in the hands of those suffering from chronic food insecurity. As argued in this chapter, the ongoing economic reforms, given appropriate content and sequencing, can be expected to generate productive employment necessary to overcome chronic food insecurity. Public support to poverty alleviation programmes and subsidized food for the vulnerable sections will have to continue but, basically, as supplementary to the broad-based, employment-oriented growth. As discussed later, the focus of such interventions in the future should be on better targeting of the beneficiaries and on cost-effective delivery systems.

Emergence of Foodgrain Surpluses

How is it that the FCI has been saddled with such embarrassingly large surpluses of foodgrains within a short period? This is a major puzzle facing the Indian economy in the recent period and staring at the policy makers, some of whom do not seem to have a clear understanding of the causes for the emergence of this phenomenon. Because of this lack of clarity, the solutions being canvassed by the ministries of food and agriculture of the Government of India, such as disbanding public procurement of foodgrains at minimum support prices, leaving the foodgrain market free to private trade, and compensating the farmers for lower market prices through direct cash payments, are quite out of line with the hard realities of the Indian situation.

Moreover, we tend to equate food security with foodgrain security. There is insufficient realization that the food basket in the country has become considerably diversified with much greater share being occupied now by non-foodgrain items such as sugar, edible oils, milk, meat, eggs, vegetables and fruits. In fact, these non-foodgrain items of food now account for over 60 per cent of consumer expenditure on food. Therefore, even if we are within an easy reach of enabling every Indian to buy enough foodgrains, we need to move quite a distance for to ensure physical as well as economic access to many of these non-foodgrain items of food, especially for the poor. The policy framework being thought of for foodgrains has to take into account the need for diversifying agricultural production to meet the emerging needs as well as for ensuring the necessary purchasing power to the poor through the generation of employment opportunities.

The sharp rise in the quantity of foodgrains procured, as well as in the stocks held, by the FCI is a very recent phenomenon. This happened within a short period beginning 1999–2000. The annual procurement for most of the years in the 1990s was around 24 million tonnes up to 1998–9, which rose to 31 and 36 million tonnes, respectively in the subsequent two years. That is, the additional procurement in these two years would have raised the stocks with the FCI by 19 million tonnes. Further, there was a decline in the off-take to the extent of 5 million tonnes in the year 2000–01 (RBI 2002). These two together explain the additional stocks of about 24 million tonnes held in 2000–01 over and above the normal stocks held in many of the previous years. It is clear from this, that the rise in procurement has been far more important than the decline in the off-take from the FCI in accounting for the rise in stocks. It is, therefore, necessary to understand the causes for the sharp rise in procurement.

The quantity of grain procured is influenced by the changes in output as well as procurement prices. It is good to remember in this context that the growth of foodgrains output has slowed down in the country during the 1990s. There was virtually no growth in foodgrains output per head. One also does not find any noticeable rise in foodgrains output in the country in recent years. This rise is not higher than the rise in the early or mid-1990s. In fact, there was a decline in foodgrains output to the extent of 6 per cent in the year 2000–01 (RBI 2001). In the case of wheat the decline was even higher at 9 per cent. Despite this decline in output, the quantity of grain procured increased by 5 million tonnes in that year. Therefore, the steep rise in procurement cannot be explained in terms of higher growth in output. However, regional concentration of growth has been conducive to increased procurement, because growth in output in the previous two years was greater in the surplus producing states of Punjab and Haryana which account for the bulk of the foodgrains procured. In the case of wheat, for example, the growth rate in these two surplus producing states was nearly double the all-India average growth rate in 1998–9 as well as 1999–2000 (RBI 2001).

What could be the factors behind the rise in foodgrain stocks with the FCI over and above the normal level, even when there is no significant increase in output in the country? One can think of two such factors: a possible decline in net exports and a steep rise in the minimum support or procurement prices (MSP). As to the net exports, recently there was some indication of a fall, for some time, because of the decline in international prices of grain. But, of late, export of grain seems to have picked up. In any case, variation in net export, by itself, cannot account for more than a small fraction of the stocks held by the FCI. This is because the net export of grain in the last seven years did not exceed 2 million tonnes per annum, on an average.

The sharp rise in procurement in the recent period may, therefore, be attributed to the steep rise in the MSP. Even the recent spurt in foodgrains output in the surplus producing regions has basically been induced by higher prices. The MSP fixed by the government have generally been higher than those recommended by the Commission on Agricultural Costs and Prices (CACP), especially in the case of wheat.

There was a 25 per cent rise in the MSP for wheat in 1997–8 with a further rise in each of the subsequent years. Altogether, the MSP for wheat was raised by 53 per cent over a period of four years, while the MSP for rice was raised by 34 per cent over the same period (CACP 2001).

The big rise in the MSP for wheat and rice could well have discouraged the private trade from augmenting its own stocks because higher market prices reduced the prospects for off-take. The sales to the FCI would have risen in such a situation. Further, in the remote regions where the FCI is not active, the private trade and the resourceful farmers can procure grain immediately after the harvest at prices lower than MSP and sell the grain so procured to the FCI. This is highly plausible because the private trade normally holds sizeable stocks of foodgrains, and these stocks fluctuate significantly from year to year in response to the changes in output and prices. For example, over the five years ending 1995–6, procurement by private trade in the country accounted, on an average, for 37 per cent of market arrivals in the case of wheat, and 47 per cent of market arrivals in the case of rice. The annual shares fluctuated between 21–59 per cent for wheat and between 40–58 per cent for rice (World Bank 1999). It is, therefore, very likely that a sizeable portion of the stocks now held by the FCI are those which would normally be held by the private trade if the procurement and market prices are not out of alignment with the supply and demand forces. If this is true, then it means the private sector is being priced out or crowded out in the market by the government in these days of marketization and privatization!

The trend of a decline in per capita consumption of foodgrains, as noted in the previous chapter, has been reinforced in the 1990s. Whereas per capita real expenditure on cereals was declining, on an average, at the rate of 0.7 per cent per annum during the 1970s and the 1980s, it declined at a much higher rate of a little over 2 per cent per annum between 1990–8 (Ravi 2001). According to the latest data released by the Central Statistical Organization (CSO), the real per capita consumer expenditure on food, including foodgrains, fell even more steeply in the year 2000–01 (*Economic Times*, 5 February 2002).

The basic difference between the period of the 1990s and the earlier period relates to the behaviour of foodgrain prices. In the earlier period, the relative prices of foodgrains were declining, which by itself, would have induced higher consumption of foodgrains. Despite this, the per capita consumption declined in this period due to the secular trend of urbanization of rural areas. During the 1990s, on the other hand, the relative prices of foodgrains were rising which, given the normal consumer behaviour, should lead to a decline in the consumption of foodgrains. Indeed, a higher rate of decline in consumption in this period suggests that the earlier trend of a decline in the consumption of foodgrains has been reinforced by the rise in their relative prices.

This is clearly demonstrated by certain statistical exercises completed recently. The Report of the Working Group on Public Distribution System and Food Security for Tenth Plan constituted by the Planning Commission shows that the rise in the foodgrain stocks with the FCI can be explained basically by the increased procurement on account of the rise in procurement prices over and above those recommended by the CACP and the reduction in consumer demand due to the rise in market prices. According to the Report, over the five year period between 1997–8 and 2001–02, when there was a steep rise in procurement prices, nearly 16 million tonnes may have been added to the FCI stocks on both these counts (Planning Commission 2001). This rise in the stocks of foodgrains with the FCI is attributed to the increase in procurement prices in the last five years. But, what would have happened to the consumption of foodgrains in the country if their relative prices remained at the average level obtaining in the 1980s? Some calculations suggest that foodgrains consumption would have been higher by at least 5 million tonnes per annum or 25 million tonnes over the five years ending 2001–02.

Policy Framework for the Future

In the light of the analysis presented here regarding the causes for the growing surplus stocks of foodgrains with the FCI, what should be the policy framework for the foodgrain sector in the country? The objectives of such a policy framework should be six-fold: (1) to consolidate the food security achieved so far in the country and strengthen it further; (2) to encourage diversification of cropping pattern so as to ensure efficiency of resource use in agriculture; (3) to enhance our competitiveness in the export market; (4) to allow a rise in the domestic consumption of foodgrains among the poor; (5) to reduce the subsidy bill for the exchequer; and (6) to reduce the costs of distribution.

There has not been any breakthrough in the growth of foodgrains output in the country in the recent period. The present surpluses with the FCI are not a consequence of a big rise in productivity in agriculture achieved through cost-reducing technological change. They are a consequence of a steep rise in the procurement prices in the recent period which, apart from rendering exports uncompetitive and discouraging the holding of stocks by the private sector, reduced the domestic consumption of foodgrains, particularly by the poor. Therefore, the proposed policy framework has to take into account the need for consolidating food security achieved so far by raising productivity through cost-reducing technological changes. Foodgrain surpluses so generated would be affordable to the poor in the country and would also be competitive in the export market. This is an important lesson thrown up by the experience of the green revolution in the country.

The experience of the green revolution in the country has also demonstrated the role of MSP in providing incentives to the farmers for sustaining productivity increases through the application of new technologies and inputs. However, the issue is: at what level should price support be provided? Minimum support price implies, by definition, a floor price below which farming becomes unviable, and as such, farmers need to be supported through purchases by the government at this price. While recommending the MSP for crops, the CACP is guided by its mandate to ensure that such prices are fair to the producers as well as to the consumers. The CACP, therefore, takes into account a number of factors, apart from the cost of production, while recommending support prices. Some such factors are: the emerging balance between the domestic supply and demand for foodgrains; the prospects for technological change; the need to ensure efficiency of resource use in agriculture, among other things, through the diversification of cropping pattern; and price movements in the country as well as in the international market. However, while fixing prices in the recent period, the government has shown scant regard for these factors which are taken into consideration by the CACP.

Views of the Department of Agriculture

It appears that the Department of Agriculture and Cooperation of the Government of India, is alive to the adverse impact of the steep rise in the procurement prices of foodgrains in recent years. The department has expressed its concern about the accumulation of foodgrain surpluses with the FCI much in excess of the requirements. It seems to have brought out the negative consequences of the present policy, such as, disincentives for the diversification of cropping pattern; inability to compete in the export market; dampening of domestic consumption; rise in food subsidy bill; and higher costs of distribution which could be reduced if there is a greater role for the private trade.

However, the department does not appear to view the present surpluses basically as a short-run phenomenon attributable mainly to the rising procurement prices. In its perception, these surpluses are of a long-term nature comparable apparently to the food surpluses in the United States of America or the European Union! Consequently, its prescriptions do not seem to reflect the need for consolidating and strengthening food security by continuing in some form the present policy for price support through public procurement at MSP. Instead, the department seems to have advocated total marketization of foodgrain trade by disbanding purchases by the FCI at MSP. The department seems to be aware that in the event of leaving the foodgrains trade totally free, the market prices of foodgrains may decline significantly. The remedy reportedly suggested by them is to directly compensate the farmers to the extent of the difference between the market price and the MSP. Alternatively, they have suggested a certain variant of the existing crop insurance scheme for protecting the farmers in the event of a fall in incomes due to variations in yields and market prices.

Under both the alternatives reportedly suggested by the Department of Agriculture, the market prices of foodgrains will be determined by the forces of demand and supply. The market prices so determined can be expected to be significantly lower than the MSP under the present reckoning at least for a few years until the supplies adjust to the market situation. The lower market prices may no doubt encourage greater domestic consumption and exports. The alternative systems may also lead to greater efficiency in distribution because of the pre-eminent role played by private trade in procurement, storage, and transportation of grain. However, they may not encourage diversification of the cropping pattern, because compensations to farmers would still be related to the area under certain crops such as rice and wheat. The subsidy outgo is also unlikely to be reduced.

The dismantling of public procurement at MSP could lead to a crash in market prices in years of good harvests and thus undermine food security so assiduously built up over a long period. Food security can be undermined due to the slow growth or decline in yields even if the area under the crops entitled to compensation increases. This is because, according to the ministry's scheme, for reasons of administrative convenience, payment of compensation is to be based not on the marketable surplus from the actual yields at the individual farm level but on average yields at the village or homogeneous area level. Therefore, the allocation of inputs by farmers would be guided by the market prices and not by the MSP. Besides, payment of compensation is an ex-post phenomenon riddled with many uncertainties at the time of decision making by the farmers regarding the inputs and technology to be applied. Therefore, compensations cannot provide incentives to the farmers for the allocation of inputs in the same way as MSP announced in advance.

Above all, both the alternative schemes for compensating the farmers are highly cumbersome even under simplified assumptions, as they involve millions of farmers for determination of their entitlements through detailed calculations at the individual farm level and for making payments. They may lead to severe moral hazards at various levels. Unlike public procurement at MSP where payments are made according to the actual and easily verifiable quantity and quality of produce sold, the payments by way of compensation may result in highly iniquitous treatment between different farmers and may thus lead to widespread discontent.

Compensations or deficiency payment may be manageable in countries like the United States of America and the European Union, where only 2–3 per cent of the population is dependent on agriculture. Besides, unlike in the developed countries, in a developing country like India, crop diversification, technological change, and rise in factor productivity hold great promise for raising farmers' incomes. These require large public investments in infrastructure, agricultural research, and extension, as well as complementary private investments. But the prospects for these would be highly circumscribed under the system of deficiency payments both because farmers would have little incentive to switch over to new practices and the rise in food subsidy bill would undermine public investment in agriculture.

The other method of compensating farmers reportedly suggested by the Department of Agriculture is through an agricultural insurance scheme. Under the National Agricultural Insurance Scheme, at present being implemented by the Ministry, farmers are protected against fluctuations in yields. Under the proposed scheme, farmers are to be protected against fluctuations in income resulting from variations in yields and prices. For various reasons, the current Agricultural Insurance Scheme is not popular with the farmers as well as many state governments. The acceptability of the new scheme is unlikely to be enhanced, as the methodology for the calculation of yield losses appears to remain the same as before.

There is a basic difference between the risk covered under the existing system of public procurement at MSP and under the proposed Agricultural Insurance Scheme. Under the existing system of public procurement, a farmer's decisions on input use are made on the basis of his expectations regarding yields on his farm with the assurance that there is no price risk. On the other hand, under the proposed insurance scheme, the farmer would be faced with uncertainty regarding the market prices at which he will be able to sell his produce. His decisions on input use could thus be constrained by this uncertainty.

Solutions

Increasing the Role of Private Trade

In view of deficiencies in both the alternative schemes reportedly suggested by the Department of Agriculture, it would be preferable to reform the existing system by reducing the role of the FCI and increasing the role of private trade. The MSP, for example, need not cover the total costs as at present. It could be moderated so as to cover only paid-out costs with some extra margin. With such a price, public procurement may become limited because the chances of the market price falling below this price may become smaller. Even with the present method of determining MSP, freezing them at the present level for a couple of years or raising them only marginally may bring about the necessary balance between the foodgrain requirements for buffer stocks, PDS, Food for Work Programme, etc., and the produce offered for sale to the FCI. Even in handling the stocks so procured, private trade can be assigned a significant role in addition to its role in handling the rest of the stocks. Besides, for improving the efficiency of operations, public procurement and distribution can be decentralized to the state level, as is being already implemented in some states, with financial assistance from the Centre.

Improving Economic Access for the Poor

Although domestic consumption of foodgrains has been restricted in the last couple of years owing to the rise in their prices, the per capita consumption of foodgrains is unlikely to increase much even when there is a moderation in relative prices. This is because of the long-term trend of a decline in the per capita consumption of foodgrains for reasons already mentioned. Eventually, as the purchasing power of the poor rises, their per capita consumption of foodgrains may rise to the average level for the whole population. If so, their consumption is unlikely to rise by more than 10–12 per cent. The demand for foodgrains in the country will, therefore, rise basically on account of population growth for quite some time until the demand for foodgrains as animal feed picks up. Past experience shows that it should be possible to increase supplies to meet this emerging demand. Therefore, it is safe to conclude that the country has already achieved foodgrain security in the sense of ensuring availability or physical access. Hopefully, we may achieve economic access too for the poor in respect of foodgrains in the near future.

However, foodgrain security, though essential, cannot be equated with food security. The share of consumer expenditure on cereals now accounts for a little less than 40 per cent of the total consumer expenditure on food in the country, the remaining 60 per cent of expenditure being incurred on items such as edible oils, sugar, milk, eggs, meat, fish, vegetables, and fruits. Even among the poor or bottom 30 per cent of the population, these non-foodgrain items of food account for as much as half the total expenditure on food. Using the same yardstick as for foodgrains, namely, to become food-secure, the per capita consumption of such items by the poor has to reach the average level for the whole population, then the consumption of such items of food by the poor will have to double for reaching this desired level. Since raising the consumption of such items by the poor to the level enjoyed by the top 30 per cent of population has to be the ultimate goal, the per capita consumption of these items by the poor has to increase three-fold for achieving this level. The demand for these items of food will, therefore, rise at a high rate on account of population growth as well as the rise in per capita income. We have, therefore, to go very far for attaining food security both in the sense of physical access as well as economic access, especially for the poor.

The experience of the green revolution in the country has demonstrated that achieving self-sufficiency or physical access to these non-cereal items of food in the country is quite feasible in the foreseeable future. Given the appropriate price signals and requisite infrastructure and technology, our farmers have shown great resilience in reallocating the available resources as well as stepping up fresh investments to meet the emerging demand for new products. Therefore, the policy framework, while safeguarding the foodgrain security already achieved, has to encourage diversification of agriculture to meet the growing demand for these non-cereal items of food.

But, achieving necessary economic access to these items of food by raising the purchasing power of the poor is going to be far more challenging than simply ensuring necessary supplies. Diversification of agriculture into non-cereal products will itself raise employment and purchasing power for the poor, to a considerable extent. This is because the potential for employment generation in dairying, horticulture, etc. is much greater than for cereals. Moreover, these activities require new and better skills and so the wage rates for such enterprises are going to be much higher. Development of agro-processing and non-farm enterprises in general in rural areas is going to be the most promising source for employment generation and for achieving effective food security in the country. The major issues bearing on the achievement of effective food security through diversification of the food sector are briefly discussed below.

Diversification of the Food Sector

Growing Demand for Non-foodgrain items

The expenditure elasticity for non-cereal food items is still quite high in India. It is thrice as high when compared to cereals in rural areas and over ten times as high in urban areas (Table 10.1).

On account of high expenditure elasticity and the decline in its relative price during the 1990s, with the rise in per capita income and expenditure, per capita consumption of non-cereal food recorded an annual growth rate of 0.80 per cent in rural areas and 0.75 per cent in urban areas, as against a decline in per capita consumption of cereals, noted earlier. Growth rates in consumption for the expenditure groups belonging to the bottom 30 per cent and the middle 40 per cent are even higher. Per capita consumption of fruits and vegetables showed the highest growth followed by edible oils (Dev *et al.* 2003). The opening up of the economy in the 1990s led to a big rise in export

Table 10.1: Expenditure Elasticities for Cereals and Non-cereal Food (Period: 1987–8 to 1999–2000)

S. No.	Commodity Group	Rural	Urban
1	Cereals	0.31	0.09
2	Milk	1.45	0.66
3	Edible Oil	0.85	0.37
4	Meat	1.02	0.54
5	Sugar	1.06	0.29
6	Pulses	0.57	0.30
7	Fruits and Vegetables	1.04	0.76
8	Other Food (other than cereals)	0.91	0.97
9	Non-food items	1.37	1.50

Source: Dev *et al.* (2003), 'Economic Liberalization, Targeted Programmes and Household Food Security: A Case Study of India', CESS–IFPRI Report (to be published), IFPRI, Washington D.C.

demand for such products. The combined value of exports of fish and meat and their preparations, fruits, vegetables, and their processed foods, which rose by about 70 per cent in the pre-reform decade, from US$ 490 million to 852 million between 1980–1 and 1990–1, rose by 270 per cent over the post-reform decade to US$ 2308 million in 2000–1 (Government of India 2002).

In response to this growing domestic and export demand for non-cereal items of food, there has been a discernible shift in the allocation of resources in Indian agriculture in the recent period away from cereals, particularly coarse cereals, to the enterprises like dairying, poultry, edible oils, meat, fish, vegetables, and fruits, etc. (Joshi and Gulati 2003). These enterprises, being labour-intensive, are suited to small holders and lead to a rise in wage employment (Chand 1996; Saleth 1999; Joshi and Gulati 2003).Thus the agricultural diversification underway in the country contributes to the achievement of effective food security in so far as the purchasing power of the lower income groups is raised. Besides, they are environment-friendly, as they are generally less land and water intensive and also the rise in the incomes of farmers growing high value products for example, vegetables and fruits results in reducing pressure for bringing more land under the plough (Chand 1996).

The bottlenecks to the realization of these benefits by responding to the growing demand, lie on the supply side. Agricultural policy in respect of price, technology, infrastructure, and institutions has so far been foodgrain-centred and has been slow to respond to the new imperatives on the supply side. Major policy initiatives are called for to bring the relative prices of foodgrains in conformity with the emerging trends in demand. Public as well as private investment has to be stepped up in agricultural research, especially biotechnology, focusing on the new activities and the unfavourable areas. Many of the new products being highly perishable, there is a need for the development and upgradation of infrastructure for roads, markets, storage, and processing. Institutional innovations would be necessary to channel more credit for such enterprises and also to provide adequate insurance cover against risk. Restrictions on the entry of big players, domestic as well as foreign, in storage, processing, and marketing have to be eased and contract/cooperative farming encouraged for reducing transaction costs, so as to attract greater investment, latest technology, and credit flow to the farmers (Joshi and Gulati 2003).

Section IV

Rural Poverty

11

Rural Tranformation in Asia

Post-reforms Trends and Perspectives

Introduction

An attempt is made in this chapter to bring out the salient features of the experience of rural transformation and poverty reduction in East and South-east Asia in the post-reform period. This experience has a special relevance for countries of South Asia, including India. This discussion would be a useful prelude to the subsequent chapters in this section focused on rural poverty in India in the post-reform period.

For nearly half a century, ever since they achieved political independence, several countries in East and South-east Asia have experienced a sustained transformation in the structure of their rural economies. There is, however, considerable variation in the pace of this transformation across countries and over different periods of time. Considering the observed rate and quality of such transformation, we propose to discuss in this chapter the experience of the following three groups of countries: East Asian countries like China and Republic of Korea belong to the first group of countries which have shown a high rate of rural transformation and speedy alleviation of rural poverty in the 1980s and the 1990s. A group of countries in South-east Asia, for example, Indonesia, Malaysia, and Thailand come next in order of performance. The performance of countries in South Asia, viz., Bangladesh, India, Nepal, Pakistan, and Sri Lanka in respect of rural development and poverty alleviation was modest and not as impressive as in the first two groups of countries.

The structural transformation of rural economies in these countries has passed through broadly three phases: In the first phase from about the early 1950s to the mid-1960s, many of them were pre occupied with restructuring of their agrarian relations by implementing land reforms and by building up basic physical and institutional infrastructure like the development of irrigation and supply of institutional credit to the farmers. The second period starting from about mid- and late 1960s was characterized by the green revolution and its gradual extension to the less endowed regions in each of these countries. The last phase, that is, the 1980s and the 1990s, is characterized by the introduction of macroeconomic reforms including structural adjustment and globalization which have had a profound impact on the transformation of their rural economies. There is, however, no hard and fast line to demarcate these three phases and there is some overlapping between them within individual countries as well as across countries. The focus of analysis in this chapter will be on the last phase of two decades.

The analysis will cover the following major facets of rural transformation: (i) growth of rural non-farm sector; and (ii) human development, population growth, and rural poverty. While discussing some of these aspects, a more specific, though brief, analysis will be attempted for China and Republic of Korea in East Asia; and Indonesia, Malaysia, and Thailand in South-east Asia. Policy perspectives for an efficient, equitable, and sustainable rural development are briefly discussed at the end.

Growth in Non-farm Rural Sector

The experience of economic growth across countries suggests that, in general, high agricultural growth is accompanied by the growth in the rural non-farm sector owing to its forward and backward linkages with agriculture. The experience in Asia in the post-reform decades of the 1980s and 1990s provides a mixed—even a contrasting—picture regarding the growth of the rural non-farm sector. These experiences seem to be largely country-specific and, therefore, mostly non-replicable, as they depend on the nature of agricultural growth, socio-economic conditions in the pre-reform period, and the quality of reform packages introduced.

For example, as discussed below, China has experienced an exceptionally high growth in both farm and rural non-farm sectors in the post-reform decade of 1980s, whereas India showed a reasonably high growth in both farm and rural non-farm sectors in its pre-reform decade of 1980s but a deceleration in both the sectors in the post-reform decade of 1990s. On the other hand, there is no evidence of a take-off in the rural non-farm sector in Thailand despite the impressive growth of its agriculture during the 1970s and 1980s under a relatively liberalized economic environment. However, common to all these experiences is the overriding importance of yield-increasing and labour-releasing agricultural growth in triggering-off the growth in the rural non-farm sector. A rise in rural demand for non-agricultural goods and services and the easy availability of labour for the production of such goods and services seem to be the key factors underlying the growth of the rural non-farm sector.

China

There was an exceptionally high rate of growth of rural non-farm sector in China during the 1980s—both in terms of output and employment (Rao 2001). There was a take-off in this sector after 1984 when deceleration in agricultural growth had set in. Corresponding to this high growth in the non-farm sector, there was a substantial increase in its share in rural gross social product and employment between 1980 and 1986 (Rao 2001). However, agriculture still accounted for 80 per cent of rural employment in 1986. Curiously, both economic liberalization, on the one hand, and the institutions, policies, and vestiges of a planned or guided economy, on the other, have combined to give a boost to the growth of the rural non-farm sector in China during the 1980s.

As discussed earlier, the growth rate of agriculture was exceptionally high in the immediate post-reform period, that is, between 1978–84. This was achieved basically through the increase in crop yields per hectare thus releasing a substantial proportion of the labour force hitherto engaged in agriculture for employment in non-farm activities. There was a big spurt in farm incomes both on account of highly favourable terms of trade and improvements in yields consequent to the introduction of the Household Responsibility System. This rise in rural demand for non-agricultural goods and services was reinforced by the more equal distribution of rural incomes. Unlike the increase in incomes of the rural rich, an increase in incomes of the poor would mostly lead to an increase in the demand for the products of the rural non-farm sector (Saith 1993). The release of the hitherto suppressed demand of the pre-reform era added to the boom in rural consumer demand.

The rise in rural incomes consequent to the agricultural breakthrough in the immediate post-reform period raised the investible capacity which was channelled more into the non-farm sector through the existing institutional framework. The improved infrastructure and higher literacy levels inherited from the pre-reform period also seemed to have served as favourable factors.

The decentralized and well-governed local institutions which have the traditions of mobilizing and allocating resources in enterprises during the planning era served as effective instruments for rural industrialization in China. They mobilized investible resources and provided various kinds of support to the rural enterprises by reducing transaction costs to them which can be quite high in a purely market-oriented rural setting. Another major factor associated with a controlled economy favouring rural non-farm enterprises is the geographical immobility of labour. This ensured sufficient availability of labour at a low cost when compared to the situation of free mobility of labour (Byrd and QuingSong 1990; Johansson and Ronnas 1996). Economic liberalization in China started with rural areas and so benefitted, in the initial stages, the rural non-farm sector more than public enterprises. The rural non-farm sector also gained indirectly from this because of its ability to compete with high-cost products.

The planned linkage of township and village enterprises with public enterprises for getting the inputs required and for the sale of their output provided an environment of certainty and stability for the rural non-farm sector.

A major issue of concern now is the sustainability or economic viability of rural enterprises in China when the liberalization process is complete and factor markets are freed. Considerations of labour cost and economies of scale may cause drastic shifts in the location of rural enterprises from rural-to-urban and from the less developed to well-developed rural areas. It appears that an efficient and sustainable rural non-farm economy is yet to evolve in China in the course of the rest of the economy getting liberalized while doing away with artificial support to the rural industry.

Thailand

The available literature points to the not-so-impressive spread of non-farm rural activities in Thailand where industry and the informal activities are concentrated in Bangkok and a few other towns. This is puzzling, as Thailand has experienced a high rate of agricultural growth during the 1970s and the 1980s, has an excellent road network, and levels of primary schooling are quite high in rural areas. The available studies attribute this insufficient rural industrialization to the nature of agricultural growth achieved, the pre-eminence of Bangkok as a centre of industrial activity, and to the protection accorded to industry by discriminating against agriculture (World Bank 1983; Siamwalla 1991; Johansson and Ronnas 1996).

Agricultural growth in Thailand has been labour-using, as it has been based on the extension of area under cultivation. Seasonality in labour demand as well as in consumer demand for goods and services is the hallmark of such a pattern of growth which is not conducive to the growth of the rural non-farm sector. The spread of yield-increasing technology can raise farm incomes and release labour for non-farm activities. The diversification of agriculture into horticultural products for which Thailand has a comparative advantage can open up opportunities for agro-processing industry in rural areas in a big way.

The industrial concentration in Bangkok because of its geographically-endowed locational advantages should be mitigated both by measures aimed at curbing such a concentration for example, reducing protection to industry, especially to units located there; and by positive measures to improve the locational advantage of the rural areas, for example, by reducing export tax on rice. Easy access to the export markets for agro-products in the developed countries can give an impetus to the growth of rural agro-based industries in some Asian countries like Thailand which have a comparative advantage in agriculture.

Rural Poverty

Absolute and Relative Poverty

Absolute poverty denotes the inability of a household to have a command over the minimum calories required for human sustenance and other basic necessities. Such households are identified as those below the expenditure group which is able to meet the normative requirement of calories. Such a group would also be incurring some expenditure on other items of basic needs. Relative poverty, on the other hand, can be perceived to be serious even when absolute poverty is low but income and expenditure inequalities are high. However, there is no unique relationship between the incidence of absolute poverty and inequality, just as there is no unique relationship between economic growth and income inequality. The decline in absolute poverty across the countries has been associated with the decline in inequalities in some cases and with the rise in quite a few other cases, depending on the socio-economic structure within which economic growth occurs and the development strategy followed. However, a decline in income or expenditure inequality, other things remaining equal, is found to result in the reduction of absolute poverty.

Incidence and Determinants of Rural Poverty

Among the Asian countries under study, there is a strong correlation between rural poverty on the one hand and a number of major economic and social development variables, on the other. The variables considered are: the access to land, population growth, overall gross domestic product (GDP) growth, agriculture GDP growth, rate of inflation, infant mortality rate, life expectancy at birth, adult literacy rate, and gross primary enrolment ratio. Several of these economic and social factors are highly inter-related. Whereas a high correlation between a set of factors does not necessarily imply a causal relationship among them, theory as well as empirical evidence suggest a definite causal relationship between some of these variables. For example, access to land and the resulting economic and social security, and high literacy levels do influence population growth rate which in turn affects economic growth and poverty via its impact on savings–investment and the development of human capital. Similarly, economic growth, human resource development (health and education), and poverty are causally related, each influencing the other.

We have seen that East Asia, China, and the Republic of Korea experienced a high overall as well as high agricultural growth (Chapter 2). They also present a picture of equal access to land, low population growth rate, low illiteracy levels, low infant mortality rate, and higher life expectancy at birth (Tables 11.1 and 11.2). Population growth rates in China and the Republic of Korea were already the lowest in the 1970s which further came down significantly nearer to one per cent in the 1980s and to one per cent in the 1990s. There is a causal nexus between economic and social security conferred by land reforms and speedy demographic transition. Equally significant is the causal relationship between slow population growth on the one hand, and high economic growth and human development, on the other.

Table 11.1: Landlessness, Population Growth, and Adult Illiteracy Rate

(per cent)

	Percentage of Rural Population without Land	Average Annual Population Growth Rate (Per cent)			Adult Illiteracy Rate 1997	
		1970–80	1980–92	1990–2001	Males	Females
	(1)	(2)	(3)	(4)	(5)	(6)
East Asia						
China	–	1.8	1.4	1.0	9	25
Rep. of Korea	4	1.8	1.1	1.0	1	4
South-east Asia						
Indonesia	15	2.3	1.8	1.6	9	20
Malaysia	12	2.4	2.5	2.4	10	19
Philippines	34	2.5	2.4	2.1	5	6
Thailand	15	2.7	1.8	0.9	3	7
South Asia						
Bangladesh	20	2.6	2.3	1.8	50	73
India	30	2.3	2.1	1.8	33	61
Nepal	18	2.5	2.6	2.4	44	79
Pakistan	30	3.1	3.1	2.5	45	75
Sri Lanka	22	1.6	1.4	1.3	6	12

Sources: 1. For columns 1, 2, and 3: ESCAP, United Nations, *Rural Poverty Alleviation and Sustainable Development in Asia and the Pacific*, 1996.
2. For column 4: The World Bank, *World Development Report*, 2003.
3. For column 5 and 6: The World Bank, *World Development Report*, 1999/2000.

Landlessness is negligible in these countries. A high proportion of small holdings in a situation where land reforms have been effectively implemented, as in the Republic of Korea, should be distinguished from a similarly high proportion of small holdings when there is high inequality in the distribution of landholdings. Ironically, the preponderance of small farms is a consequence of the success of land reforms in one situation and of its failure in another. In the former, the preponderance of small holdings is inevitable, especially when there is an acute scarcity of land, as in the Republic of Korea. In the latter situation, other things remaining equal, holdings of the large majority of small farmers would be smaller in size, and there would be economic and social deprivation in terms of lack of access to credit, inputs, and technology.

Table 11.2: Infant Mortality Rate and Life Expectancy at Birth

	Infant Mortality Rate (Per 1000 Live Births)		Life Expectancy at Birth (1997)	
	1980	1997	Males	Females
East Asia				
China	42	32	68	71
Rep. of Korea	26	9	69	76
South-east Asia				
Indonesia	90	47	63	67
Malaysia	30	11	70	75
Philippines	52	35	67	70
Thailand	49	33	66	72
South Asia				
Bangladesh	132	75	58	58
India	115	71	62	64
Nepal	132	83	58	57
Pakistan	127	95	61	63
Sri Lanka	34	14	71	75

Source: The World Bank, *World Development Report*, 1999/2000.

What is even more serious, the socio-political clout enjoyed by the large land owners perpetuates the dependency syndrome for the rural poor. Agricultural wages are driven down to low levels on account of the larger supply of labour as well as the oligopsonistic practices followed by a small number of big land owners (Gaiha 1993). For the same reason, the rates of interest charged on credit, particularly consumption credit to the poor, could be exorbitant and rents on land leased out to the poor households could be high (Bharadwaj 1974). Thus, the indirect impact of land reforms by way of influencing the factor markets in rural areas in favour of the poor and raising their socio-political clout would be no less important than better access to land as an income-earning asset.

Gross domestic product growth rates were close to 10 per cent in these countries in the 1980s and continued to be high in the 1990s. Agricultural growth rates in the Republic of Korea appear comparatively lower, but they have to be viewed in conjunction with overall economic growth rates to see their impact on rural poverty. However, agricultural growth in the Republic of Korea was well above the population growth rate in the 1970s as well as the 1980s.

The rate of inflation was brought down significantly in the Republic of Korea from around 17 per cent during the 1970s to well below 10 per cent in both the countries during the 1980s (ESCAP 1996). Thus a combination of access to land which ensured social and economic security to the poor, low population growth, and high economic growth rates—overall as well as agricultural—and low rate of inflation resulted in the low incidence of rural poverty in these countries. The incidence of rural poverty is the lowest in these East Asian countries (Table 11.3). As discussed below, such interrelationships between these factors appear equally glaring in all the three groups of countries.

Table 11.3: Rural Poverty (Head-count Ratio)

	Initial (Pre-reform) Year		Later Year	
	Year	Rural Poverty	Year	Rural Poverty
	(1)	(2)	(3)	(4)
East Asia				
China	1978	30.3T	1998	4.6
Rep. of Korea	1967	33.7	1988	6.5
South-east Asia				
Indonesia	1984	21.0	1999	27.1T
Malaysia	1984	18.4T	1989	15.5T
Philippines	1977	66.0	1997	50.7
Thailand	1976	36.0	1992	15.5
South Asia				
Bangladesh	1984	50.0	1995–6	39.8
India	1983	49.0	1999–2000	26.8
Nepal	1988	61.0	1995–6	44.0
Pakistan	–	–	1991	36.9
Sri Lanka	1983	51.0	1995–6	25.0T

Note: T denotes total, that is, rural and urban combined.
Sources: 1. For initial year: ESCAP, United Nations, *Rural Poverty Alleviation and Sustainable Development in Asia and the Pacific*, 1996.
2. For later year: The World Bank, *World Development Report*, 1999/2000 and 1999/2003.

Countries in South-east Asia account for the next higher incidence of rural poverty in both the periods. Landlessness is greater in this group of countries than in the first group. Considering that a smaller land holding in this group indicates greater deprivation than in the first group where land reforms have been implemented effectively, if the landless and the small holders are combined, the extent of deprivation, that is, the proportion of such population to total rural population, ranged from around 50 per cent in Malaysia to about 75 per cent in Indonesia and Philippines (ESCAP 1996). Population growth rates in this group of countries were higher during the 1970s (over 2 per cent). They declined over the 1980s, but were still closer to 2 per cent in two cases and over 2 per cent in the other two cases. They experienced high economic growth rates of 6–8 per cent during the 1970s which, however, decelerated in the 1980s. However, except in Philippines, growth rates continued to be quite high, being as high as 8 per cent in Thailand. Agricultural growth rates were well above population growth rates (1.5 per cent higher) in both the periods. Except in Philippines, inflation rates were brought down significantly to low levels (ESCAP 1996).

These countries thus show a relatively moderate performance in respect of access to land, population growth, economic growth, rate of inflation, and the incidence of rural poverty.

The incidence of rural poverty in the South Asian countries was much higher than in most countries of South-east Asia during the 1980s. The rural head-count ratio was 61 per cent for Nepal and, except in Pakistan, it was a little over 40 per cent in the rest of the countries in the region. These estimates of rural poverty (head-count ratio) given in Table 11.3 may not be strictly comparable across countries because of the possible differences, among others, in the poverty norms used. However, a World Bank study, on the basis of a global poverty line at US$ 370 per person a year in constant 1985 Purchasing Power Parity (PPP) prices, showed that in 1990 the percentage of population below the poverty line was 49 in South Asia as compared to 11.3 in East and South-east Asia (World Bank, *World Development Report* 1992, p. 30). In South Asian countries, landlessness amounts to 20–30 per cent as against below 15 per cent in South-east Asia (except Philippines). Except in Pakistan, the incidence of small holdings varies from 50 per cent to 66 per cent. Thus the combined incidence of landlessness and small holdings ranges from 50 per cent in Pakistan to over 80 per cent in other countries (ESCAP 1996). Except in Sri Lanka, population growth rates were nearer to those of South-east Asian countries in the 1970s. However, they were higher in Pakistan. During the 1980s, population growth rates in these countries slowed down but, on the whole, were still higher than those in South-east Asia.

Growth rates of GDP in South Asia were significantly lower than in South-east Asian countries in the 1970s. They accelerated in most cases during the 1980s, but, on the whole, were not as impressive as in South-east Asia barring Philippines. Except in Sri Lanka, they were significantly lower than the population growth rates. They accelerated over the 1980s roughly to the levels experienced in South-east Asia, but per capita growth was still not as impressive as in many countries of South-east Asia.

Further, South Asian countries had very little success in bringing down inflation rates, except Bangladesh. Rates of inflation were nearer or higher than 10 per cent over the 1980s (ESCAP 1996). This experience points to better macroeconomic management in East and South-east Asia than in South Asia.

Altogether, the South Asian countries present a picture of greater deprivation or assetlessness, slower overall growth, slower agricultural growth, especially in per capita terms, higher inflation, and higher incidence of rural poverty than in East and South-east Asia. However, except in Pakistan and Nepal, population growth slowed down during the 1980s and the 1990s, and overall as well as agricultural growth rates accelerated in the 1980s. Whereas in the 1990s, overall GDP growth rates improved in these countries, there was, in general, a slow down in agricultural growth rates. Rural poverty declined but the incidence was still quite high. This is to be viewed against the backdrop of asset deprivation and slow overall and agricultural growth rates during the 1970s.

Social Development

Infant mortality rates which were already among the lowest in East Asia in 1980 declined further and continued to be among the lowest in the late 1990s, especially in the Republic of Korea. Decline in infant mortality rate was comparatively slow in China which could be attributed to some retrogression in health policy in the post-reform period. There is a significant decline in the infant mortality rate in Indonesia and all the other South-east Asian countries. Yet, they are still high in Indonesia (at 47) when compared to other South-east Asian countries. Except in Sri Lanka, they were quite high in the South Asian countries in 1980 and, despite the decline, were still very high in the late 1990s.

Life Expectancy at birth was well over 60 years for males and over 70 years for females in 1997 in East and South-east Asia. For most South Asian countries, however, it was around 60 years. In Sri Lanka, however, it was over 70 years for both males and females.

Adult illiteracy rates for males in 1997 were quite low in East and South-east Asia. For females too, except in China, Indonesia, and Malaysia, they were quite low. However, they were distinctly higher in South Asian countries, especially for females.

Gender Discrimination

Gender discrimination in respect of social development is quite high, especially in countries of South Asia. In 1975 the female–male ratio for life expectancy at birth was less than 1 in countries of South Asia except Sri Lanka, whereas it was above 1 for all the other countries. By 1992, it improved but continued to be lower than 1 for Nepal (ESCAP 1996). In 1997, it was above 1 for most countries, but for Nepal it was slightly lower (Table 11.2).

In respect of adult literacy, gender discrimination was the highest in South Asian countries in 1975. The female–male ratio was 35 per cent for Bangladesh; 40 per cent for India; 34 per cent for Pakistan; and as low as 15 per cent for Nepal. In 1993, this discrimination reduced in all the countries but the South Asian countries still showed the lowest female–male ratio (below 50 per cent), the lowest among them being for Nepal (ESCAP 1996).

The above analysis regarding the factors associated with rural poverty across the countries of East, South-east, and South Asia shows that, in the first place, the levels and changes in rural poverty are highly correlated with the levels and changes in the indicators of economic and social development. Second, these movements suggest a strong causal relationship among many of these variables. Third, the performance of the countries of East Asia is most impressive in respect of rural poverty reduction as well as improvement in the associated economic and social development factors, while the countries of South Asia show the lowest performance. Even the gender discrimination seems to be highly correlated with levels of rural poverty and levels of socio-economic development.

Rural Poverty: Household Level Characteristics

Access to Land

Landlessness and the limited access to land is a glaring feature of rural poverty. It is also the foremost characteristic, as much else influencing rural poverty depends on the access to productive assets. A survey by the Bangladesh Institute of Development Studies shows that poverty incidence is 78 per cent for households with no cultivated land and 71 per cent for those with less than 0.5 acre. Ninety per cent of the hard-core poor own less than 1.5 acres and 53 per cent have no cultivated land. Similarly, in India the incidence of poverty is the highest among the agricultural labour households who have very little access to land (*Asian Development Review* 1992).

Even in a country like the Republic of Korea where the decline in rural poverty has been rapid and where labour-intensive growth has been an important factor accounting for the decline in rural poverty, one of the most obvious and direct personal causes of whatever rural poverty that still remains is landlessness. About 88 per cent of landless households were identified as poor in a sample survey. Although about 38 per cent of poor farmers owned land, the majority of farms were smaller than 0.5 ha. The average ownership of land by poor farmers was 0.1 ha compared to 0.8 ha for the non-poor. Although the poor rented land, the area operated was usually small. Further, a case study in 1987 showed that possession of farmland has been a critical factor in determining the poor for the past two generations: 72 per cent of the current rural poor originate from the landless households (*Asian Development Review* 1992).

In Philippines, wherever the concentration of land is relatively high, the incidence of poverty is also high. Incidence of poverty shows greater association with concentration of land ownership than with size of holding. This could be attributed, in part, to the eviction of former tenants resulting in landlessness. However, given the concentration of land, high population growth, and limited employment opportunities outside agriculture can also be held responsible for the widespread poverty in rural areas. In Sri Lanka, on the other hand, most households have access to land which has been a critical determinant of rural poverty. A majority of poor farmers have access to land with holdings less than 1 acre. In Thailand, even though the concentration of land is high, there was a substantial access to land per head, including that leased in, on account of encroachment on forest land, which itself is attributable to landlessness and lack of land reform.

Demographic Factors

The poor households in all the countries studied have a larger family size with greater dependency ratio. In Bangladesh, the extremely poor and moderately poor households have a larger number of children below 10 years of age, fewer members in the income earning age group, and a high child–woman ratio. Similarly in the Republic of Korea, the poor have larger families and higher dependency rate than the non-poor. Female headed households represented 11 per cent of total households in the villages in a case study, 77 per cent of whom were identified as poor. Other important personal causes of rural poverty in Korea include poor health and nutritional status.

In Philippines, as in Korea, the rural poor tend to belong to relatively young age-groups, have a large family and low educational attainment. They are also characterized by high underemployment. In Sri Lanka, the incidence of rural poverty is found to increase with the increase in household size. About 40 per cent of households in poverty have seven members or more. The incidence of poverty is the lowest among ages 60 or more. As elsewhere, in Thailand the rural poor tend to have larger family size, fewer income earners, and household heads with lower education. They lack basic amenities such as proper toilet facilities, piped water supply, and electricity.

Literacy

In Bangladesh, nearly 86 per cent of adult members in the extremely poor households were illiterate compared with 47 per cent in the non-poor households. The proportion of students of school-going age (6 to 15 years old) was 53 per cent for males and 43 per cent for females for the extremely poor as compared to 70 per cent and 62 per cent for the non-poor households. In Korea, a low level of education was a distinctive characteristic of the rural poor. A case study showed that none of the poor household heads received high-school education. Compared with the national average of 8.6 years in 1985, the rural poor had an average of 3 years of schooling. In Thailand, health and primary education are satisfactory, while secondary education for the poor is a problem.

Access to Credit, Inputs, and Technology

In Bangladesh, there is little difference in the extent of use of modern technology like the use of high yielding varieties of seeds across size of holding. In the case of chemical fertilizers, however, large farmers use more per acre than small farmers, on account of their better access to resources. Similarly, in Philippines, the poor have inadequate access to modern technology partly due to lack of access to credit. Rural poverty is common where agricultural productivity is low and where droughts and typhoons occur frequently. Even in Korea, lack of access to agricultural technologies and low level of education are important causes of rural poverty.

Poverty and Inequality

The head-count ratio is insensitive to changes in expenditure distribution among the poor and to the level of deprivation for the poor or the distance of their average expenditure from the poverty line expenditure. Therefore, in addition to the head-count ratio, certain distributionally sensitive measures of poverty have been extensively used. Income gap, Poverty gap, Foster-Greer-Thorbecké (FGT) measure of poverty, and Sen Index are some such measures often used. Income gap, for example, is measured as the average income shortfall of the poor expressed in proportion to the poverty line income. Poverty gap is measured as the arithmetic mean of the income shortfall in proportion to the poverty line over the whole population. This measure is sensitive to both the number of the poor and their degree of poverty (Balisacan 1992).

Estimates of these measures derived from household expenditure surveys for these countries show that they broadly correspond to the trend of head-count ratios. That is, the intensity of rural poverty in terms of the distance of the average expenditure of the rural poor from the poverty line expenditure as well as the inequality in expenditure among the rural poor are generally higher where the rural head-count ratio is higher. Second, the picture regarding rural income or expenditure inequalities in relation to the incidence of rural poverty is mixed, some countries showing a rise in such inequality with the decline in rural poverty with others showing a decline. Third, relative poverty or the per capita expenditure of the rural poor as a proportion to the average per capita consumer expenditure in the economy as a whole, has in general tended to rise. This inequality is rooted in rural–urban inequality in expenditure which has risen with the rise in GDP per capita.

In India, Bangladesh, and Philippines, the distributionally sensitive measures like the Sen index of poverty show a pattern similar to head-count ratio. In India, the severity of poverty is indicated by the fact that the bottom 20 per cent of rural households accounted for about 90 per cent of rural poor. In Indonesia, since 1976, the Gini coefficients have gradually decreased both for rural and urban populations. However, from 1976 to 1987, the rate of increase in current monthly expenditures has been higher in rural than in urban areas. In Korea, the size distribution of farm household income is more equitable than that of non-farm household income. This is explained by the diminishing importance of rice paddy among the larger farmers and the increasing importance of non-farm labour force and agricultural capital formation among smaller farmers in the 1980s. Relative poverty or relative deprivation defined as the rural farm household income below one half of the average household income, has become an issue of concern in the Republic of Korea, as the development gap has become wider between rural and urban areas. Relative poverty has thus declined at a much lower rate than absolute poverty. In Philippines, there was an increase in personal income inequality in rural areas between 1961 and 1971. Adoption of modern technology was initially concentrated among large farmers. This together with highly skewed distribution of agricultural landholdings and the slow growth of non-farm employment opportunities in relation to labour force growth, explains the rise in inequality. Despite this, the head-count ratio declined. In Sri Lanka, between 1980–1 and 1985–6, all the income groups other than the highest decile experienced a decline in their respective shares in total income. The Gini concentration ratio has increased, though at a lower rate for the rural sector (Asian Development Bank 1992).

China

There was a dramatic reduction in rural poverty in China from about one-third of rural population in 1978 to about 8 per cent in 1996. Much of this reduction was achieved in a short period of seven years between 1978 and 1985 following the liberalization of the economy (ESCAP 1996). This is explained by the rapid, broad-based rural development, encompassing farm as well as non-farm sectors. Surprisingly, however, further reduction in poverty has been slow after the mid-1980s despite high overall economic growth. Absolute poverty is now almost entirely restricted to resource-deficient remote upland areas in the interior provinces of northern, northwestern, and southwestern China.

The key factor responsible for the sluggish reduction in rural poverty after the mid-eighties is the absence of reasonable agricultural growth and rural enterprise development in upland areas on account of low level of infrastructure and low level of application of yield-increasing technology (ESCAP 1996). Rural enterprises have a comparative advantage in the wealthier areas on account of inexpensive access to national and international markets. Migration of excess labour from the less developed areas to those booming with economic activity—already in evidence in a big way—offers one possible solution to the poverty problem in the backward areas. Efforts are also on to better integrate these backward areas with the rest of the economy through infrastructure and human resource development. This experience shows that in the post-liberalization era, even in a country like China with its impressive record in respect of poverty reduction, development strategy, and macroeconomic policies involving a reduced role of the state could undermine poverty alleviation efforts.

Republic of Korea

By successfully implementing land reforms, significantly reducing population growth and by adopting export-oriented and growth-pole development strategies since the 1960s, the Republic of Korea has been able to achieve a very high growth and reduce absolute poverty significantly. The farm poverty head-count ratio declined dramatically over a period of two decades from 33.7 per cent in 1967 to 6.5 per cent in 1988, despite an annual rate of inflation of over 12 per cent during this period (Chung and Oh 1992).

The country has reached a stage where the focus of macroeconomic policy has shifted from the alleviation of absolute poverty to reducing relative poverty and inequality. Towards this end, paradoxically, the policies being advocated are those which seek to protect agriculture, curb the concentration of economic power in the hands of a few industrial conglomerates, and foster small and medium industries. These objectives are to be achieved, among other means, through greater investment in human resource development and infrastructure building with a view to providing greater opportunities for upper social mobility for the poor (Chung and Oh 1992).

Indonesia

As a consequence of high agricultural growth in the pre- as well as post-reform period, the decline in the incidence of rural poverty was faster from around 21 per cent in 1984 to around 14 per cent in 1993, as against a decline from 9.3 per cent to 8.7 per cent in urban areas (World Bank 1990; Tjondronegoro *et al.* 1992). Indonesia's success in poverty reduction is explained, in a significant measure, by the achievements in the pre-adjustment period in the area of agriculture, particularly rice, and the development of physical and social infrastructure in rural areas, which provided a strong impetus to economic growth in the adjustment period. Although the number of landless is significant, a large number of poor belong to the category of small holders, who benefited significantly from the two rounds of devaluations, which also led to the rise in farm wages (Thorbecke 1992, p. 20). The prevailing low inequality in expenditure meant that overall income growth is easily translated into income increases at the lower levels leading to poverty reduction. Thus about half of those rising above the poverty line in rural areas by 1987 belonged to the category of small holders (World Bank 1990).

The nature and speed of government's policy response to the external shocks was an important factor accounting for high growth and reduction in poverty in Indonesia. In reducing development expenditures, those on sectors having a bearing on poverty such as agriculture, human resource development and transfers to lower-level governments were protected even as there was a freeze on civil service wages and salaries.

It appears that major declines in poverty were witnessed in rural Java and the remaining poverty is now concentrated in eastern areas of Indonesia and certain specific locations in Java. A major programme of agricultural resettlement known as transmigration provided employment to a considerable part of Java's incremental labour force.

However, there is a growing concern about the reversal of the earlier trend of a decline in income inequality and about growing regional disparities in development. Therefore, in addition to growth there is a need for poverty alleviation programmes targeted to specific regions and groups. There is also a need to step up the export of labour-intensive manufactures and agro-processed products. Further, human resource development is required for exploiting the emerging opportunities for the poor in the services sector.

Thailand

The inequalities in the distribution of land are significant in Thailand. Yet, the encroachment of forest area by the poor for cultivation with the tacit support of the government led to a significant reduction in poverty. However, the decline in poverty in Thailand has been associated with a rise in inequality in income distribution. The poor are mostly farmers accounting for more than three quarters of the total number of poor (ESCAP 1996).

Since rural Thailand has good infrastructure and the literacy levels are high, rural poverty can be reduced significantly by raising farm yields, by diversifying agriculture and by expanding rural non-farm activities. Raising the educational levels of the poor in rural areas is another promising avenue for reducing poverty and inequality as this may induce the outward migration of labour force which now appears excessive in rural areas.

Malaysia

In Malaysia, contrary to the general expectation, the consequences of the stabilization measures for the poor did not turn out to be harsh basically on account of the dynamism of growth built over the 1970s and a strong pursuit of policies for equity between various ethnic groups under the New Economic Policy (NEP). The income inequality as measured by the Gini ratio declined significantly between 1970 and 1984, mainly because of the decline in rural poverty among the Malay or Bumiputra population (comprising half of the country's population), from over two-thirds in 1970 to only a quarter in 1984. It is thus interesting that despite the macroeconomic adjustment during 1984–7, poverty continued to decline, though at a slower pace, reaching the level of 17 per cent in 1987. This was due entirely to the decline in rural poverty on account of the rise in the incomes of paddy farmers. These are predominantly poorly educated Malay, working in smallholder agriculture or as estate workers (Demery and Demery 1992). These farmers were beginning to realize the productivity potentials that previous public investments in rural infrastructure had facilitated.

The stabilization measures in the adjustment period, that is, between 1984 and 1987, attempted to protect the share of social sector spending at the level obtaining in 1979. In real terms, the expenditures for education and health rose, on an average, by 5.7 and 3.7 per cent, respectively. The allocation within sectors was not biased against programmes favouring the poor (Demery and Demery 1992).

Policy Perspectives: Emerging Issues of Concern

The analysis in this chapter brings out the primacy of access to land in influencing the incidence of rural poverty, intensity of poverty and inequality; and the favourable impact of high agricultural and overall growth as well as low rates of inflation on rural poverty. In all these respects, the performance of East Asian countries like China and Republic of Korea stands out prominently as most effective, while the performance in most countries of South Asia is least impressive.

The Asian experience with rural poverty reduction discussed above suggests that where land is not equitably distributed, the role of labour-intensive growth—agricultural and overall—becomes important for neutralizing the adverse impact of the inequitable distribution of land and for reducing population growth. The role of trade and investment and technology transfer assume added significance in this situation. However, appropriate policy framework and measures may be needed for achieving labour-intensive growth, especially in the non-agricultural sector, as at present the dependence of the labour force on agriculture seems excessive.

This experience also underlines the importance of reducing inflation rates by adopting appropriate macroeconomic policies for reducing rural poverty.

Over a period of time, the disparities between groups of countries in this Asian region in respect of social development have probably narrowed down to a greater extent than in the case of incidence of rural poverty and levels of economic development. This is to be expected because the impact of public investment and public policy on the levels of social development is more immediate and direct. Since many of these economic and social factors interact with each other by reinforcing the beneficial impact, it would be prudent for public policy to undertake concerted measures on all these fronts for maximizing the benefits arising from these mutually interactive processes and for breaking the vicious circle of poverty and social and economic backwardness.

The foregoing survey of changes in the rural economy of selected regions of Asia also suggests that there is a significant potential for efficient, equitable, and sustainable transformation of rural areas which is yet to be exploited. Infrastructure and human resource development in the less developed areas, technological changes in agriculture to overcome the green revolution fatigue and improving export prospects for agro-products come out as some major issues of concern. Ensuring gender equity, arresting the degradation of environment and effective governance through decentralized development are other major areas of concern.

The role of governments in the developing countries of Asia is extremely important in creating these conditions which are necessary for deriving full benefits from the favourable macroeconomic environment created in many of these countries during the 1980s and the 1990s.

12

Trade Liberalization and Rural Poverty

Introduction

The Uruguay Round agreements on agriculture have to be viewed in the context of the ongoing liberalization of economies in South Asia, including India, where poverty is widespread and which in fact account for the large majority of the poor in Asia. The agreements of the Uruguay Round will give further impetus to economic reforms in these countries by speeding up trade and investment flows and accelerating technological change. On the other hand, the benefits from the Uruguay Round agreements for the poor in these countries would be visible only when the impact of the ongoing economic reforms together with other measures to augment infrastructure and skills begin to yield results in terms of improving supply elasticities and employment.

Apart from providing an impetus to trade, investment, and technological change, the Uruguay Round agreements lend greater certainty and predictability to the global environment surrounding trade and investment, thus enabling individual countries to plan more effectively for the future. This is extremely important for orderly growth and poverty reduction in the newly developing economies whose capacity to withstand the vagaries of international trading environment is low.

Consequences of the Uruguay Round Agreements

The available studies show that the immediate or short-run impact of the implementation of the Uruguay Round agreements could be to raise the world prices of certain agricultural commodities, particularly of food staples like rice and wheat, despite some increase in their output (ESCAP 1995). This is on account of the increased demand following reduced tariffs and stepping-up of trade in grains. The long-term impact of these price changes on the poor would depend upon the induced increase in output and employment as well as on the extent to which the poor are net buyers of foodgrains. In situations where agricultural output is sufficiently responsive to price changes, the employment and incomes of the rural poor may increase significantly and in view of the softening impact of the increase in the supplies of foodgrains on prices, the urban poor may also not be adversely affected.

Of greater importance, however, is the capacity of the poorer countries to take advantage of the liberalized trading environment and produce for export agricultural commodities for which the demand is likely to be elastic for example, meat, milk products, and horticultural products through value addition by undertaking agro-processing. As mentioned above, the price environment is likely to be favourable for undertaking these activities. Further, studies show that the welfare gains from technological change in the economies of the region, that is, from the increase in productivity of resources induced by trade and investment following the Uruguay Round, would amount to several times the static gains or gains from the scenario without induced technological change (ESCAP 1995). The willingness and the ability of the poorer Asian countries to undertake long-term measures to strengthen the supply side factors in agriculture by investing in infrastructure and by improving agricultural research and extension will thus hold the key to deriving full benefits from the Uruguay Round. Studies show, moreover, that agricultural trade liberalization and a significant reduction in subsidies in the developed countries may, in all likelihood, result in lowering land prices in those economies and raising them in the developing economies. The land owning farmers in the developing Asian economies, including small holders, will stand to benefit from the rise in land prices (ESCAP 1995).

Under the Uruguay Round agreements, food security stocks and domestic food aid fall in the list of items placed in the so-called 'green box', the domestic supports on which are excluded from the agreed budgetary reductions. Further, the Uruguay Round decision on measures in favour of least developed countries calls for financial support for a country if hardship is caused by the rising prices for imported food. Moreover, the participants agreed to ensure that the implementation of the Round does not adversely affect the availability of food aid to meet the needs of developing countries.

The consequences of the Uruguay Round agreements for the rural poor depend not merely on their possible impact on agricultural growth and employment but on wages and employment in the economy in general following complete Uruguay Round trade liberalization including the phasing out of the Multi-fibre Agreement (MFA). The latter may result in lowering the world prices of textiles and clothing somewhat owing to the opportunities for export opening up in the low-cost regions. Despite this, the exports of textiles and clothing from Asia will increase significantly, so that the countries in the region will be in a better position to finance their food imports despite the rise in their prices. The increase in the output of textiles for exports will generate additional employment for the urban as well as rural poor on a significant scale, resulting in a rise in wages and thus enabling many of them to cross the poverty line. This has been dramatically illustrated by the Bangladesh experience even as the Uruguay Round agreements were in progress, when the share of garments in exports rose from less than 1 per cent to 40 per cent within a short period, drawing the rural poor, especially women, into this industry. It has been estimated that the additional welfare gains for the countries of Asia from complete liberalization of trade including the phasing out of the MFA, could be more than twice as high as the welfare gains arising from global agricultural liberalization only (ESCAP 1995).

Commodity Specialization and Regional Interdependence

In a liberalized trading framework, individual countries tend to specialize in the production of commodities in which they have a comparative advantage, so that the resulting rise in welfare and reduction in poverty would be consistent with, and indeed due to, economic efficiency. However, measures of comparative advantage at any point of time with given technology and factor prices do not provide satisfactory guidelines for policy, especially for the developing economies experiencing fast growth and hence facing the prospect of rapid changes in technology and factor prices (ESCAP 1996).

The scenario regarding the comparative advantage of individual agricultural commodities within the Economic and Social Commission for Asia and the Pacific (ESCAP) region seems to have altered significantly over the last two decades. In the case of rice, for example, Thailand was not only the single largest exporter in the ESCAP region in the mid-1970s, but accounted for as high as around 97 per cent of exports from the region. However, its share in the region's rice exports came down to one-third in 1992, while countries like Pakistan, India, and China increased their shares significantly (ESCAP 1995). It appears that with economic growth and modernization in the Asia-Pacific region, there are not only shifts in the comparative advantage in respect of individual commodities within countries, but a larger number of countries are able to specialize in a wide range of commodities. It would be prudent, therefore, to leave open the specifics concerning commodity specialization within countries which are best resolved by the emerging patterns of production and trade, while emphasizing only the desirability of openness in trade and the need for individual developing countries, especially those in South Asia, to step-up agricultural infrastructure and to strengthen agricultural research and extension.

Notwithstanding the limitations of judging the long-run comparative advantage that the individual countries may enjoy in respect of specific commodities, the emerging trends regarding production and exports of various commodities seem to indicate that Thailand, China, Vietnam, and South Asia may have an advantage in respect of rice, Australia in wheat, China and Thailand in fruits and vegetables, and the South-east Asian countries in vegetable oils. In Bangladesh and the eastern Gangetic Plains of India where rural poverty is widespread, rice—because of its high labour-intensity—seems to be emerging as a major poverty-alleviating crop. Horticulture and floriculture appear to hold similar potential in Nepal and the dry, upland areas in India, provided public investments are stepped up for infrastructure towards agro-processing and marketing, and the necessary financial and technical assistance is extended to small farmers so as to enable them to withstand competition from the bigger farms and corporations (ESCAP 1996). Further, the development of horticulture in such areas requires soil and moisture conservation through watershed development on a community basis. This is how the poverty alleviation objective is easily integrated with concerns for the protection of environment. However, for the low-income countries, including those in South Asia, agricultural liberalization *per se* may not be sufficient to alleviate poverty, and welfare gains may not be significant in the absence of measures for the upgradation of infrastructure and for technological change to raise the productivity of resources.

The complementarity between the countries of the Asia-Pacific region is indicated by the fact that the bulk of the trade flows are intra-regional. For example, the top five importers of cotton exports from Australia and Pakistan are ESCAP countries. The top four importers of Malaysian vegetable oils are ESCAP countries, as are the top three importers of China's fruits and vegetables (ESCAP 1995). This inter-dependence may persist because, apart from agro-climatic differences, there is a wide variation in the levels of development between the countries of the region and currently the rates of growth among them also diverge significantly. To illustrate, the fast growing regions like East and South-east Asia provide a huge market for exports from other ESCAP countries. Therefore, pursuing open regionalism by further liberalizing trade and investment and by refraining from undertaking protectionist measures, for which pressures seem to be building up in some countries, would be in the best interests of countries in the region.

Access to Developed Country Markets

In recent decades, high agricultural protection in developed countries has severely limited the access of foreign producers, most especially those from developing countries, to domestic markets of the former countries. As in past industrialization episodes, the rapid industrialization in East Asian countries has accompanied a decline in the competitiveness of agriculture. In Japan, South Korea, Taiwan, and more recently, Malaysia and Thailand, this has been perceived as a threat to domestic food security. The familiar response to this perception has invariably involved the erection of barriers against imports competing with domestic production (ESCAP 1996).

Unfortunately, the worldwide liberalization of agricultural trade intended by the Uruguay Round of multilateral trade agreement may not be as great as expected (World Bank 1995). While the agreement did result in significant reform of the rules of agricultural trade, it has fallen short of actually reducing the high agricultural protection in Organization for Economic Cooperation and Development (OECD) countries (except Japan). In addition, most of these countries applied binding tariffs much higher than the tariff equivalents of border protection prevailing in the base period. They also applied non-tariff barriers in the form of sanitary and phyto-sanitary (SPS) measures.

Expanding access to developed-country markets is probably the most effective and sustainable way of delivering development 'assistance' to developing countries. But in ensuring the expansion of markets for the products of more advanced countries, developing countries will also have to undertake policy reforms aimed at enhancing efficiency of resource allocation and fostering sustainable economic growth (ESCAP 1996).

13

Attack on Poverty and Deprivation

Role of Structural Change and Structural Adjustment

So far, the strategy for the removal of poverty in India consisted of a series of poverty alleviation programmes (PAPs) designed to widen the income-earning opportunities for the poor and enhance their socio-economic status. When we talked of structural changes in the 1950s and the 1960s, we usually had in mind land reforms, credit reform, introduction of Panchayati Raj, and other such measures which not only improved the income-earning power of the poor and the under-privileged but also raised their bargaining power vis-á-vis the big land owners, money-lenders, traders, and contractors. The series of special programmes launched in the 1970s to strengthen the income-earning power of the small and marginal farmers, scheduled castes and tribes and those in the backward regions constituted such interventions by the state in the absence of which the poor would have been left entirely to the mercy of the market forces. Similarly, the endowment of assets to the poor for self-employment under the Integrated Rural Development Programme (IRDP), the special programmes for wage employment and those for the women such as Development of Women and Children in Rural Areas (DWCRA) were designed in the 1980s to empower the poor. More recently, measures such as the reservation of jobs for the weaker sections and the activization of Panchayati Raj institutions with reservations in them for women and other weaker sections through the 73rd and 74th Amendments of the Constitution have been designed to trigger social change by releasing the creative energies of the weak and the underprivileged while at the same time protecting them from the operation of market forces.

One would prefer to bracket all these measures as those inducing structural changes in varying degree. This is because they seek to enhance the socio-economic power of the poor through conscious public intervention in the market and thus to modify the market forces in their favour which would otherwise work to their disadvantage. Such measures should be distinguished from the populist measures which merely act as doles and do not enable the poor to stand on their own or fight for their rights.

Thus all interventions in favour of the poor which alter the relative socio-economic position of different entities operating in the market can be termed as those which induce structural changes. Such changes can be induced by autonomous forces such as the peasant movements for the redistribution of land and enforcement of tenurial rights or the organizations of rural labour fighting for higher wages and better living conditions. However, structural changes induced by state intervention have become increasingly important over a period of time, though it is necessary to remember that in a democratic polity, state action is itself determined by the wishes of the people expressed through electoral and legislative processes as well as by the pressures exerted by the poor through their organized strength.

The interventions by the state enumerated above are basically redistributive in nature. Some of them are confiscatory as in the case of redistribution of surplus land acquired from the large landowners after the imposition of ceiling on land holdings. However, most of the measures are not confiscatory, but represent preferential share for the poor out of the incremental income, wealth, credit, and jobs from the society mobilized and allocated through the mechanism of the state. Confiscatory reforms are a rarity in the post-World War situation, especially in democratic societies.

The largest of confiscatory reforms were witnessed in East Asia including in the Peoples' Republic of China and Japan in the immediate post-war period under authoritarian regimes subscribing to diametrically different ideologies. Confiscatory reforms are revolutionary and are, therefore, far-reaching in their consequences. They accelerate structural changes by at once abolishing the privileges enjoyed hitherto by a few, thus severely undermining their socio-economic clout, even as the socio-economic position of the large majority is lifted up. This explains why the reduction in poverty has been dramatic in such societies, growth rates in gross domestic product (GDP) have accelerated, and contrary to expectation, based on Simon Kuznets' hypothesis (Kuznets 1966), growth has been associated with decline in inequality. Historically, most other countries including India in the post-war climate have been destined for redistributive reforms of a gradual or evolutionary nature. The obvious consequence is the uneasy co-existence of different interest groups, which explains the slow rate of structural change, slow reduction in poverty, and indeed slow rate of growth in output.

From the gradual structural changes in the post-war period, we are witnessing a transition to 'structural adjustment' as a guiding principle of economic policy in the post-cold war period. Historically, these phenomena are not accidental but are germane to the respective periods. However, the immediate question of interest for us is whether the process of structural adjustment underway is going to retard the already slow pace of structural change and thus postpone the eradication of poverty and deprivation to an indefinitely long period. It is argued here that this need not be so and indeed for various reasons the process of structural adjustment, properly conceived and implemented, is becoming a necessary, though not sufficient, condition for accelerating the process of structural change so as to eradicate poverty.

Whereas structural changes of the type enumerated above involve state intervention to alter the relative socio-economic position of different groups with a view to turning the markets friendly to the poor, structural adjustment involves freeing markets and minimizing state intervention in certain spheres of economic activity with a view to turning the economy market-friendly. The idea is to allow the market signals to determine the allocation of resources and provide incentives for the absorption of cost-reducing technologies in an open and competitive setting. This would enhance the productivity and efficiency of resource-use in the economy, thus stepping up the growth rate and resource generation.

It can be seen easily that in activities where direct management by the state has led to gross inefficiencies and huge financial losses, disengaging the state from such activities and handing them over to the users of services where possible or to the private sector can at once improve the health of the economy and augment the resources of the state, which it can deploy for programmes designed to effect structural changes so as to eradicate poverty. In fact, the capacity of the state to intervene massively in favour of the poor has been undermined by the huge losses incurred by the state undertakings and enterprises on account of the perpetuation of inefficiency and low productivity and the inability to recover costs by charging economic rates from the users of services. The major beneficiaries from such underpricing or hidden subsidies are the affluent sections who have the capacity to pay.

Whereas 'structural changes' as defined above are concerned with equity, 'structural adjustment' is concerned with efficiency. The achievement of equity or social justice depends, among other things, on the availability of resources with the state which can be generated only through the increase in productivity arising from the efficient use of resources in the economy. Therefore, at this stage of development, the goals of equity and efficiency are highly complementary.

The East Asian experience in the post-war period offers a classic illustration of how structural changes directed at improving the socio-economic position of the weaker sections can, by turning markets in favour of the poor, contribute to a significant reduction in poverty and inequality, even as growth rates in GDP are raised to very high levels (Chapter 2).

The reduction in absolute poverty in East Asia between 1970 and 1990 has been dramatic. The proportion of population below the poverty line in this region comprising Peoples' Republic of China, Indonesia, Korea, Malaysia, Philippines, Thailand, and Indochina declined from 35 per cent to 10 per cent over this period (Johansen 1993; see also Table 11.3). In India, on the other hand, the poverty ratio is estimated to have declined from 54 per cent in 1972 to 35.5 per cent in 1990–1 and 26 per cent in 1999–2000. On a roughly comparable basis, the absolute number of poor in India in 1990–1 were as many as 298 million as against 180 million in the whole of East Asia, including 100 million in China. Further, the key social indicators viz., life expectancy, infant mortality, adult literacy, and population growth show these countries to be in a much better position than India in 1990 when economic reforms were launched (Chapter 11). It is known that many of these countries were no better than India in the 1950s and the 1960s in respect of per capita income and the levels of social development.

How does one explain the dramatic transformation of these societies on equitable lines? A series of structural changes and right priorities in development had already placed many of these economies on a high growth path with wider or equitable sharing of benefits much before they had to undergo the process of structural adjustment beginning in the early 1980s. If one were to generalize their experience, abstracting from inter-country variations, the literature on the subject converges on the following: The diffusion of primary education was the single most important factor accounting for the reduction in poverty and income inequality, as, in general, human capital represented by primary education turns out be the most important variable explaining growth, followed by physical capital and total factor productivity (World Bank 1993a). This process of transformation was very much aided by the outward orientation of quite a few of these economies, particularly the smaller ones. Also, the prospects for trade were encouraging which they turned to their advantage by stepping up labour-intensive exports.

There are, no doubt, inter-country variations in the East Asian experience but they do not seem to invalidate the overall conclusion regarding broad-based growth. For example, high growth in Indonesia was triggered-off by the development of oil and liquefied natural gas industries and the Organization of the Petroleum Exporting Countries (OPEC) price increases in the 1970s. But many other countries with the same advantages did not show similar demographic transition, high and broad-based growth. Indonesia, like other East Asian countries, gave a high priority to universal primary education, agriculture, and rural development and, again, like other East Asian countries, did not allow public expenditures to be cut for these sectors in the wake of fiscal stabilization attempted in the 1980s (Wing Thye woo *et al.* 1994).

It is clear from this that several East and South-east Asian countries were well prepared to absorb the shocks of stabilization and structural adjustment measures undertaken in the 1980s. Indeed, their stabilization periods did not last longer than a couple of years, that too without experiencing severe cuts in essential public expenditures and without resulting in high rates of inflation for prolonged periods. Their inflation rates in most cases during this period were less than 10 per cent—nearer 5 per cent than 10 per cent. Because of such favourable initial conditions in these countries, the adverse impact of economic reforms on the poor was minimal.

However, the performance of East Asian countries in respect of environmental protection does not seem to be encouraging, despite their better resource position and significant reduction in poverty. East Asia has the highest rate of deforestation and highest intensity of energy use per unit of GDP among the developing regions. It also faces serious problems of sanitation in urban areas and soil degradation in rural areas (World Bank 1993b). Low poverty levels cannot be a source of comfort if quality of life deteriorates. Moreover, environmental degradation signifies inter-generational inequity, the improved standards of living for the present generation being achieved at the cost of the levels of living for the future generation. Nevertheless, in view of better resource position, these countries can be expected to mitigate the stress on environment, in the years to come, with better awareness of the problem.

The success of East and South-east Asian economies with pre-reform growth and improved distribution of income as well as with structural adjustment in the post-reform period is attributed, in a significant measure, to the flexibility in labour market involving free mobility of labour, wage flexibility etc. This is in contrast to the distortions in labour market in countries of South Asia introduced, in no small measure, by the restrictive labour legislation (Khan 1994). It must be noted, however, that structural changes involving, among other things, early demographic transition resulting in the supply of labour lagging behind the demand, constituted the foundations for the emergence of flexible labour market conditions in East Asian countries. On the other hand, protective labour legislation is often resorted to in situations where the dynamism of growth is lacking and the demographic transition is slow resulting in the supply of labour outstripping the demand.

The period of 1990s may not be long enough to be able to capture the full impact of ongoing economic reforms in India. It is not too short a period either, considering particularly the low tolerance limit in a populous, poor, and democratic country like ours (Gupta 1994). While assessing the impact of economic reforms in India on the poverty situation so far, we need to keep in mind some of the favourable factors operating in the economy, especially in the immediate pre-reform period.

Certainly, being late comers in this venture, we can be wiser, if we choose to, as considerable amount of experience has been accumulated on the consequences of the ongoing package of economic reforms for the poor. In fact, 'Adjustment with Human Face' has now become an accepted precept with the World Bank and the International Monetary Fund (IMF). Without this wisdom born out of experience, the consequences for the poor would, perhaps, have been worse. But, the real shield has been provided by the checks inherent in an active democracy with a free press and perhaps also by the presence of a large number of social scientists (Stuijvenberg 1994). Moreover, India has been extremely lucky to have been blessed with a series of normal monsoons and good harvests in the 1990s. At least three good harvests experienced in the pre-reform period gave favourable lagged effects. Certain counter factual policy simulations suggest that with a rainfall deficiency of 10 per cent in 1992–3 and 1993–4, the average inflation rate would have been up by another 3 per cent, current account balance would have deteriorated and foreign exchange reserves would have been substantially lower (Bhattacharya *et al.* 1994).

Acceleration in the growth of rice output during the 1980s, especially in the eastern region, had a favourable impact on the poverty situation. There has been a rise in real wages in agriculture in the poorer regions in response to the rise in employment opportunities in the rural sector. Further, the need for a 'safety net' for the rural poor had been recognized even in the pre-reform period by putting in place a number of PAPs, although their implementation needs considerable improvement.

As expected, on the basis of the experience of several other countries, the most favourable impact of economic reforms has so far been on the balance of payments. The growth rate of the economy had revived after three years of reform. Again, as expected, the impact on poverty and income distribution in the immediate post-reform period seems to have been, on balance, adverse. The most distressing feature in this context is the inflation rate of 10 per cent or more for a greater part of the three and a half year period following reforms. This is unprecedented. We did experience a higher rate of inflation than this twice—in the early 1970s and the early 1980s—but over a much shorter period. This is because, we could contain the revenue expenditure and raise tax revenues more effectively on the earlier occasions than in the early 1990s when capital and social expenditures became a major casualty.

Overall, it appears that the impact of economic reforms so far on the poor in India has not been as adverse as in the countries of Latin America or sub-Saharan Africa. At the same time, the impact has not been as favourable as in East Asian countries like China and Indonesia. However, the full impact of economic reforms in India is yet to be felt, not to speak of the fact that these reforms have yet to run their full course. Even so, concern for monitoring such impact arises because poverty is still widespread in India and its tolerance limit is low.

The slow down in plan expenditures has particularly affected the social sectors through an impact on state plans, especially in the immediate post-reform period. Net domestic investment as a proportion of GDP had gone down from 19.2 per cent in 1989–90 to 15.6 per cent in 1993–4. The percentage share of states in public sector outlay went down from 39.7 per cent to 34.4 per cent over the corresponding period. It is true that for the rural development sector, as a whole, there has been a significant increase in allocations from about 3000 crores in 1991–2 to around 7000 crores in 1994–5. In the case of education, health and other social sectors too the central budgetary support had gone up in absolute terms. However, since education and health, are largely financed in the state plans, their share in the total budgetary outlays for the Centre and states together have either declined or remained constant (Chapter 14). Again, in view of the declining share of state plans and the poor resource position of the larger and more backward states, the state plan outlays had fallen far short of the targets, particularly in states like Bihar, Orissa, and West Bengal leading to considerable shortfalls in agriculture, irrigation, and social sector outlays (Nayyar 1994).

The consumer price index for agricultural labourers witnessed an increase of 50 per cent in the first half of 1990s, while the per capita availability of foodgrains declined (Government of India, *Economic Survey 2002–03*). Further, there has been a significant increase in the issue prices of both rice and wheat supplied under the public distribution system (PDS), over a period of four years. As a consequence, the difference between the free market and the PDS prices had narrowed down significantly resulting in reduced off-take from the PDS and the accumulation of stocks with the government (Table 13.1).

In the case of wheat, as the difference between the wholesale price and PDS price narrowed down in 1994–5 and 1995–6 due to the steep hike in the issue price, the off-take dropped to less than half of the allocations. Again, a similar position was repeated in 1999–2000 and 2000–01 when there was a steep hike in issue prices—this time affecting those above the poverty line (Table 13.1).

In respect of rice, on the other hand, the divergence between the wholesale price and the PDS issue price was greater until the mid-1990s. As a result, the off-take of rice in relation to its allocation was better than in the case of wheat. Even so, because of the successive rise in the PDS issue prices, the off-take of rice remained well below the allocations. But, when the issue prices of rice were raised significantly—to the levels higher than even the wholesale prices—towards the close of the 1990s for those above the poverty line, the off-take fell steeply to half the level of allocations (Table 13.2).

The estimates from the National Sample Survey (NSS) data show that the absolute number of rural poor rose from 232 million in 1987–8

Table 13.1: Wheat: PDS Issue Price Relative to Wholesale Price and the Off-take Relative to Allocation

Year	Wheat				
	WSP	PDS Issue Price	WSP/PDS × 100	(Million Tonnes) Allocation	Off-take
1992–3	392	280	140.0	9.25	7.47
1993–4	382	330	115.8	9.56	5.91
1994–5	419	402	104.2	10.80	4.83
1995–6	435	402	108.2	11.31	5.29
1996–7	509	402	126.6	10.72	8.52
1997–8	581	450* (250)	129.1	10.11	7.08
1998–9	646	650* (250)	99.4	10.11	7.95
1999–2000	710	682* (250)	104.1	10.37	5.76
2000–01	658	830* (415)	79.3	11.57	4.07
2001–02	–	610* (415)	–	13.14	5.68

Note: * For those above poverty line (APL);
Figures in parentheses indicate prices for those below poverty line (BPL) including those covered under Antyodaya.
Source: Government of India, *Economic Survey, 2002–03*.

Table 13.2: Rice: PDS Issue Price Relative to Wholesale Price and the Off-take Relative to Allocation

Year	Rice				
	WSP	PDS Issue Price	WSP/PDS × 100	(Million Tonnes) Allocation	Off-take
1992–3	514	377	136.3	11.48	9.55
1993–4	594	437	135.9	12.41	8.87
1994–5	679	537	126.4	13.32	8.03
1995–6	704	537	131.1	14.62	9.46
1996–7	686	537	127.8	15.10	11.14
1997–8	673	700* (350)	96.1	12.83	9.90
1998–9	745	905* (350)	82.3	12.94	10.74
1999–2000	844	905* (350)	93.3	13.89	11.31
2000–01	1250	1130* (565)	110.6	16.26	7.97
2001–02	–	830* (565)	–	17.23	8.16

Note: * For those above poverty line (APL);
Figures in parentheses indicate prices for those below poverty line (BPL) including those covered under Antyodaya.
Source: Government of India, *Economic Survey, 2002–03*.

to 244 million in 1993–4, against the earlier trend of a decline in the absolute number of poor (Chapter 14). Further, between 1990–1—the year when the reform started—and 1992, the distribution of consumption both in the rural and urban areas deteriorated. The consumption shares of individuals in both the lowest three deciles and middle 4 deciles declined while that of top three deciles increased, representing a reversal of the trend observed since 1987–8 (Gupta 1994).

It is possible that apart from the rise in the consumerism among the upper income groups, the fiscal compression affected the consumption of lower income groups adversely, especially in rural areas, on account of a slow down in public investment as well as social spending. Also, the reduction in fertilizer subsidy may have reduced the yields and on-farm incomes of small and marginal farmers by restricting the use of fertilizers, especially because they have little marketable surplus to sell at higher food prices, even as they have to pay more for the purchase of foodgrains (Gupta 1994).

If the immediate impact of economic reforms on the poor has, on the whole, been adverse in India, it is mainly because, unlike in East Asian countries, the socio-economic position of the poor continues to be vulnerable. The persistence of poverty and destitution is attributable basically to the delayed or slow pace of structural changes. As such, the poverty situation would have been serious even without economic reforms.

So far, we have considered mainly the impact of stabilization measures on the poor. It can be argued with some justification that these are the inevitable short-term consequences and that one should wait for the beneficial long-term effects, especially those arising from measures for structural adjustment. It is, therefore, necessary to reflect on the manner in which the measures for structural adjustment, especially those directly affecting agriculture, are likely to alter the poverty situation.

A major consequence of structural adjustment would be the improvement in the incentive framework facing the farmers consequent to opening up the economy to competition, internal as well as external. As expected, the terms of trade for agriculture vis-á-vis industry have improved (Chapter 5). This may raise rural investment and employment. Stepping up the output of agro-based products, especially those relating to horticulture and floriculture, which have a favourable demand, domestic as well as for export, can raise income and employment in the dry land areas where poverty is widespread.

However, the required infrastructure needs to be provided and steps have to be taken to ensure that small and marginal farmers benefit fully from such opportunities. Further, the poor in general need to be protected from the rise in the prices of essential commodities like foodgrains consequent to opening up of trade and changes in the exchange rate, through the well-targeted PDS.

Another major consequence of structural adjustment would be the improvement in the resource position of the state governments on account of better cost recovery from the users of services like irrigation, rural electricity, and public transport etc. In view of competitive populism among the political parties, this can be achieved only by gradually handing over the management of these services to the user-groups where possible, and by privatizing them where necessary. Generation of financial resources can be expected to be greater on account of better cost-recovery as well as improved efficiency in resource-use.

The contribution of PAPs is generally measured in terms of their direct and immediate impact by way of increase in the incomes of the beneficiaries. However, their indirect and long-term impact in terms of tilting the socio-economic structure in favour of the poor and the deprived is equally significant. For example, studies have shown that the Employment Guarantee Scheme in Maharashtra has contributed immensely to empowering women and bringing together the poor from various castes and communities, thus triggering desirable changes at the household as well as at the village level (Government of India 1991). To give another example from Andhra Pradesh, the mass literacy campaign gave rise to a powerful but unanticipated movement led by women for banning Arrack, a harmful intoxicant, and resulted in silent struggles for the general upliftment of the poor, apart from changing the behavioural patterns.

Further, it can easily be seen that the Employment Guarantee Scheme in a drought-prone area, by providing assured income, has the potential of freeing the worker from dependence on the big land owner and the money-lender. It can also induce the poor to send their children to school. The schemes for the abolition of bonded labour and child labour and for the provision of universal primary education are highly interdependent and can succeed better when 'virtuous circles' for social change are initiated. Already, there is evidence to show that the rise in wages and reduction in poverty over the 1980s had led to greater enrolment of children in schools, resulting, in turn, in slowing down the growth of labour force and higher wages (UNDP 1993).

Poverty alleviation programmes have been launched in India from time to time as an immediate or short-term response to the discontent from the poor, as the benefits of economic growth were not percolating to them sufficiently. So far, we have not been able to evolve and project coherent strategy for structural transformation on egalitarian lines. The so-called 'safety net' for the poor to cope with the adverse consequences of 'structural adjustment' is also in the nature of a palliative devoid of a positive thrust for socio-economic transformation. This lack of vision and political will explains why even the implementation of the existing PAPs has been grossly inefficient.

Already, there is a feeling of alienation among the poor, because new economic policies are being perceived as benefiting mainly the rich and the privileged. Moreover, the aggressive projection of globalization can demoralize the national psyche as the perception of increasing dependence on external sources gathers momentum. The expectation that the ongoing measures for structural adjustment will, by themselves, result in equitable development would be belied much sooner than the earlier idea that the benefits of economic growth will automatically trickle down to the poor. It is high time, therefore, that our policy makers came forward with an integrated package of measures for socio-structural transformation affecting the lives of the common people and place them high on the national agenda on par with the ongoing measures for structural adjustment and muster the necessary political will to implement them effectively.

The objectives of such a package should be to ensure social and economic security, enlarge freedoms and opportunities for the poor, speed up demographic transition, and build human capital, with a view to forging and strengthening the mechanisms for equitable or redistributive growth. We shall spell out briefly the major elements of such a package. These are by no means original or new, nor are they exhaustive.

First, the land base of the poor should be strengthened by extending long-term loans on liberal terms for the purchase of land to those interested in cultivation, by giving preference to women farmers. There is evidence of increasing feminization of agriculture, due to the male labour getting into non-agricultural occupations. Even the incidence of child labour among girls is increasing with an increasing number of boys going to schools (Government of India 1991). Female labour and female-headed households belong to those forming a hard core of rural poverty.

Second, the existing wage and self-employment programmes should be expanded by integrating them with area development as well as with programmes for environmental protection such as watershed development. Self-employment programmes need to be extended in a big way to urban areas also, in view of growing urban poverty (Papola 1993). Incidentally, the deficiencies in infrastructure, leakages etc., encountered in the implementation of the IRDP, would be less serious in urban areas.

Third, we should accord much greater priority to universal primary education than before with a view to achieving the goal within the shortest possible period. The associated minimum needs programme such as provision of primary health services, drinking water etc., needs to be pursued with similar vigour. The programmes for improvement of female literacy and the abolition of child labour need to have time-bound targets. Their link with the expansion of employment opportunities and universalization of primary education should not be lost sight of.

Fourth, with the opening up of trade in agricultural commodities, the need for strengthening the PDS for foodgrains has become imperative. Strict targeting of food subsidies for the genuinely poor can alone sustain the programme on an expanded scale.

Fifth, since all these programmes need to be undertaken on a much larger scale than at present, the commitment of resources has to be correspondingly at a much higher scale. The structural adjustment measures at the state level for cost-recovery from the beneficiaries of services have to be pursued boldly, by confining input subsidies only to the weaker segments. Tax reforms should be such as to raise the revenues significantly by broadening the base and improving the collections. These reforms should bear some rational relationship to the enhanced commitments for social expenditures. It would be necessary to ensure that the share of states in the Centre's tax revenues does not go down on account of the sluggish increase of the shareable revenues.

Finally, effective implementation of the programmes for poverty alleviation and social development requires the active participation of beneficiaries in their designing as well as implementation. The revival of local self-governing institutions with reservations for the weaker sections, following the 73rd and 74th Amendments of the Constitution, offers considerable prospects in this direction. However, political will is required to devolve to these institutions the necessary functions, resources, and power over administration.

Unless the tasks mentioned above are placed high on the national agenda by mobilizing the requisite resources and mustering the necessary will for social engineering, it would be difficult to prevent the market forces, unleashed under the existing package of economic reforms, from further marginalizing the weaker sections. It is indeed a tragedy in the sphere of social policy that the mindset wedded to efficiency is often blind to considerations of equity, while, conversely, the mindset committed to equity is often indifferent to issues of efficiency. As mentioned earlier, there is little trade-off between these goals at this stage of development in India. The need for evolving a package of reforms, which will reconcile the goals of efficiency with concerns for equity, is imperative.

14

Economic Reforms and Rural Poverty

Post-reform Experience

Introduction

In this chapter we shall discuss the impact of economic reforms on rural poverty in India in the post-reform period. It would be useful to examine this for the immediate post-reform period as well as for the decade of 1990, as a whole. The latter would allow for a more adequate, if not fuller, response to the reforms launched in the early 1990s. To begin with, the experience in the pre-reform decade of 1980s is discussed briefly so as to provide a comparative picture.

Experience in the Pre-reform Decade (1980s)

From the Planning Commission or official estimates, one finds a significant declining trend in the incidence of rural poverty, in terms of head-count ratio (HCR), during the 1980s. This is consistent with the observed rise in real wages in rural areas in most parts of the country in this period (Jose 1988). Another favourable development during the 1980s was the decline in the relative prices of foodgrains due to the rise in total factor productivity. Consumers seem to have benefited relatively more than the producers from these productivity gains, particularly in the case of rice and jowar, the demand for which is relatively inelastic (Tyagi 1990). However, there has been a significant decline in the elasticity of employment with respect to agricultural output throughout the green revolution period even in some of the less developed areas (Bhalla *et al.* 1991). The decline in employment elasticity in agriculture despite the 'abundance' of unorganized labour, and the reduction in rural poverty ratio despite the declining employment elasticity deserve explanation.

According to a study group of the National Commission on Rural Labour, factor-substitution induced by the rise in wages seems to have been far more important in reducing employment elasticity than the character of technological change which by itself has, on the whole, been labour-using (Bhalla *et al.* 1991). However, factor substitution itself is traceable, in part, to the suitability of new technology to the infrastructurally developed areas where wage rates were already high. On the other hand, the demand for labour in the low-wage areas has risen slowly, until recently, on account of the lack of infrastructure like assured irrigation as well as the non-availability of technology suited to such regions. Availability of credit on liberal terms for the purchase of labour-substituting machines, the prices of which have risen slowly relative to the prices of agricultural commodities and wages, has also been responsible for increasing substitution of capital for labour (Government of India 1991a; Binswanger and Khandker 1992). Part of the decline in employment elasticity is attributable to the steep decline in self-employment, presumably among marginal and tiny holdings. Moreover, it is common knowledge that there is aversion to manual labour even among small farmers belonging to upper castes who are also keen to get rid of wage-labour. In some places even small farmers having surplus labour demand machines for transplantation and even aerial spraying for pesticides! (Rao 1994). The unwillingness to get on with hired labour or the inability to ensure adequate effort from them gets reflected in the high cost of management and supervision.

The rise in real wages in agriculture in the country is not explained by the growth of agricultural output which continues to be modest in per capita terms, but is explained basically by the shift of labour force from agriculture to non-agricultural occupations (Bhalla *et al.* 1991). The expansion of self-employment as well as wage-employment activities under the poverty alleviation programmes during the 1980s appear to have contributed significantly to the rise in agricultural wages by increasing the opportunities for off-farm employment. The allocations to poverty alleviation programmes across regions were made roughly in proportion to the incidence of rural poverty. These employment programmes seem to account for at least 60 per cent of incremental employment generated in rural areas in the 1980s (Rao, Ray, and Subbarao 1988).

In the light of this experience, it would be interesting to again go over the debate on agricultural change and rural poverty, following the pioneering analysis by Montek S. Ahluwalia (1978) and developed further around the unfinished paper by Dharm Narain (Mellor and Desai 1986). The benefits of agricultural growth can trickle down to the rural poor basically through labour-absorption in the process of agricultural growth. These are the direct effects. The indirect effects are represented by the expansion of employment in the rural non-farm sector induced by the rising agricultural incomes, fall in the relative prices of foodgrains and the achievement of self-sufficiency in food which enables the expansion of poverty alleviation programmes. The econometric exercises on the effect of agricultural growth on rural poverty were focused on knowing whether this relationship was positive and statistically significant (Ahluwalia 1978). The magnitude of this impact as such did not appear to matter much in these initial exercises. The observed relationship reflected both the direct and indirect effects of agricultural growth and there was hardly any attempt to know the magnitude represented by the direct effects, let alone identifying the factors accounting for direct effects. In terms of insights for policy, therefore, such equations hide more than they reveal.

In view of the steep decline in employment elasticity in agriculture, it appears that the direct contribution of agriculture, by way of labour-absorption, towards the reduction of rural poverty has been less than its indirect contribution through the expansion of off-farm employment opportunities, achievement of food security in the sense of self-sufficiency and the decline in the relative prices of foodgrains. This experience does not imply, however, that the potential for labour-absorption in agriculture has been exhausted. Indeed, the experience does suggest that by focusing on public investment and on appropriate technology packages for the low-wage areas, it should be possible to raise substantially the wages and incomes for the rural poor.

For example, several states in the eastern and central regions experienced higher than average growth in foodgrains output during the 1980s. The growth in fertilizer consumption during the 1980s in the eastern region was substantially higher than the all-India average growth. As per the estimates of the Planning Commission as well as the alternative estimates by B.S. Minhas, L.R. Jain, and S.D. Tendulkar (Minhas *et al.* 1991), the percentage share of the eastern and central regions in the number of rural poor in the country which had gone up between 1970–1 and 1983 showed a decline between 1983 and 1987–8, as against a rise in the share of some of the developed states. This means the annual rate of decline in rural poverty ratio (HCR) among many of these eastern and central states was higher than the average for the country as a whole. This evidence is indicative of the significant impact of agricultural growth in the labour-abundant, low-wage areas in reducing rural poverty in the 1980s.

Experience in the Immediate Post-reform Period

The estimates on poverty for 1993–4 showed that the incidence of poverty or the proportion of people below the poverty line was lower than that in 1987–8. However, according to official estimates (Table 14.1), the annual rate of decline in the incidence of poverty over this period was lower than in the preceding decade (Rao 1997), despite a series of good monsoons and the spread of the green revolution to the poorer states in eastern India.

Table 14.1: Trends in Poverty in India, 1977–8 to 1993–4

(per cent)

Region	Poverty (Head-count Ratio)			Growth Rate (Annual)	
	1977–8	1987–8	1993–4	1977–8 to 1987–8	1987–8 to 1993–4
Rural	50.60	39.23	36.66	–2.51	–1.12
Urban	40.50	36.20	30.51	–1.12	–2.81
All India	48.36	38.47	35.04	–2.26	–1.54

Sources: Rao (1997); World Bank 1997.

Further, as shown in Table 14.2, according to the official estimates based on the NSS data, whereas there was a decline in the absolute number of rural poor by 32 million persons between 1977–8 and 1987–8, there was a reversal of this declining trend in the immediate post-reform period, as the number of rural poor rose by 12 million persons in 1993–4.

Table 14.2: Number of Poor

(millions)

	Rural	Urban	Total
1977–8	264	65	329
1987–8	232	75	307
1993–4	244	76	320

Source: Government of India, Planning Commission, Poverty Estimates based on National Sample Surveys.

We have seen that the perceptible decline in poverty in the 1980s was the combined result of acceleration in the growth rate in GDP, spread of green revolution to the poorer areas, increased allocations for poverty alleviation programmes and strengthening of the public distribution system (PDS) for foodgrains. In the immediate post-reform period or the early 1990s, however, the growth rate in gross domestic product (GDP) had come down significantly; the rate of inflation was high, persisting around 10 per cent for four consecutive years; and the expenditure on social sectors including the poverty alleviation programmes slowed.

The consumer price index for agricultural labourers increased by 50 per cent over the five years ending in 1993–4. This is because, among other things, the drive to reduce food subsidies led to a steep increase in the issue prices of foodgrains supplied under the PDS. The difference between the free market and the PDS prices narrowed significantly, leading to reduced off-take from the PDS and a decline in the per capita availability of foodgrains (Rao and Radhakrishna 1997; Radhakrishna *et al.* 1997). These factors may explain the slow pace of reduction in poverty in this period as compared to the greater part of the 1980s.

On the other hand, the impact of economic reforms on the urban poor seems to have been favourable since the rate of reduction in urban poverty is greater than that in the previous decade (Table 14.1). It would be interesting in this context to investigate the response of the urban informal sector, on which the bulk of the urban poor depend, to the reforms undertaken so far.

Employment in the Rural Non-farm Sector

We noted in Chapter 11 that high growth of rural non-farm sector was responsible for the speedy reduction of rural poverty in several East and South-east Asian countries in the post-reform period. The experience in India so far does not appear to be encouraging in this respect.

For India, the estimates regarding growth of output or income in the rural non-farm sector are not available. However, one can get an indication of the performance of this sector from its employment growth. There was a deceleration in employment growth in the rural non-farm sector during 1988–94, for both males and females, as compared to the pre-reform period covering 1978–88 (Dev and Sharma 1999). However, since there was a severe drought in 1987–8, public works programmes—basically for the construction of roads and buildings—were undertaken extensively in large parts of the country. This component of employment being transient, the observed growth rates in rural non-farm employment could give an exaggerated picture for the period ending the year 1987–8, even as they underestimate employment growth in the period beginning from the year 1987–8 (Dev and Sharma 1999).

However, growth in rural non-farm employment even when construction is excluded shows a significant decline during the period 1988–94 when compared to 1978–83, and a moderate decline in comparison to 1983–8 (Rao 2003). This decline in employment is significant for males even when compared to 1983–8. Also, it appears that the dependence of female labour on agriculture has increased in the post-reform year of 1993–4 when compared to 1987–8 (Bhalla, Sheila 1998; Dev and Sharma 1999). Since productivity and wage rates in the rural non-farm sector are significantly higher than in agriculture (Chadha 1993; Bhalla, Sheila 1998), the above facts indicate a deterioration in the incomes of the rural non-farm sector in the immediate post reform period. This is not surprising in view of the continued decline in public investment in agriculture and the squeeze in public expenditure on rural development in general following fiscal compression in the post-reform period.

Factors Accounting for the Rise in Poverty in the Immediate Post-reform Period

The impact of economic reforms on poverty would appear to depend on the initial conditions—the socio-economic structure, the underlying dynamism of the economy and the severity of the crisis itself in the immediate pre-reform period—as well as on the content of economic reforms and the quality of measures adopted to cope with the crisis. In general, an egalitarian socio-economic structure and a high rate of growth of GDP resulting in structural transformation of the economy in the pre-reform period would seem to have a favourable impact on the poverty situation in the post-reform period (Killick 1994). Indonesia provides a classic case where despite stringent adjustment measures adopted in the early 1980s involving significant devaluation of the currency in two rounds, the growth rate of the economy, even though it decelerated, continued to be quite high in per capita terms. Agricultural growth too, despite slowing down, remained far above the population growth rate. As a result, the HCR or the proportion of population below the poverty line continued to decline significantly in the immediate post-reform period, despite a severe fiscal squeeze (Thorbecke 1992; World Bank 1990). Indeed, as noted in Chapter 11, devaluation by itself contributed to a significant decline in rural poverty, as agricultural commodities produced mainly by small holders accounted for a substantial share in the export basket.

The above experience suggests that in a country like India where the socio-economic structure is not as egalitarian as in most East Asian countries and where the structural transformation of the economy was not conspicuous in the pre-reform period, the poorer sections of the society could be expected to be particularly vulnerable to the shocks of adjustment. For example, agricultural exports which steadily declined in importance over the plan period, constituted less than 20 per cent of total exports in the immediate post-reform period, so that the devaluation of the rupee resulted in raising the cost of living of the rural poor more than in raising their incomes as farmers and wage earners.

It is clear from the analyses done in the mid-1990s that the slow rate of decline in the incidence of poverty (HCR) in the immediate post-reform period with a rise in the absolute number of poor in India is attributable not so much to the measures for structural adjustment as to those aimed at achieving macroeconomic stabilization (Gupta 1995; Nayyar 1996; and Prabhu 1996). For one thing, structural reforms yield results over the medium and longer term whereas the impact of stabilization measures is felt immediately, even though their consequences too would extend to the longer period. Second, thanks to the popular pressures inherent in a democratic polity against too fast a reform, some of the measures of structural nature which could result in large-scale unemployment, for example, privatization of public enterprises and an easy 'exit' policy, could not be pushed through (Stuijvenberg 1996).

Stabilization measures may have affected poverty and inequality in the immediate post-reform period in two important ways: First, through the direct impact of fiscal measures and second through the rise in the prices of essential commodities like foodgrains consequent to the reduction in subsidies (Sen 1996). Significant reduction in taxes and a uniform reduction in subsidies for the rich and the poor alike may have altered the distribution of income in favour of the richer sections. Slashing of public expenditures, particularly capital and social expenditures, especially in states where poverty is widespread, could have a dampening effect on employment and wages. As argued below, the adverse impact of these cuts in public expenditure seems to have been greater in rural than in urban areas. Second, the persistence of a high rate of inflation, particularly in respect of essential commodities, resulting from devaluation, rising revenue deficit, and the ineffective supply management, seems to have eroded the real incomes of the poor, especially of the rural poor who are insufficiently covered by the PDS. Persistence of a high rate of inflation seems to have been more significant than the slow rise in employment in affecting the levels of living of the poor in this period.

Reducing tax rates and improving the collection of revenues through better compliance as well as stricter administration are integral to the reform process. Import duties, excise duties, and taxes on income were reduced significantly in the immediate post-reform budgets. Whereas the negative impact of cuts in tax rates on public revenues is immediate, there is considerable time-lag in the enlargement of revenues following tax reforms and better administration. Moreover, there was severe resistance to the implementation of another equally important item on the reform agenda, viz., reducing subsidies by targeting them to the deserving sections. On balance, therefore, there was a significant slow down in the growth of revenues. Thus, the tax-ratio or the proportion of total tax revenues (net to the Centre) to GDP at 6.7 per cent in 1994–5 was lower than 7.9 per cent in the five years preceding reform. On the other hand, the reduction in subsidies in the central budget was modest—from 2 per cent of GDP in the immediate pre-reform period to 1.4 per cent in 1994–5 (Rao 1995).

The bulk of the revenue expenditure on items like interest payments, subsidies, defence, and general administration has been inflexible. As a consequence, the revenue deficit which constituted 2.6 per cent of GDP in the five years preceding reform rose to 3.7 per cent of GDP in 1994–5 (Rao 1995). With the drive to reduce fiscal deficit in a situation of rising revenue deficit, the axe has inevitably fallen on capital and social expenditures, a good part of which are incurred at the state level through the transfer of resources. Besides, the slow growth of revenues from union excise duties and income tax following the cut in tax rates has meant a significant erosion of resources for states, as, statutorily, the latter have a significant share in these revenues (Prabhu 1996). The position of the less developed or low-income states became even more vulnerable because, under the existing arrangements, the per capita transfers to such states from these tax revenues are higher than for the developed states.

The cuts in tax rates and the failure to target subsidies to the poor seem to have led to a rise in inequality in consumer expenditure (Gupta 1995). This is to be expected, because the incidence of even indirect taxes like the union excise duties is progressive, so that the reduction in tax rates results in a rise in the disposable incomes of the upper income groups. On the other hand, an untargeted reduction in subsidies on fertilizers resulted in a significant decline in the use of fertilizers by the small and marginal farmers, who do not have enough surpluses to sell and could not, therefore, benefit to the same extent as surplus farmers from the significant rise in the procurement prices for foodgrains in the post-reform period. There was thus a virtual stagnation in the consumption of fertilizers in agriculture in the immediate post-reform period: 12.4 million tonnes of nutrients in 1993–4 as against 12.5 million tonnes in 1990–1 (Government of India 1995a). This stagnation is traceable mainly to the reduced application on small and marginal farms. The application of fertilizers per hectare on these farms being significantly higher than on large farms (NCAER 1991), the quantity used by them could be expected to be particularly sensitive to the rise in prices. It is highly probable, therefore, that the incomes of small and marginal farmers went down on account of the rise in the cost of fertilizers and their reduced application, contributing to the slow reduction in rural poverty.

There has been a decline in the share of expenditures on rural development and social services, especially at the state level, consequent to fiscal compression. Whereas the slow down in these expenditures would have adversely affected the well-being of the poorer sections, social consumption is not accounted for in the measurement of poverty, which is based on the private household expenditure. The expenditure on poverty alleviation programmes, i.e., on publicly provided wage and self-employment, could not be protected wholly in face of the significant squeeze on the overall expenditure (Gupta 1995). The combined outlays of the Centre and the states on rural development and social services at 6.7 per cent of GDP in 1994–5 were significantly lower than 7.3 per cent of GDP in the immediate pre-reform year (Guhan 1995). However, it is public investment in rural infrastructure which has been the main casualty of stabilization measures. For example, real public investment in agriculture continued to decline significantly in the post-reform period (Government of India 1995b). Investment in other rural infrastructure such as rural electrification, roads, and markets has also been adversely affected. There was thus a shift of employment towards low-paid jobs which could be poverty-induced (Kundu 1996). This is consistent with a negligible rise in real wage rate for the unskilled labour and its significant decline for skilled labour in agriculture in the immediate post-reform period.

The above discussion suggests that stabilization measures may have affected the rural poor more than the urban poor basically through the reduced demand for rural labour, which is critically dependent on public expenditure (Sen 1996). It has been argued that the rise in rural poverty in India in the immediate post-reform period should be attributed basically to factors which are not directly linked to economic reform, such as a dip of 2.5 per cent in agricultural output in 1991–2, the depletion of stocks of foodgrains with the government, the rise in the procurement prices of foodgrains etc. (Tendulkar and Jain 1995). It may be noted, however, that rural poverty declined even in 1987–8—one of the worst drought years in recent history. The deficiencies in respect of supply management as well as the failure to generate adequate employment through public works even when the drought is moderate are explained basically by the fiscal squeeze which was part of the ongoing economic reform process (Dev 1995). What is more important, the available evidence shows that despite some reduction in agricultural output in the immediate post-reform year, employment has not declined in the primary sector, whereas non-agricultural rural employment, which is particularly sensitive to public expenditure, declined significantly in the immediate post-reform period (Dev 1995).

Experience in the Post-reform Decade of 1990s

Rural Poverty

If we consider the experience over a longer period of a decade after the reforms, that is, the 1990s, the socio-economic indicators bearing on poverty give a relatively favourable picture when compared to the immediate post-reform period. This is on account of the improvement in per capita GDP growth and also due to some recovery in public expenditure on agriculture, rural development, and social sectors.

The real GDP growth rate at 6.1 per cent between 1992–3 to 2000–01 was higher than in the pre-reform decade (RBI 2003a). What is more, since there was a decline in population growth rate during the 1990s, there was clearly an acceleration in per capita GDP growth rate. We have seen in Chapters 2 and 11 that, across Asian countries, the reduction in rural poverty bears a stronger correlation with the GDP growth than with agricultural growth *per se*. An overview of experience in India with regard to changes in the incidence of poverty since 1950 reveals a strong impact of economic growth on poverty reduction (Ravallion and Datt 1996).

As noted in Chapter 5, there was a slow down in the annual growth rate of GDP from agriculture and the allied sectors from 3.1 per cent between 1981–91 to 2.76 per cent between 1991–2001. Since the growth rate of rural population declined from 1.79–1.65 per cent between 1991–2001, the per capita growth rate in agriculture GDP was still positive at 1.11 per cent per annum in the post-reform decade, though lower than in the pre-reform decade. It is now well established, following the study by Montek S. Ahluwalia (1978), that a rise in agricultural output per head would lead to a decline in the incidence of rural poverty (HCR).

However, due to the declining employment elasticity in agriculture and the slow growth of rural non-farm sector, the growth rate of rural employment was slow, around 0.5 per cent per annum between 1993–4 and 1999–2000 as compared to 1.7 per cent per annum between 1983 and 1993–4 (Dev 2003).

Despite the slow growth of employment, the growth of real wages in agriculture was significant in the 1990s as in the previous decade. This is to be expected considering that the growth of agricultural output per head was positive and that there was increasing diversification of agriculture towards high value activities for which productivity and wage rates would be high. However, there is conflicting evidence about the rate of rise in real wages in agriculture. On the basis of information on agricultural wages in India from the Ministry of Agriculture, Angus Deaton and Jean Dreze show that the growth of real agricultural wages in India declined from 5.5 per cent per annum during the 1980s to 2.5 per cent per annum over the 1990s (Deaton and Dreze 2002). They, nevertheless, underline the poverty reducing impact of growth in agricultural wages in the 1990s. On the other hand, according to K. Sundaram, on the basis of the evidence from the NSS Employment and Unemployment Surveys, the real wages for males as well as females rose, on an average, at a higher rate in the 1990s over the 1980s. For casual wage labourers in rural India, the annual rate of rise in the 1980s for males ranged between 2.3–2.8 per cent in most cases and for females it ranged between 2.7–4 per cent, whereas in the 1990s, the corresponding figures were 2.8–3.8 per cent in the case of males and 3–5 per cent in the case of females. This evidence, according to Sundaram, 'offers no support for the hypothesis of a slow-down in the rate of growth of average daily wage earnings of adult casual labourers during the 1990s relative to that between 1983 and 1994' (Sundaram 2001).

The rate of inflation relevant for the rural poor came down significantly during the second half of the 1990s when compared to the immediate post-reform period: The All India Consumer Price Index Numbers for Agricultural Labourers which rose at the rate of 12.5 per cent per annum between 1986–7 and 1994–5 fell to 6.1 per cent per annum between 1995–6 and 1999–2000 (Government of India 2003, *Economic Survey 2002–2003*).

Public expenditure on rural development, in so far as it is targeted to the rural poor, has a direct impact on their incomes. Per capita real expenditure on rural development (at 1993–4 prices) at state level had declined by 21 per cent in 1995–6 when compared to 1990–1 but rose again by 1999–2000, representing a rise of 4 per cent over 1990–1 (Dev and Mooij 2003). The recovery was sharper for the poorer states. These states—Bihar, Madhya Pradesh, Orissa, Rajasthan, and Uttar Pradesh—together experienced a cut of 30 per cent by 1995–6 in their per capita real expenditures on rural development when compared to 1990–1. But their expenditures in 1999–2000 were 21 per cent higher than in 1990–1 (Dev and Mooij 2003).

The favourable factors enumerated above may have resulted in reducing the incidence of rural poverty in 1999–2000 when compared to 1993–4. We give in Table 14.3 the official estimates as well as those of Deaton and Dreze after making adjustments for the changes in the questionnaire design and revising poverty line (Deaton and Dreze 2002; also see, Sen 2000).

Both the official and the adjusted estimates show that the incidence of poverty was significantly lower in 1999–2000 when compared to 1993–4. But the official estimates show a faster rate of decline in poverty in the post-reform period when compared to the period between 1987–8 and 1993–4. However, in the Planning Commission's own admission, the official estimates for 1999–2000 are not comparable with those in the earlier period. The adjusted estimates by Deaton and Dreze show the pace of poverty decline to be more or less the same in both the periods. The Poverty Gap Index which measures the aggregate shortfall of the consumption of the poor from the poverty line, has also declined in the post-reform period, in line with the decline in the HCR.

Table 14.3: Poverty: All India Head-count Ratios

(*per cent*)

	1987–8	1993–4	1999–2000
Rural			
Official	39.4	37.1	26.8
Adjusted	39.4	33.0	26.3
Urban			
Official	39.1	32.9	24.1
Adjusted	22.5	17.8	12.0
		All India Poverty Gap Index	
Adjusted			
Rural	9.4	7.0	5.2
Urban	4.8	3.7	2.3

Source: Deaton and Dreze (2002).

There are alternative estimates, apart from those by Deaton and Dreze, which show a slower rate of decline in poverty in the post-reform period when compared to the 1980s. Whereas the official estimates show a 10 percentage point decline in rural poverty during 1993–4 to 1999–2000, Deaton and Dreze show a decline of 6.7 percentage points; Sundaram and Tendulkar (2003) show a 5.3 percentage point decline; and Sen and Himanshu (2003) show a decline of only around 3 percentage points. Changes in the number of rural poor also vary from a decline of 50 million (official estimates) to an increase of 1.5 million (Sen and Himanshu 2003) during 1993–2000 (for details regarding the assumptions and adjustments made in these studies for making the estimates comparable, see Appendix A14).

It may be concluded that the rate of decline in the incidence of poverty in the post-reform period has not been higher than in the pre-reform period. In all probability, the rate of decline has been lower in the post-reform period.

To understand the mechanisms for the decline in rural poverty in the post-reform period , despite a slow down in per capita GDP growth from agriculture and slow growth in rural employment, one needs to trace out the possible trickle-down effects of accelerated GDP growth for the rural poor, for example, migration of rural labour to avail of more remunerative employment opportunities, remittances, etc. It appears, nevertheless, that accelerated GDP growth in the post-reform period did not translate itself into accelerated poverty reduction.

A striking feature of the post-reform experience brought out by Deaton and Dreze is the increase in inter-state inequalities in the growth of per capita state domestic product (SDP), in the average per capita consumption expenditure (APCE) and the rate of reduction in rural poverty. This was marked by increasing divergence, that is, the richer states in general registered a much higher growth in GDP than the poorer states. These findings are consistent with the earlier finding by Montek S. Ahluwalia regarding the rise in inter-state inequalities in SDP growth in the post-reform period (Ahluwalia 2000).

Contrary to the experience of the 1980s discussed above, the annual rate of reduction in rural poverty in the 1990s was significantly lower in the poorer states than in the better-off states (Deaton and Dreze 2002). All the states where real wages have grown at a higher rate than the all-India average of 2.5 per cent per annum, for example, Gujarat, Karnataka, Kerala, and Tamil Nadu have experienced sharp reduction in poverty. On the other hand, the entire eastern region (Assam, Orissa, West Bengal, and Bihar), Andhra Pradesh, and Madhya Pradesh where the growth of agricultural wages was low, experienced lower reduction in rural poverty (Dev 2003).

Deaton and Dreze also bring out the increase in rural–urban as well as intra-urban inequalities in per capita consumption expenditure in the post-reform period. This has important implications for the incidence of poverty or the HCR, as, other things remaining the same, the rise in inequality in per capita expenditure would lead to a rise in the HCR. Thus, according to them, 'the all-India HCR in 1999–2000 was 1.3 percentage points higher than it would have been (with the same growth rate of APCE) in the absence of any increase in inequality' (Deaton and Dreze 2002). In other words, another 13 million people (out of the population of a billion) would have been lifted above the poverty line if there was no rise in income inequalities in the post-reform period.

Poverty Among the Socio-economically Disadvantaged Sections

The incidence of poverty (HCR) continued to be higher than the average among the socially disadvantaged sections in 1999–2000: Among the population belonging to scheduled castes (SCs) in rural areas, it was 36.3 per cent or 9 percentage points higher than the national average of 27.1 per cent. It was even higher for the scheduled tribes (STs), that is, 45.9 per cent. Looking at the distribution of the rural poor among different socially disadvantaged sections in 1999–2000, we find that SCs account for 27.3 per cent; STs 17.5 per cent; and other backward castes for 36.8 per cent. Thus as many as 81 per cent of the rural poor belonged to the socially disadvantaged sections (Radhakrishna and Shovan Ray 2003).

Occupation-wise, agricultural labour accounted for 46.8 per cent of the rural poor; rural artisans for 12.3 per cent; and non-agricultural rural labour for 7.8 per cent. Thus, the class of rural wage labour—which is socio-economically disadvantaged—constitutes over two-thirds of the rural poor. If we add to this category, the poor belonging to the class of self-employed in agriculture among small and marginal holdings who depend essentially on family labour (28.1 per cent), rural labour accounts for the overwhelming proportion of the rural poor (Radhakrishna and Shovan Ray 2003). In view of the predominance of rural labour among the rural poor, it would be interesting to examine in some detail how the prospects for the rural labour are affected by the ongoing economic reforms. This is attempted in the following section.

Economic Reforms and the Prospects for Rural Labour

Rural Labour Scene: Major Features

The rural labour force, whether in agriculture or non-agriculture, has been growing at a faster rate than the population growth in rural areas. There has been a steep decline in the proportion of self-employed households in agriculture. It appears that the continued sub-division of holdings among the small and marginal farms is rendering some of the self-employed labour force redundant on the farms who are joining the ranks of wage labour. In non-agriculture, employment, particularly of females, in certain household industries has been declining under the impact of the technologically efficient and modern industries. These facts underline the need for greater employment generation in rural areas.

With regard to the prospects for employment in rural areas, the position has not been encouraging. The National Sample Survey (NSS) data for the 1970s, 1980s, and the 1990s reveals that there has been a sharp deceleration in the growth of employment in rural areas over the years (Papola 1992; Dev 2003). Agriculture is still the single most important source of employment, as nearly two-thirds of the total workforce is still dependent on agriculture, and such workforce accounted for 77 per cent of the rural poor in 1993–4. As mentioned before, the growth in employment in this sector in relation to the growth in agricultural output, that is, employment elasticity, has been declining sharply (Bhalla *et al.* 1991). Part of this decline in employment elasticity may be attributable to the decline in labour among marginal holdings whose productivity is low. But there is also a significant trend towards the substitution of capital for labour in agriculture.

Is this substitution attributable to the high cost of labour? By any standards, the agricultural wage rates, particularly in backward areas, are not high even though they have shown some rise since the 1980s. In most cases they are still below the legally fixed minimum wages. This is what can be expected when labour is assetless and largely unorganized. But then, capital has become cheaper, particularly considering the factor endowments in the rural areas. For example, public financial institutions extend loans for farm machinery and other agricultural investments at concessional rates. As much as 70 per cent of such long-term credit for agriculture from commercial banks is accounted for by large farmers who employ the bulk of the hired labour (Chapter 8). The rise in the substitution of capital for labour in agriculture seems to be due not so much to the rise in wage rates as to the availability of capital at a low cost.

This has been happening despite the increasing migration of rural labour from the backward regions, where the productivity of labour is low, to the agriculturally developed pockets. Thanks largely to the highly uneven levels of development across regions, there are now over 10 million labourers on the move in rural areas (Government of India 1991a). And paradoxically, the labour which used to be bonded within the village where it works, is getting out of that bondage in search of better employment outside and in this process getting bonded to contractors and other middlemen who extend loans for subsistence in the intervening period. Bondedness is now spreading to non-agricultural activities like carpet weaving, match works etc. where child labour is extensively employed. Tribals dispossessed of their land or displaced from forests without having any skills for new employment are increasingly joining the migration streams (Government of India 1991a).

The backward areas are generally characterized by a low level of rainfall which is highly uncertain or variable so that low level of employment and low level of wages are associated with high uncertainty of employment. Even as self-employment has been declining in agriculture, the proportion of workers regularly employed has come down significantly. The increasing casualization of labour has added to the uncertainty of employment in rural areas.

A silver lining in this otherwise dismal picture for rural labour is the rise in real wages for agricultural labour since the 1980s. Interestingly, the rise in wages has been relatively greater in the less developed regions and also for female labour (Jose 1988). The increasing adoption of new agricultural technology in the eastern Gangetic Plains as well as in the rain-fed upland areas during the 1980s could be an important factor responsible for this rise in wages. These areas are also characterized by the out-migration of labour. However, it seems, the rise in agricultural wages is attributable mainly to the rise in the demand for labour in non-agricultural activities notably construction and services (Bhalla *et al.* 1991). Despite this, the per head earnings and consumption levels of rural labour have increased only marginally in real terms on account of the decline in the number of days worked per labourer in a year.

The rural labour families have very little access to the minimum needs like primary education, health care, potable water, and foodgrains from the fair-price shops. Further, rural labour is denied most of the social security benefits like old age pension, maternity and sickness benefits, and compensation for accidents. The benefits from the meagre allocations made in our country for social security accrue largely to the well-organized urban workers who constitute a small fraction of the total workforce in the country (Government of India 1991a). It is now widely recognized that the degradation of the environment has impacted more severely on the rural poor, particularly women and children, on account of the shortages of drinking water, fuelwood, and fodder.

Thus, even though there are some signs of improvement in the levels of living since the 1980s, rural labour has been largely bypassed by the processes of socio-economic development over the last five decades, despite its immense contribution to the development of agriculture and of rural areas in general. It is, therefore, necessary to identify the major structural, institutional, and planning deficiencies for this state of affairs before we discuss the possible impact of the ongoing economic reforms on the living conditions of rural labour.

Factors Underlying the Poverty of Rural Labour

Assetlessness and high population growth are the two major causes for the increase in the number of people offering themselves as wage labour in rural areas under unfavourable terms. Despite the two rounds of land reforms after independence, only about 1 per cent of cultivated land in the country could be redistributed to the landless. This lack of assets has led to the rise in the supply of wage labour as well as to the weakening of its bargaining power. The biggest asset that the rural labour possesses is its 'labour power' which is, however, highly insecure on account of high incidence of sickness, high infant mortality, and the disabilities of old age. Hence, the high value placed by them on the number of children. This has, in turn, eroded the modest gains in employment and wages.

On the other hand, the demand for labour has been lagging behind its supply. The growth of employment in rural areas has decelerated from 2.5 per cent per annum during the 1970s to 1.7 per cent over the 1980s, and 0.5 per cent in the 1990s. This is on account of the slow rate of public investment in agriculture and the slow pace of land-augmenting technological change in the less developed areas. Further, the technological upgradation of rural industries and improvement in rural infrastructure in general have considerably lagged behind the improvements in agricultural practices. Moreover, despite interregional migration of labour, highly uneven levels of regional development have resulted in less than optimum levels of employment and income for rural labour, both because of the rise in capital-intensity in the developed pockets and the existence of untapped potential for labour absorption in the less developed regions.

Impact of Economic Reforms on Rural Labour

Economic reforms, among other things, by freeing the factor markets are expected to bring the prices of factors of production, such as capital and labour in alignment with factor endowments. This implies that in the Indian rural setting, where capital is scarce and labour is abundant, the relative prices of these factors would be such that there would be incentive to employ more labour in relation to capital. This, in conjunction with the higher rate of investment expected in the economy as a result of economic restructuring, should result in higher growth of employment. However, such a reasoning overlooks the emerging nature of demand for goods and services unleashed by the market forces in a society where the distribution of income and wealth are highly unequal and where economic inequalities are reinforced by social inequalities. Elitist consumption goods for example, durable consumption goods are generally capital intensive and, therefore, if income distribution and consumption patterns are changed drastically as a result of liberalization and marketization, the prospects for labour use may not be as encouraging as is expected on the basis of simplistic reasoning centring round the relative factor prices. Also, there is a general aversion on the part of entrepreneurs to employ labour—a human and social entity and, therefore, an 'uncertain' and 'undependable' factor, to economize on which they would be willing to incur higher cost in terms of greater capital intensity. The above factors may indeed explain why economic reforms have so far yielded dismal results in terms of employment generation in India.

To assess the possible impact of the ongoing economic reforms on the livelihood of rural labour, it would be useful to distinguish the effects of stabilization measures from the impact of structural adjustment, although the efforts are on to proceed simultaneously on both the fronts. In any case, major reforms of a structural nature directly affecting agriculture have not been introduced so far. It is, nevertheless, true that rural labour cannot remain unaffected by the structural adjustment measures undertaken in non-agriculture.

The rural labour, particularly in the less developed areas, is affected by stabilization measures in two fundamental ways. One is the reduced rate of public investment in agriculture and social sectors like minimum needs including primary education, health care, and drinking water. It has been observed time and again in planning exercises and performance evaluations in India that infrastructure development like irrigation, rural electrification, and development of roads and markets, bears the highest correlation with the overall growth of employment in the economy, particularly because public investments in such infrastructure stimulate private investment. In the less developed areas, the increase in employment and the rise in wages generally go together, as both are impelled by the rise in the demand for labour.

Since agriculture, rural development, irrigation, and social sectors are basically in the domain of the states, they have become the first victim of stabilization measures. It is true that central outlays on poverty alleviation programmes have, by and large, been protected but in view of the erosion of states' resources, these outlays can be protected at the state level only at the cost of other essential outlays for agriculture and social sectors so that the overall impact on rural employment is likely to be adverse.

The other important consequence is the rise in the prices of essential commodities like foodgrains. This has acted more harshly on the poor. As expected, stabilization measures have no doubt brought down the overall rate of inflation somewhat, but, despite half a dozen good harvests in succession, the impact has not been as quick and significant as on the earlier two occasions, viz., mid-1970s and the early 1980s. In fact, for quite some time, the rise in the prices of foodgrains and agricultural commodities in general during the 1990s was higher than that in the rest of the prices, representing a reversal of the trend noticed in the 1980s.

The processes of structural adjustment underway in the economy have a direct as well as indirect bearing on the rural poor. To take the indirect effects first, more resources may flow into agriculture, as its relative profitability improves consequent to the improvement in the terms of trade between agriculture and industry. Rural labour may benefit from such a situation in so far as it results in the rise in employment and wages.

However, as against this, one has to note the possible backlash effects of structural adjustment on rural industries and employment. If our search for appropriate technology for rural industries did not meet with conspicuous success in the last 50 years, it is highly unlikely that it would hold any great promise in the context of growing competition that certain rural industries may face from the technologically modern and efficient enterprises enjoying economies of scale. The threat of 'new poor' entering the rural labour market looms large not only on account of the possible displacement of some of the rural industries but also due to the 'exit' of inefficient enterprises and the possible rise in capital intensity in the industrial and services sectors consequent to the changes in the composition of demand for goods and services. This process would be accentuated if the existing ceiling on land holdings is relaxed, as part of the reform process, to encourage the entry of the corporate sector in agriculture. Such a course would unduly raise capital intensity in agriculture and entice the small and marginal farmers to sell their lands thus swelling the ranks of rural labour.

To summarize, the impact of stabilization measures on rural employment and welfare has, in general, been negative. The liberalization of the economy and the opening up of trade in agricultural commodities would, in all probability, stimulate growth in agricultural output. To what extent this would translate itself into growth in rural employment would depend crucially upon public investments in infrastructure in the less developed and low wage areas and the policy of ceilings on land holdings. Otherwise, capital intensity in agriculture and in the rural sector would rise, especially in the developed regions, with negligible effect on further employment generation in the rural sector as a whole. This uncertainty coupled with the backlash effects of technological upgradation on rural industries and the rise in the relative prices of foodgrains makes one circumspect about the prospects for the rural labour in the country in the wake of economic reforms. The latest evidence shows that, despite mild acceleration in GDP growth in the post-reform period of the 1990s, there has been a sharp deceleration in employment growth during the same period. The employment elasticity in the primary sector has become virtually nil in the post-reform period while the employment elasticity in the secondary and tertiary sectors has also declined. Thus, jobless growth has already become a serious problem in the Indian Economy (Bhattacharya and Sakthivel 2003).

At the moment the major issue concerning rural labour and the rural poor at large is how to cope with the possible adverse consequences of economic reforms. If the 'trickle-down' theory had to be discarded under the development strategy followed so far, the prospects of benefits trickling down to the poor appear even more remote with greater marketization and privatization, unless the growth rate of the economy gets pushed up to an unbelievably higher level. Apart from measures for human resource development, social security, and basic needs, the provision of employment guarantees and public distribution of essential commodities to the vulnerable sections of the society are called for (Government of India 1991a).

The Employment Guarantee Programme conceived well and implemented effectively would result in raising the market wages and thus facilitate the enforcement of minimum wages. In view of the rise in income and staying power of rural labour, it would be easier for the government to implement programmes such as the abolition of bonded labour and child labour and improving the enrolment as well as reducing the drop-out rate of children in the schools. Thus the indirect benefits of employment guarantee by way of rise in market wages, empowerment of labour, and enhanced potential for sustained employment may be greater than the direct benefit in terms of employment generated under the programme. It would also be necessary to identify the newly emerging activities in rural areas in response to economic restructuring underway and support programmes for training in skills for such activities.

However, some of the critics regard such initiatives as 'populist' which will result in raising the fiscal deficit (Narasimham 1993). But such programmes, if properly implemented, can contribute substantially to human resource development, improving agricultural productivity, promoting equity or social justice and protecting the environment. Therefore, reconciling the efficiency goals with considerations of social justice is the foremost challenge facing the ongoing process of economic reforms.

Social Sector Expenditure

As shown in Table 14.4, the various measures of social expenditure indicate a decline or very little rise in the first half of 1990s. There was a significant rise in these expenditures, when seen in per capita terms, in the second half of the 1990s. Even so, the growth of social expenditures in the post-reform period of 1990s, as a whole, decelerated greatly when compared to the pre-reform decade of 1980s. Per capita social sector expenditures (on social services plus rural development) by the Centre, at 1993–4 prices, which rose at the rate of 14.1 per cent per annum between 1980–1 and 1989–90, registered a much lower growth of 6.3 per cent per annum between 1992–3 and 2002–03. Similar expenditures by all the states together registered a decline from 9.3 per cent per annum to 6.3 per cent per annum over the same period (Dev and Mooij 2003).

The above trends in public expenditure on social sectors are consistent with the slow progress in certain social indicators over this period. Although the annual rate of decline in illiteracy rate was significantly higher in the 1990s (2.8 per cent) when compared to that in the 1980s (1.5 per cent), this was mainly due to refocusing of

Table 14.4: Social Sector (Social Services and Rural Development) Expenditure Centre and States

Average Annual for the 5-year Period	As % of GDP	As % of Agg. Pub. Exp.	Per Capita Exp. (Rs) in 1993–4 Prices
1987–8 to 1991–2	6.95	24.97	601.2
1992–3 to 1996–7	6.39	25.21	647.6
1997–8 to 2001–2	7.04	26.43	914.0

Source: Dev and Mooij (2003).

expenditure on education in favour of primary education. Infant mortality rate declined by 1.5 per cent per year during 1990s, as against 2.9 per cent per year during the 1980s. The decline in total fertility rate by 1.8 per cent per year during the 1990s was only marginally higher than 1.7 per cent per annum during the 1980s (Deaton and Dreze 2002).

Fiscal Trends in the Post-reform Period

The continued decline in public investment in agriculture and slow recovery in public expenditure on social sectors, including rural development, are traceable to the failure of economic reforms to mobilize public revenues by stepping up the tax–GDP ratio and reducing the subsidies, for example, on irrigation and electricity for pumping water. Also, fiscal reforms have not been able to reign in inessential public expenditure, for example, unusual hike in the salaries for government employees.

The acceleration in the growth of per capita GDP in the post-reform period indicates the rise in taxable capacity. Despite the rise in taxable capacity, the tax–GDP ratio has declined significantly in the post-reform period: The tax–GDP ratio for the Centre (before transfers to the states) which was around 10.5 per cent of GDP in the quinquennium preceding reform, came down to around 8.7 per cent of GDP during the quinquennium ending 2001–02 (Government of India, Ministry of Finance, 2002; RBI 2003b). On the other hand, own tax revenues of all states combined stood at around 5.4 per cent of GDP in both the periods (RBI 2003c). The decline in tax effort by the Centre to the extent of nearly 2 per cent of GDP (which amounted approximately to Rs 45,000 crores in 2001–02) is explained basically by the failure to tax income from services—a sector responsible for the acceleration of GDP in the post-reform period.

Following the reduction in marginal rates of taxation, the growth of revenues from personal income tax for the Centre accelerated from 15.4 per cent per annum during 1980s to 17.4 per cent per annum during the post-reform period of 1990s. However, the growth of revenues from union excise duties decelerated from 14.6 per cent to 10.7 per cent over the same period. The growth of revenues from these two sources combined, which are shareable with the states, declined from 14.7 per cent per annum during the 1980s to 12.2 per cent per annum during the 1990s (computed from the Budget Papers of the Government of India for various years). Since the devolution or shares from these revenues for states were fixed by the finance commissions, the decline in the growth of these revenues led to a decline in the growth of revenues for the states, especially for the poorer ones, as the per capita devolution recommended for them is higher than that for the better-off states. As a result, the tax–GDP ratio for states, inclusive of devolution, came down from around 8 per cent in the immediate pre-reform years to 7.4 per cent in 1998–9.

On the expenditure side, the pay hike for the employees at the Centre led to similar hikes at the state level resulting in the rise in fiscal deficits at both the Centre and the states, despite the slow growth of expenditures on agriculture, rural development, and other social sectors. The gross fiscal deficit of the central and state governments combined, which rose to a high of 9.4 per cent of GDP in 1990–1, came down to 7 per cent in the immediate post-reform years, but rose again to a high of 9.5 per cent or more since 1999–2000 (RBI 2003b).

It is clear from the above that fiscal reforms both for raising revenues and reducing inessential expenditures are a prerequisite for protecting and raising the social expenditures for reducing poverty. It is also clear that the Centre has a greater responsibility for raising revenues and for containing inessential expenditure.

Implications for Policy

The above analysis suggests that the deterioration in the living conditions of the poor in India in the immediate post-reform period could have been avoided if the policy package and the measures adopted had taken due account of the vulnerability of the prevailing socio-economic structure, especially in rural areas, to the shocks of adjustment.

Considering the magnitude of the problem, the oft-repeated remedy in terms of 'adjustment with human face' involving certain ameliorative measures for those adversely affected by reforms appears no more than a palliative. Measures for the structural transformation of the rural economy by raising agricultural growth, significantly stepping up non-farm rural growth to absorb labour force shifting from agriculture, and human resource development have to be given a high priority in the development strategy (Ravallion and Datt 1996). Indeed, in view of the possible rise in the prices of essential commodities consequent to liberalization of trade and the fiscal limits to subsidizing the public schemes for poverty alleviation, greater employment generation in the process of growth becomes essential (Lipton 1995).

Strengthening the resource position of the poorer states for investing in physical and social infrastructure where the private sector is not forthcoming becomes critical for poverty eradication through structural change. This means, the content and pace of tax reforms have to bear a meaningful relationship to the requirement for resources. For example, the revenues from direct taxes on income can almost be trebled even with the existing tax rates, if the tax administration is streamlined and made stricter (Government of India 1991b).

Since redistribution of land is not politically feasible and the implementation of top–down subsidy-oriented poverty alleviation programmes is not likely to be effective, economic and social empowerment of the poor has to be achieved basically through productive employment and human development. This requires, apart from social development, rapid, broad-based, labour-intensive growth. Going by the East Asian experience, this implies that India should aim at an annual average growth rate in GDP of 7–8 per cent together with agricultural growth rate of around 4–5 per cent over the next decade.

Another major implication is that although public investment in infrastructure has to increase, it needs to be increasingly augmented by private investment and the management of publicly provided infrastructure needs to be de-bureaucratized and de-politicized by involving the private sector and users of services, such as through water user associations in canal networks. This is necessary to improve the efficiency of services as well as to recover the costs from the users. Finally, as discussed earlier, there is a need to improve the efficiency of delivery systems for rural development by empowering the locally elected institutions.

15

Poverty Alleviation Programmes and Their Integration with Overall Development

Introduction

In view of the inadequate impact of agricultural and overall economic growth on the alleviation of poverty, a strategy of direct attack on poverty through various poverty alleviation programmes (PAPs) targeting those below the poverty line has been in operation in the country, especially since the early 1980s. The efficiency of these PAPs in terms of their design as well as implementation has been a major policy concern with a view to ensuring maximum income generation for the poor from the expenditure incurred on the programmes.

Beyond the immediate issue of maximum income generation for the poor from the given expenditure, a major long-term concern in this field relates to the integration of the PAPs with overall development. In this context, the integration of the poverty alleviation objective with the overall development strategy has to be distinguished from the issue of integrating specific PAPs with development. The former is concerned basically with questions like investment priorities (for example the relative importance to the wage-goods sector, such as agriculture), choice of techniques (with implications for the magnitude of employment generation) and location of projects (in low wage or less developed areas versus developed areas), so that the growth process leads to adequate employment and income generation for the poor. In brief, this approach seeks to maximize the 'trickle-down' effects for the poor from the growth process consistent with economic efficiency. The latter approach, that is, integration of PAPs with overall development seeks to ensure that the existing or modified PAPs, as they operate, subserve the goals of overall development such as the sustained increase in gross domestic product (GDP) through the increase in the productivity of resources, augmenting the employment generating potential in the economic system, conservation of environment, technological upgradation, and human development (Rao 1992).

These two approaches are not mutually contradictory but reinforce each other. In fact, the failure to integrate the poverty alleviation objective with the overall development strategy has necessitated the launching of specific PAPs under the strategy of 'direct attack' on poverty. The proliferation of PAPs, on the other hand, without adequate integration with the overall goals of development, has led to the inefficient use of the large chunk of resources allocated to PAPs on account of weak linkages with growth, low potential for sustained employment generation and insufficient impact on social development and protection of environment. This trend, if unchecked, can undermine the objectives of economic growth as well as poverty alleviation. The first issue, still a live one, is extremely important, but the present chapter is basically concerned with the latter issue of integrating the PAPs with overall development.

'Dichotomy' between Agricultural Growth and Rural Poverty Alleviation

The link between agricultural development and poverty alleviation was clearly visible in the first few years of planning in India when land reforms and irrigation development were given a pre-eminent place. With the introduction of new technology in the mid-1960s, increasing yield per hectare of cropped area rather than increasing cropping intensity, which has higher employment elasticity, became the central concern and the locus of agricultural growth shifted to the developed regions and the prosperous farmers. Although there was some reversal of this trend in the 1980s, the employment elasticity in agriculture for the country as a whole has declined significantly, the elasticity becoming even negative in the traditional green revolution belt.

The failure of agricultural growth to make a sizeable dent on rural poverty has led the policy makers to focus attention on the strategy of 'direct attack' on poverty through PAPs. In this process, the tendency to view agricultural development programmes as different from those for poverty alleviation and vice versa has become quite pronounced. Those concerned with raising agricultural productivity are preoccupied exclusively with technologies and input combinations that raise yield per hectare and with the 'progressive farmers' and developed regions where the results are quick and substantial. They are not as much concerned with small farmers or with extending technologies and practices which increase employment in areas where poverty is widespread. On the other hand, in the pursuit of poverty alleviation programmes such as the Integrated Rural Development Programme (IRDP) and Jawahar Rozgar Yojana (JRY), etc., one does not find adequate concern for undertaking activities such as soil conservation, water harvesting, drainage, and construction of field channels which raise agricultural productivity. In fact, in the field one often finds each department considering the other as a rival competing for staff and other resources. This approach is detrimental to raising agricultural productivity as well as to alleviating rural poverty on a sustained basis.

PAPs: Overview of Experience

Agriculture in India continues to be a decentralized activity where millions of individual farmers take decisions in a free institutional setting regarding investment, crops to be grown, input mix to be used, and the amount of produce to be sold, within the infrastructural and policy environment provided by the government. Because of this, the allocation of resources by the farmers has, by and large, been efficient even though the direct impact of this on poverty alleviation has not been significant. Indeed, there are certain negative effects on the environment owing to the adverse externalities arising from this decision-making process, such as those associated with the extension of cultivation to the hill slopes and marginal lands.

In contrast to the decision-making process in agriculture, PAPs represent essentially top–down ventures heavily dependent on the bureaucracy. As a consequence, the felt needs of the people do not get sufficient attention and the activities chosen are very often ill-suited to the local resource endowments. In the absence of market institutions and owing to the infirmities in the working of the non-market institutions like the government departments and representative local institutions, together with the extreme reluctance to involve non-governmental organizations (NGOs) in the designing and implementation of PAPs, a number of intermediaries are found to operate in a clandestine manner between the government and the beneficiaries. This has resulted in large leakages and inefficiencies in the implementation of PAPs.

Despite these inefficiencies, the contribution of PAPs to the observed reduction in rural poverty has been significant. In regions where agricultural growth is slow and poverty is widespread, the various PAPs accounted for more than half the incremental incomes of the rural poor in the 1980s (Rao, Ray, and Subbarao 1988).

Over a period of time, there has been a significant shift in the composition of self-employment activities under IRDP away from primary sector activities such as animal husbandry towards secondary and tertiary sector activities where the capital–output ratios are generally lower and the leakages are much smaller. Moreover, contrary to the fears expressed regarding the economic viability of the poorer household enterprises (Rath 1985), the concurrent evaluation studies show that the lower income households have been able to achieve better results than upper income households, both in terms of lower capital–output ratios and smaller leakages (Rao and Rangaswamy 1988). The performance of IRDP was found to be distinctly better in the infrastructurally developed regions where the awareness levels and bargaining power of the beneficiaries are higher (Subbarao 1985).

However, the self-employment activities are weakly integrated with area development planning, resulting in lack of flexibility in both the selection of activities suiting local resource endowments and devising methods for implementation. Wage-employment programmes are also insufficiently integrated with plans for area development. The assets created are mostly of the type which do not have a potential for sustained increase in employment over a period of time. Further, the upper income groups in the rural areas seem to have been the major beneficiaries from the assets created, whereas the assets created exclusively for the benefit of the poor such as housing and irrigation for marginal farmers are relatively few (Hirway *et al.* 1991).

Potential for Integration of PAPs with Overall Development

The integration of PAPs with agricultural development can be made effective by strengthening the land-base for the poor, particularly the women, through the effective implementation of the existing legislation on land reform. Since there is an active land market in the countryside where farmers having access to resources are able to augment their landholdings, it would be desirable to advance long-term loans on liberal terms to the landless poor for the purchase of land. The decision of the Government of India to permit loans for purchase of land under the IRDP is a step in the right direction, but it is rarely followed up.

The existing policy of containing population growth is not strictly a poverty alleviation programme but unless it is integrated with income generating programmes and social development for the poor, it would be difficult to motivate the poor to limit the size of their families. The official policy has so far treated population growth as essentially exogeneous to the developmental process. However, the experience over the plan period in different parts of the country has shown that the decline in fertility levels is very much influenced by the levels of social and economic development such as age at marriage of girls, infant mortality rate, literacy levels (particularly for females), and income levels.

Given the appropriate land and population policies, there are three major potential areas for integration of PAPs with overall development: (i) stepping up existing wage-employment programmes in rural areas for capital construction in agriculture and for eco-development; (ii) stimulating the growth of household and small-scale rural industries by integrating them with the existing self-employment programmes like IRDP; and (iii) acceleration in the pace of social development in rural areas. The rest of this chapter is devoted to the examination of various programmes in these three areas from the point of view of their integration with overall development.

Major Wage Employment Programmes

We shall briefly review the two major wage employment programmes, viz., JRY and the Employment Assurance Scheme (EAS). The JRY was launched in the last year of the Seventh Plan by merging the two ongoing wage-employment programmes, viz., National Rural Employment Programme (NREP) and Rural Landless Employment Guarantee Programme (RLEGP). In the planning as well as execution of works under JRY, an important role was assigned to different tiers of panchayats, the Centre's contribution to the expenditure being 80 per cent and the states' share 20 per cent. Unlike the previous programmes which could not cover a large number of villages, the JRY was being implemented in all the villages in the country. Central assistance to the states for JRY was distributed roughly in proportion to the number of rural poor in each state.

The above pattern of allocation does not appear to impose any major constraints on the integration of this wage-employment programme into the overall development of the area. Funds are allocated broadly according to the social and economic backwardness of the area or roughly in proportion to the needs for infrastructure development, physical as well as social. Districts and gram panchayats are free to pool resources to take up works for the common benefit. However, there is no provision for diverting even part of the outlays meant for self-employment programmes like IRDP towards wage-employment or vice versa. This significantly limits the possibilities for integration of PAPs with overall development. This is because, according to the available studies, self-employment programmes like IRDP have usually proved to be more productive and better integrated with overall development in regions which are infrastructurally developed. On the other hand, less developed regions are in greater need of labour-intensive works for infrastructure development. Despite this limitation, it is important to recognize that even under the existing pattern of allocation, there is significant scope for integrating PAPs with overall development and this potential has not been fully exploited so far.

A significant feature of the programme in its actual operation, contrary to its original objective, was the accent on asset-creation like school buildings with a very high ratio of material to labour cost. Moreover, in violation of the guidelines, the works were executed in most cases by contractors who relied on mechanized equipment and outside labour. On the positive side, creation of durable community assets seemed to have the support of the local people. Further, the active involvement of panchayats contributed to improved awareness and the development of leadership at the local level (Government of India, Planning Commission 2000). In the light of this experience, JRY was restructured as the Jawahar Gram Samridhi Yojana with effect from April 1999 for creating community village infrastructure to increase employment opportunities on a sustained basis.

The EAS represents another significant initiative. According to this scheme, those who are in need and seeking employment were to get assured wage employment for 100 days during the lean agricultural season. The scheme, when it started, was to be implemented in over 1700 backward blocks situated in drought-prone, desert, tribal, and hill areas in which currently the revamped public distribution system (RPDS) was in operation. In course of time, EAS was extended to other blocks, and by 1997–8, the scheme was being implemented in as many as 5448 rural blocks in the country.

While undertaking works, priority was to be given to water and soil conservation, agro-forestry, horticulture, silvipasture, and minor irrigation works. These are best undertaken in the framework of watershed development in which mini or micro watersheds are taken up for systematic treatment by using technologies that are area-specific, cost-effective, ecologically sound, and locally acceptable.

The EAS was thus easily amenable to integration with programmes for area development such as the National Watershed Development Project for Rain-fed Areas (NWDPRA). The latter seeks to ensure sustainable production of biomass and restoration of ecological balance through employment-oriented production systems like multiple cropping, agro-forestry, and horticulture. Besides this, a centrally-sponsored scheme to associate scheduled tribes (STs) and rural poor in afforestation of degraded forests is also in place, with tribal people being entitled to usufruct in full. The enormous potential for integrating the employment objective with eco-development is evident from the fact that the reclamation of about 40 million hectares of waste land for bio-mass production can generate over 50 million person-years of work.

However, a number of infirmities in the EAS began to surface in the course of its implementation. Since the allocations under the programme were open-ended, the richer and the more enterprising states cornered bulk of the funds under the programme. To rectify this, with effect from April 1999, the allocations to the states were made on the basis of poverty. Like the JRY, the works were being increasingly executed by contractors with a high material to labour ratio. It was also found that figures of employment generation were far from genuine, and muster rolls were not being maintained by the village panchayats. What is worse, contrary to its avowed objective, bulk of the funds were being used for constructing school buildings, anganwadis etc. instead of for eco-development activities such as watershed development, de-silting of tanks, and afforestation. Even the Ministry of Rural Development in its revised guidelines no longer permits watershed development on the ground that it takes more time to complete (Government of India, Planning Commission 2000).

Thus for all practical purposes, the distinction between JRY and EAS disappeared except that the former was being implemented through panchayats. The employment generated was also not sizeable as these two programmes together generateed not more than 5 per cent of the working days for those below the poverty line. Therefore, the contribution of these wage employment programmes to poverty alleviation as well as overall development is extremely limited both on account of inadequate allocations as well as failure to adhere to the original guidelines.

It is necessary to integrate the nutritional objective with employment generation goals. Even a rise in employment and wages need not necessarily result in improvement of nutritional levels of the poor if the prices of foodgrains rise simultaneously or they become inaccessible. In view of this, in the earlier wage-employment programmes it was stipulated that part of the wage payment be made in kind in terms of certain quantity of foodgrains. But under JRY this was made optional with the result that the off-take of foodgrains under this programme came down drastically. This is due to the reduced availability of foodgrains for the programme rather than the preferences of wage-labour. In view of this experience, there are serious moves now for restoring the earlier practice of paying part of the wages in terms of foodgrains.

It is clear from the findings of various evaluation studies that the constraints to the integration of wage-employment programmes with overall development relate to the wrong choice of activities as well as the ineffectiveness in implementation of the activities chosen. The choice of activities in the framework of area planning may result in improved priorities and better sequencing of activities but the problem of the quality of execution would still remain. The existing policy proposes to dispense with the contractor system in the execution of wage-employment projects under the PAPs because of low generation of employment from the given investment levels, as the contractors' margins are high and the material-wage ratio tends to be high. Moreover, whereas the contractor system may be efficient in the execution of certain activities like construction of houses, school buildings, and roads, it is ill-suited to undertaking activities like eco-development involving peoples' contribution and sequencing of various activities in an integrated framework, requiring sustained interest by the community in the supervision and monitoring of activities over a long period of time.

Self-employment Programmes

Three major initiatives were taken by the government during the Sixth and Seventh Plans for self-employment of the rural poor. They are:

IRDP, Training of Rural Youth for Self-employment (TRYSEM), and Development of Women and Children in Rural Areas (DWCRA).

Training of rural youth for self-employment is designed to provide technical skills and to upgrade the traditional skills of rural youth belonging to families below the poverty line, so as to enable them to take up self-employment ventures under IRDP or wage employment. Under DWCRA groups of women are granted assistance to take up viable economic activities with a one time grant for each group to be used as a revolving fund. In view of encouraging results, this programme got a major fillip during the Eighth Five Year Plan, and to this day, it stands out as the most successful among the ongoing PAPs. This is basically explained by the fact that this programme is run exclusively by women and on a group basis.

It appears from the various evaluation studies as well as from our discussions with the field-level functionaries and peoples' representatives that the integration of self-employment programmes with overall development is even weaker than that of the wage employment programmes. Consequently, not only is their contribution to overall development meagre but income generation for the poor also falls short of expectations. This is on account of asset formation under IRDP falling very short of the level warranted by the outlays as well as the choice of activities not being in consonance with the emerging consumer demand.

The Mid-term Appraisal for the Ninth Five Year Plan brings out the various deficiencies of IRDP, especially the large-scale corruption and leakages. These have arisen because, as mentioned earlier, the relative importance of self-employment and wage-employment programmes is made almost invariant in different parts of the country despite the significant differences in infrastructural development of the regions. Consequently, in areas of poor infrastructure with insufficient linkages with input supplies and marketing of output, there are considerable inefficiencies and wastages in the operation of IRDP, while in the infrastructurally developed areas the existing potential for efficient and remunerative self-employment is not fully exploited. Again, as mentioned before, the bureaucratic processes, on which the government's self-employment programmes are heavily dependent, do not adequately ensure the selection of activities which are in consonance with the emerging demand. The access to technical and financial assistance and inputs is also far from adequate.

The DWCRA too has suffered on account of selection of unviable activities and lack of investment. Therefore, during the Eighth Plan period, formation of thrift and credit societies was envisaged which will be entitled to receive matching contributions from the government. It was also proposed that TRYSEM should to be better integrated with development by: (a) assessing training needs in terms of activities which can either be started under IRDP or in fields where wage-employment opportunities are likely to increase; (b) improving the skill endowment of trainees; and (c) organizing groups of persons in a particular productive venture and bringing them together for training. Besides training in skills, training in entrepreneurship (that is, management, accounts, etc.) was also proposed to be covered for self-employment ventures by involving banks in the identification of trades and beneficiaries.

In view of the serious deficiencies brought out by various evaluations of self-employment programmes, it was decided to merge them into a single self-employment programme, viz., the Swarnajayanti Gram Swarozgar Yojana (SGSY) with effect from April 1999. Social mobilization of the poor by organizing them into self-help groups (SHGs), their capacity building, cluster approach in planning their activities, and special safeguards for the weaker sections such as that 50 per cent of the groups formed should be exclusively of women, 40 per cent of Swarozgaris assisted should also be women and that SC/ST constitute 50 per cent are the main features of the reconstituted programme.

However, since the features outlined above are not entirely new, there is every reason to guard against the failures of the earlier programmes by continuing to pursue solutions which appeared clear even earlier. For example, within agriculture, the potential for self-employment has been increasing in non-crop activities like livestock production, dairying, fisheries, and forestry, the demand for which is income-elastic. This calls for considerable investment in the improvement of the cattle population and grazing land as well as land reclamation and development of fisheries and forests. Recent trends in employment also indicate a significant rise in employment in the informal rural (non-agricultural) sector, comprising household and small-scale manufacturing, services, and construction, the demand for which is highly income-elastic. It is necessary to identify, at the micro level, such newly emerging enterprises and their requirements for training in skills, finance, and marketing infrastructure. The best way to integrate self-employment programmes with overall development is to reorient them towards these newly emerging fields.

Many of the livestock-based enterprises are not land-intensive and, as such, typically suit the marginal holdings and the landless. However, these activities, in general, require government support for resources, training in skills and marketing. Since the demand for these products is income-elastic, they are highly complementary to growth in general. The banks need to play a much greater role than at present, not only in providing credit directly to the poor but also in supporting pilot projects for identifying productive activities for the poor, providing extension services and carrying out evaluations, so that the experience available is used for selecting projects capable of being replicated. Since many of these activities are capital-intensive and skill-intensive, though not land-intensive, those who have access to resources and technical services may be quick to invest in such ventures and pre-empt the market for those products. It is, therefore, important to devise appropriate institutions for public investment as well as for the provision of various technical services on a preferential basis for the enterprises run by the poor.

To the extent possible, these self-employment activities should be organized on a group or cooperative basis, as envisaged, so that the risks for the individuals are reduced and economies of scale inherent in some of these activities are fully realized while, at the same time, group initiative and effort of the poor is promoted to check exploitation by middlemen. The general level of consciousness and educational level among the poor is much higher now than three decades ago when economists in India actively debated the subject of cooperatives for the poor. Besides, purely in the economic sense, the indivisibility phenomenon is becoming increasingly important in many of the activities with modern practices or where technical services are important. Thus the group or cooperative endeavour can offer greater economic returns now than before, partly through better use of modern equipment and technical services but also because of better access to resources and knowledge, and the pressure that the members of the group can bring to bear on the seats of power.

Minimum Needs Programme and Measures for Social Development

Social or human development through the provision of minimum needs such as elementary education, adult education, primary health facilities, potable drinking water, public distribution of foodgrains, and housing has a direct bearing on poverty alleviation both by improving the levels of living or quality of life of the rural poor and by generating employment for the rural youth in the provision of such services. Compulsory primary education will help, among other things, to eradicate child labour and thus ensure the physical and mental development of children. In general, social development by raising the skills and awareness of the rural poor, will enable them to bargain for better terms in the rural markets for wage labour, credit, and land, and will eventually result in slowing down population growth. Thus apart from reducing poverty, the measures for social development will prepare the rural poor for effective participation in the developmental process in the future.

Upgrading the skills of the rural artisans through training will significantly contribute to overall development by overcoming shortages of skilled personnel. The skills to be upgraded should depend on the type of artisans in each area and local demand for them. The training programmes and duration will have to be flexible to suit local requirements. In view of the training requirements for agricultural labourers and rural artisans on a large scale, and the need to co-ordinate them and plan the requirements in a comprehensive manner, the National Commission on Rural Labour recommended that a district training institute be established in each district staffed by competent trainers (Government of India 1991).

The integration of the minimum needs programme and social development programmes with overall development does not pose any major problems in respect of choice of activities or *inter se* priorities. Their contribution to development depends virtually on the quality of implementation of such programmes. For example, the literacy rate would be low despite high rate of enrolment of children if there is a high drop-out. Similarly, despite a wide territorial coverage by primary health centres, the achievements in terms of decline in the infant mortality rate and birth rate have been low for want of adequate staff or medicines. Further, in the case of water supply, the quantity and quality of water supplied is relevant rather than the number of villages covered. In view of the above, it is necessary to shift the emphasis from mere targeting to achieving qualitative results.

Conclusion

An attempt has been made in this chapter to examine the potential as well as the prospects for integrating the major PAPs in rural areas with overall development. The potential for such integration is quite high, both by way of better choice of activities and more effective implementation of the activities chosen. Devising appropriate institutional mechanisms for planning the activities under PAPs within the framework of area development planning through the Panchayati Raj institutions and, more particularly, for their effective implementation constitutes the biggest challenge in the drive for eradication of poverty in rural areas. Considering the past experience, the improvement on this score is bound to be a time-consuming process.

Implementation of socio-economic measures designed to bring about structural changes in rural society, improvement in literacy and awareness levels of the poor and progress towards group endeavour on the part of the poor themselves will determine the pace of success in the implementation of PAPs. The dilemma faced is, therefore, clear and unmistakable: PAPs are needed most under conditions of widespread poverty, prevalence of unorganized activities, illiteracy, and ignorance. It is precisely these conditions which render planning and, more so, implementation of these programmes most difficult. These programmes can be better implemented as income levels rise and the staying power of the poor improves and as their literacy and awareness levels rise.

Section V

Sustainable Rural Development

16

Sustainable Rural Development

Some Conceptual Issues and the Indian Experience

Some Conceptual Issues

Until recently, agricultural economists in India had not been particularly concerned about environmental issues. Therefore, to present a stylized or schematic framework arising from their work would be rather presumptuous. Agricultural economists in general became sensitized to the severity of the problem of ecological degradation in India since the early 1980s, through their exposure to the grass roots situation and interactions with non-governmental organizations (NGOs) and administrators.

The most popular and accepted definition of 'sustainable development' is the one given by the World Commission of Environment and Development, called the Brundtland Commission (Brundtland *et al.* 1987): 'Sustainable development is development that meets the needs of the present without compromising the ability of future generations to meet their own needs'. This is a highly elastic definition, which may be why it is so popular. Among economists, it is well accepted that issues bearing on environmental degradation must be seen in the context of development.

It is incorrect to look at environment and development in a static framework. This is because development, by itself, opens up opportunities for ecological conservation, for example, in terms of the choice of technology. Today's technology may be highly resource-using, but newer technologies which can be evolved as a result of development may be resource-conserving. In agriculture, for instance, better technology has meant the availability of options in terms of input substitution whereby natural inputs can be substituted by others which do not exhaust the natural resources. Furthermore, equitable development—development accompanied by social justice—will enhance the ability of the poorer population to withstand the rigours of life. It will improve their staying power, thereby reducing pressure on the environment, for example, on land, water, and forests.

This definition of sustainable development does not centre around the so-called 'trade-off' between present and future consumption. It does not rigidly say that the concern for meeting present needs will necessarily undermine the capacity of future generations to meet their needs. It only says that methods for meeting the present needs should not be at the cost of the future generation's ability to meet its needs. To give a simple example, in drought-prone areas, the management of resources is such that even the present needs are not met. People, in fact, migrate to other regions to meet their immediate needs.

Yet, we have seen models—Ralegaon Siddhi, Adgaon or Sukhomajri—places which lie in the very same dry belt, where, due to proper management of resources, not only has the capacity to meet basic needs of the present generation improved, but they have also been able to preserve the stock of natural capital or even enhance it for future generations. This complementary relationship between the present and the future arising from the methods of management of resources is extremely important and is not precluded in this definition. But, at the same time, it should be noted that it is only places like Sukhomajri, Adgaon, or Ralegan Siddhi, which have been lucky to have motivated and committed leaders, who have been able to organize the people to manage their resources in a sustainable way. Otherwise, the overall situation is depressing.

This definition does not also look at the capabilities of future generations merely in terms of the capabilities of the present generation. It allows for the improvement of knowledge. Technologies which may not be known or available at present, may become available only to future generations. Therefore, it talks about the ability of future generations to meet their requirements. We have to allow for the possibility that with technological improvements, more choices will be open for the future generations. The abilities of the future generations are, therefore, not to be looked at purely from a static angle, that is, in the light of present knowledge and present stock of resources.

Operationally, there are three major indicators of sustainability in agriculture in the drought-prone areas. The first is the groundwater-table. In all the drought-prone areas evaluated recently, the water-table has gone down significantly. In the last ten years, it has, in fact, been going down at a faster rate (Government of India, Planning Commission 2000). This means, the rate of extraction of water has been much higher than the rate of percolation or recharge. Over a period of time, there are indications that the in situ or on-the-ground conservation of rainwater has declined. It is generally found that, on an average, only 30 per cent of rain water is being conserved, while 70 per cent is going waste (Dasgupta 1993; Government of India, Ministry of Rural Development 1994). Even in areas where rainfall is only 300 mm or so, 70–80 per cent of the rainwater is going waste. There are a number of areas where, over a period of time, as a result of devegetation and deforestation, the run-off has increased and the recharge has declined. The gap between recharge and extraction has clearly widened. However, in similar areas where NGOs are working, 60–70 per cent of rainwater is conserved. Tanks are full of water and crops are thriving.

Related to the above is the problem of deforestation. Even today, despite all the ongoing social forestry and afforestation programmes, the forest cover on a net basis has been going down, though at a diminishing rate.

And finally, with declining fodder availability in many drought-prone areas, the carrying capacity of land for animals has also declined. There has been a change in the structure of livestock—the number of heads of cattle is rapidly giving way to sheep and goats. The demand for cattle has been going down partly because of tractorization, but also because the carrying capacity of land has been going down. Animals who are better absorbers or whose conversion ratio—feed–meat or feed–milk ratio—is better, are becoming popular. Animals considered 'inefficient' from this angle have been declining in numbers.

If these major indicators are taken into account, degradation of land has become severe. Some of the recent studies reveal the negative impact of the degradation of land on agricultural productivity growth (Evenson, Pray, and Rosegrant 1999). In many states, thus, development of agriculture is becoming increasingly unsustainable.

What are the basic reasons for this? Population growth and the pressure arising from population is often mentioned in this context. If population growth slows down, per capita income will increase. But with the increase in per capita income, the demand for products which exert pressure on the environment and on natural resources, such as meat, wool, and timber for housing, will increase at a faster rate, because the demand for all these products is highly income-elastic.

Income-elasticity of demand for these products is, in fact, much higher than for jowar (*sorghum*) or bajra (millet) which are extensively grown in dry land areas. And, if population growth is less, then certainly the demand for cereals like jowar or bajra will be less and the area used for growing these crops will also be less, but, by the same token, the pressure on the environment will increase because of the demand arising from high income. Growing urbanization and export demand will also exert pressure on the environment.

A number of studies have shown that areas experiencing lower population growth in the country are also the ones where there has been out-migration due to the degradation of the natural resource base of the region (Rao 1994a). Labour often migrates out of such areas and settles down in the irrigated areas. Thus, in these areas, population growth is found to be lower than the national average, while in other areas where there are no obvious environmental degradation problems, population growth is higher than the national average as there is a lot of in-migration. Arid and semi-arid western Rajasthan is an exception where growth in human and animal population has been much higher than the state average.

The pressure from population growth and poverty is still significant but, clearly, its importance has been declining relative to the pressure of demand from affluence. The poor are increasingly becoming the victims of natural resource degradation in the form of shortage of fuel, fodder, and drinking water rather than being the perpetrators of such degradation.

Globalization of Indian agriculture will no doubt exert pressure on the natural resources. But in so far as it does away with the implicit taxation of agriculture and thus improves the resource position of the farmers and attracts greater investment, it would make it easier to reduce input subsidies and augment water resources in a sustainable way.

We have seen that, by and large, a population-centred explanation is insufficient to understand environmental degradation. We have to look at income and other factors along with the breakdown of traditional institutions which used to manage the natural resources. One would not like to idealize these pre-independence institutions, which were undoubtedly authoritarian, where village authorities had enough power to regulate the activities of the human and animal population and ensure compliance with rules designed to protect the environment. It is also true, however, that this was in the context of low population growth which was a favourable factor.

As traditional institutions broke down, a vacuum was created. There was a period of experimentation, after which the Panchayati Raj institutions started functioning in some states, particularly, the western states of Gujarat, Maharashtra, and Rajasthan in the 1950s and the 1960s. But very soon, they too became defunct. So the vacuum created by the collapse of traditional institutions has not been adequately filled by new institutions. This is a very important factor accounting for the degradation of natural resources. And this is also where the perception of economists comes in. The price policy or the subsidy framework, which was followed for agricultural activities and for the rural areas in general, has been such that there was no incentive to conserve natural resources. In fact, there was every incentive to overuse and deplete them.

Moreover, in these areas, wages are generally low and so is agricultural productivity. The poor have to depend upon moneylenders for consumption loans as institutional loans are not designed to meet consumption demand. Rents are also very high. It is, thus, a situation of low wages, high rents, high interest rates, and high poverty. In other words, it can be described as a poverty syndrome which exhibits symptoms of powerlessness and low productivity of resources. In a situation like this, the poor place a high value on the present consumption. They place a greater value on using resources intensively at present because they are hard-pressed for meeting their immediate consumption needs. They do not have enough to invest either for augmenting their resources or for improving the productivity of their resources.

Therefore, unless there is intelligent public intervention, both on the resource ownership side as well as on the developmental and pricing side, people will continue to place a high value on present consumption ignoring the need to conserve the resources for the future. This is what is referred to as high 'time preference' and is most inimical to environmental protection. Sustainability or sustainable development becomes operationally effective only when the time horizon is longer.

Take the case of groundwater. Throughout the greater part of the western belt of India, from a purely economic angle, there is an inefficient use or wastage of this scarce resource. One is surprised to find water-logging near water pumps even in areas where the rainfall is barely 300 mm. This occurs because someone may have switched the pump on and gone away, unconcerned about the wastage of water because electricity which is used to run the pump is priced at a flat rate per pump set. Thus, we find that the marginal cost for using a scarce resource like water is zero, which is highly detrimental to environmental protection.

From the Taxation Enquiry Commission of 1953, to the most recent Report of the Committee headed by A. Vaidyanathan (Government of India, Planning Commission 1992), volumetric rates for surface water have been recommended. While it may not be possible to immediately introduce volumetric rates all over the country for all the irrigation projects, it is possible to do so for quite a few of these projects. But no beginning has been made in that direction even after 50 years. Several technicians have estimated that as much as 50 per cent of our water resources are wasted (Chapter 7). With proper pricing of water, it should be possible to increase crop output per unit of water.

Some experts think that even without investing any more in irrigation for the next 20–30 years, it would still be possible to increase our agricultural output. According to them, with proper outlets, proper management, and proper pricing, we can increase our output six-fold from the existing volume of water (Rao 1997a). While that may be an exaggeration, there is no doubt that a lot of surface water is being wasted because of defective delivery systems and pricing.

This is true even for fertilizers, although our environmental problems in rural areas do not arise from the excessive use of chemicals. The average level of use of fertilizers and pesticides in India is quite low when compared to the West, but without subsidies or with less subsidies, chemical fertilizers would be used even more thinly. In fact, in certain years of good rainfall in some backward areas, the high demand for fertilizer coupled with low supply, usually results in the creation of a black market for fertilizers, which in turn, is the result of its excessive use in the other more developed areas of the country, where subsidy levels are much higher. Even with reduced subsidies or higher prices for fertilizers, output can increase significantly with the given quantity of fertilizers, without increasing irrigation, because the productivity per unit of fertilizers would be greater at lower levels of application over a wider area (Chapter 6).

In periods of drought, the subject exercising the minds of planners and administrators is usually how to regulate and restrict the number of wells as a solution to the problem of shortage of drinking water. But a reduction in the number of wells would only lead to the redistribution of water. It would not make much difference to the water-table if the number of wells is reduced by, say, 10–20 per cent or if new wells are not allowed to be dug in problem areas as long as the pricing of water remains unchanged, because there would be excessive withdrawal of water from the existing wells. Instead, there should be a consensus among political parties that they would not oppose any system which advocates the rational pricing of water. It is a matter of great importance to try and develop a consensus amongst the political elite on these issues.

Today, as a result of globalization and the free flow of information, farmers in India know that, when compared to them, farmers in the US, Europe, and Japan enjoy higher levels of subsidies. Their subsidy levels are as high as 20–30 per cent of their farm output, while in India they are only about 7–8 per cent of farm output. But, then, our resources are scarcer, which could be put to more productive alternative uses. We could invest our money in irrigation, rural electrification, on the public distribution system (PDS), and on poverty removal. This is where creating resource literacy among the people becomes important.

In conclusion, there are a few issues which are critical while developing any future strategy for sustainable development of rural areas. If all the money that has been spent on employment generation, such as drought relief or famine relief work, the Jawahar Rozgar Yojana (JRY), etc. had been properly spent, we would have had a very different picture. We would have had Sukhomajris, Adgaons, and Ralegaon Siddhis all over the country. These resources would have been sufficient for taking up afforestation projects which would, in turn, have conserved our soil and moisture and at the same time would have provided productive employment to the rural poor. These projects would have also ensured the enrichment of our natural resource base. But, we have failed to do this. This is, in fact, a case of state as well as market failure. Private actions driven purely by the profit motive have resulted in the destruction of the environment. The state has failed because it could not plan appropriately by involving people at the grass roots level. Therefore, the first important requirement is to plan appropriately on a watershed basis which generally involves a village or a few villages in some cases. But largely the plans will have to be village-centred and watershed-centred. The treatment of soil has to follow sequentially—from the catchment area to areas lower down (Government of India, Ministry of Rural Development 1994).

Second, there is no coordination between different government departments. For example, the forest department does its work and the minor irrigation department does its own without any coordination between them. In the case of irrigated areas, since the entire activity is oriented towards raising productivity at the individual farm level, it is the farmers who act as coordinating agents. In the process, however, they incur heavy costs of coordination. But in the unirrigated, dry areas where conservation requires cooperation among individual farmers, the role of the coordinator has to be taken up by the state. In such cases, therefore, coordinated planning becomes essential.

Third, it is important to involve the local people in the preparation of plans. Otherwise, typically, the implementation of official plans is thwarted by the local people whose perception of the plan's effects differs from that of the administration. On the other hand, where the beneficiaries have been involved right from the planning stage to the implementation stage, one finds that the projects have been successfully implemented. This is possible because only those activities are undertaken which the people themselves consider to be profitable. The local people, thus, would have an interest in protecting and sustaining these activities.

Finally, because of their greater dependence on natural resources, rural women have acquired substantial knowledge about the plant species, their uses, and conservation techniques. Moreover, poor rural women are often found to be better conservators as the adverse impact of degradation of natural resources on them is direct and immediate. Policy initiatives are, therefore, called for to enlist the participation of the rural poor, especially women among them, for the protection and regeneration of degraded areas (Dasgupta 1993). Several NGOs in the region are involved in the activities relating to the conservation of the environment with the participation of people. Public policy needs to be more alive to the need for involving such NGOs in the programmes for the conservation of natural resources.

The involvement of the local people can be brought about either through voluntary organizations (NGOs) or through elected panchayats. There is occasionally a debate about whether the village panchayats, as they are constituted now, can be vehicles for ensuring sustainable development or whether one can depend only on NGOs. However, modalities have to be worked out for collaborative ventures between elected institutions, NGOs, and administrators.

Sustainable Development of Agriculture in India

We have discussed in the previous section the widely accepted definition of sustainable development given by the World Commission of Environment and Development called the Brundtland Commission (Brundtland *et al.* 1987). To recapitulate, this definition looks at 'sustainability' in a dynamic framework. Development by itself may open up opportunities for conservation of natural resources through the evolution and adoption of appropriate technologies. Moreover, this definition is inclusive in that it allows for equitable development which would improve the staying power of the poor, thus reducing their pressure on environment. Further, this definition is not centred around a trade-off between the present and the future. It is thus possible, for example, to conceive of practices for managing resources which enhance the capacity of the present as well as future generations to meet their needs (Rao 1997a).

In the context of agriculture, this definition entails strategies and policies that augment existing land and water resources through investment; technologies for increasing the productivity of these resources; and pricing policies as well as management practices that economize on the use of such inputs. This requires awareness on the part of the people at large about the causes and consequences of environmental degradation and appropriate institutions for the participation of the users of resources in the decision-making processes. Sustainable development is thus a holistic concept calling for measures on several fronts for achieving its objectives effectively.

We have discussed in the previous chapters the linkages between growth in agriculture, reforms, and poverty alleviation. But how has the growth in agriculture and reduction in poverty impinged upon the health of natural resources? What implications would it have for sustainable use of resources?

The variables bearing on the sustainable use of natural resources do not suggest that the processes of degradation underway would have been reversed. For example, the subsidies on power for pumping water, the very low user charges for canal irrigation and the subsidies on fertilizers, which are responsible for the overexploitation of natural resources as well as for retarding technological changes for conserving resources, are still on the increase.

We have estimates about the rate at which agricultural output has been growing in the country during the plan period. We also have fairly good estimates of growth in various inputs used for achieving this growth in output. But do we have equally dependable estimates regarding the costs imposed by this growth on the environment? The answer is perhaps 'No' despite the laudable scholarly efforts being made in this direction. Nevertheless, there is a consensus among experts that the agricultural growth we have achieved has entailed identifiable costs to the environment which, in principle, can be quantified. These costs include deforestation, degradation of land, depletion of groundwater, and loss of bio-diversity.

In the first two decades of planning, that is, during the 1950s and 1960s, agricultural growth was achieved mainly through the expansion of area under cultivation by reducing area under fallows and through deforestation. It appears that at least half the deforested area during this period was brought under the plough. The green revolution launched in the country in the late 1960s was land-saving and so the pressure on land began to ease. But, at the same time, water and fertilizers became major inputs and, as such, much of the degradation caused to the environment in the subsequent period such as water-logging and salinity, depletion of groundwater, and unbalanced use of chemical fertilizers and pesticides are associated with the green revolution.

Despite these adverse consequences, it appears that, on balance, land-saving technological change represented by the green revolution was the single most important factor contributing to sustainability (Rao 1997b). Extension of cultivation to marginal lands and to area under forests has been halted. Of late, there has been a rise in area under fallows. The amount of fallow area is highly correlated with area irrigated, suggesting that the progress of yield-increasing technology has reduced pressure on marginal lands (Ray 1992; Reddy 1991). A study for the ecologically fragile Himalayan region (Himachal Pradesh) shows that farm diversification through horticultural crops, which are land-saving as well as labour-using, in so far as it leads to a rise in the incomes of farmers, results in reducing pressure on land for growing field crops and for grazing their livestock. It also reduces pressure for deforestation (Chand 1996). The rapid displacement of bullocks by tractors, and cows by buffaloes in prosperous irrigated areas also points to a similar trend (Rao 1994a). However, the concentration of cattle among land-scarce small holdings and the rapid increase in the number of small ruminants like sheep and goats are exerting pressure on the environment, especially in the dry areas (Rao 1994a).

On account of the shortage of fuel wood in the 1970s, its prices rose at double the rate at which the prices of foodgrains were rising. This price rise and the social forestry programme launched by the government in this period to meet the fuel wood crisis seem to have evoked a positive response from the farmers. The eucalyptus-based farm forestry in the relatively well-endowed agricultural plains and certain exotic species coming up in degraded private and public lands in the dry regions of the country, appear to have contributed to easing the fuel wood crisis (Natarajan 1995). This is evident from the fact that the price of fuel wood became steady in the 1985–90 period. The programmes for participatory forest management in certain states, for example, West Bengal, Andhra Pradesh, Madhya Pradesh, Rajasthan, and Uttar Pradesh, by giving usufructuary rights to the local people, as well as social forestry programmes in the country have contributed to easing fuel wood shortages. The recently revamped programme for watershed development towards soil and moisture conservation in dry land areas seems to be making a favourable impact owing to its participatory character. As a consequence of all these developments, the annual rate of deforestation has declined from over 1 million hectares in the 1970s to a little over 0.1 million hectares in the 1990s (Centre for Science and Environment 1998).

Although the pressure to increase the area under cultivation has considerably eased, the challenges of stepping up agricultural output in a sustainable way are quite daunting. This is because, the gross domestic product (GDP) from agriculture needs to grow at a minimum rate of 4–5 per cent per annum for sustaining an overall growth in GDP of 7–8 per cent per annum over the next decade and beyond. The opening up of trade and the rise in domestic demand for agro-products as a result of the rise in per capita income are likely to be the most important factors causing pressure on natural resources. The pressure from population growth and poverty is still significant, but its importance has clearly been declining relative to the pressure of demand arising from affluence.

Luckily, the country has the potential for achieving this rate of agricultural growth in a sustainable manner without causing undue pressure on its natural resources. There is a large potential for raising productivity per unit of land by augmenting both surface and groundwater resources and indeed for raising the productivity of inputs as a whole through the widespread application of yield-increasing and input-saving technologies.

Thus, land-augmenting technological change, that is, the application of seed–water–fertilizer technology is likely to be the single biggest factor in easing pressure on natural resources both by improving productivity from these limited resources and by reducing rural poverty and hence the pressure from the rural poor on natural resources. Besides, the development and use of biotechnology can contribute to the protection of the environment by raising yields in ways that are both cost-effective and environmentally sound. It will also lead to an improvement in the quality of animals and thus facilitate the reduction in their numbers. These areas of agricultural research and extension, therefore, deserve to be given a high priority by the governments in the region.

Out of the total potential from major and medium irrigation projects, about 40 per cent of the area still remains to be exploited. Further, nearly 25 million hectares can probably be added under minor irrigation sources including from groundwater sources (Rao 1994b). Moreover, about 25–50 per cent of irrigation water presently in use can be saved through improved management practices without reducing yields and such savings in water would in fact raise yields substantially in respect of several crops (ICAR 1997). Further, in the arid and semi-arid areas, as mentioned in the previous section, only about 30 per cent of rainwater is conserved whereas the NGOs working in the same areas are able to conserve 60–70 per cent of the rainwater. The levels of chemical fertilizer use and crop yields in India are substantially lower than those in East Asia, pointing to the large unexploited potential for raising yields by applying the high-yielding technology and by extending even the known technology to the less developed areas in central and eastern parts of the country, as nearly two-thirds of the irrigation potential remaining to be exploited is located in such areas.

However, despite the existence of a large potential, the growth of agriculture has slowed down in the post-reform period of the 1990s. This is explained by the slow growth of inputs like irrigation water and fertilizers and the declining contribution of total factor productivity (TFP).

The subsidies on canal irrigation and on power for pumping water are leading to the overexploitation of existing water resources, resulting in water logging and salinity on the one hand, and depletion of groundwater, on the other. Higher subsidies on nitrogenous fertilizers have resulted in an adverse NPK ratio which has reduced the productivity of fertilizers, apart from causing damage to soils. Extensive and improper use of pesticides on account of subsidies and inadequate extension services are also causing degradation of the environment.

As discussed in Chapter 5, the contribution to growth from the productivity of inputs (TFP) which had risen to a little over 40 per cent in the post-green revolution period, declined to about 30 per cent in the late 1980s. This is explained by the slow pace of technological change for raising yields and for saving inputs. Further, as explained in Chapter 6, despite a high rate of return on investment, agricultural research has been underfunded. The annual growth rate in real public expenditure on agricultural research and education, having accelerated in the post-green revolution period, has slowed since the mid-1980s, hovering around only about 0.5 per cent of the agricultural GDP in the early 1990s, as against 1 per cent projected for the Ninth Plan by the Indian Council of Agricultural Research.

Effective strategies are needed to put agriculture on the path of sustainable development. First, there is a need to step up public and private investment in infrastructure, for example, irrigation, rural electrification, rural roads, warehousing, and agro-processing. Second, increase in TFP through the use of water-saving as well as environment-friendly, bio-technologies has to become a predominant source of agricultural growth. Such a strategy alone can reduce pressure on natural resources and can minimize the pollution from the excessive use of chemical inputs.

The level of research expenditure in India at present is sub-optimal or significantly lower than desired in the central and eastern states of Bihar, Madhya Pradesh, Orissa, Uttar Pradesh, and West Bengal, where productivity is low and poverty is widespread. The research expenditures are also not in tune with the diversification of agriculture and are not quite environment-friendly. Livestock, horticulture, agro-forestry, and dry land areas receive sub-optimal expenditures (Pal, Jha, and Singh 1997).

Whereas soil and moisture conservation would raise the profitability of investment in research for unfavourable areas, it is equally true that the availability of improved technologies would make conservation of natural resources attractive to the farmers. Evolution of new technologies for marginal lands by giving priority to frontier areas of research like biotechnology which are environment friendly is likely to contribute significantly to the sustainable use of resources.

Under the revamped watershed development programme for marginal lands, the adverse externalities of individual actions are sought to be minimized, as, under the new strategy the farmers are fully involved in the preparation as well as implementation of plans for watershed development. The involvement of the poor in the reforestation of degraded forests with proper user rights for them under the joint forest management (JFM), as implemented in some states like West Bengal, Orissa, and Andhra Pradesh holds great promise for the regeneration of the environment.

The performance of watershed development programmes in rain-fed areas shows that to sustain interest and participation of farmers in soil and moisture conservation, it would be necessary to improve economic returns on the investments made in the conservation of resources (Shah 1998). This can be done by introducing new yield-increasing technologies and new products like horticulture which have favourable demand and are also environment-friendly. Indeed, since irrigated areas have so far received greater attention for research and extension, the rain-fed or unfavourable areas are now showing higher marginal returns than irrigated areas from government investments in technologies and infrastructures. Since unfavourable areas in India account for a large proportion of total agricultural land and population, the poverty reducing effects of such investments are also larger in unfavourable areas (Fan and Hazell 1997).

These tasks would require reforms at the national, state, and panchayat levels. At the national level, the macroeconomic reforms underway need to be extended to agriculture by opening up trade and by removing restrictions such as on domestic trade and on agro-processing. These reforms by improving the terms of trade for agriculture and by opening up new opportunities for production and trade, will provide incentives for greater private investment in augmenting agricultural infrastructure. They will also provide incentives for making agriculture competitive through the adoption of cost-reducing technologies.

Experience shows that strengthening of publicly provided infrastructure, especially power, in the medium term, holds the key to inducing private investment and thus deriving full benefits from the ongoing macroeconomic reforms. This brings us to the set of reforms at the state and panchayat levels, where there needs to be a thorough restructuring of institutions for the management of infrastructure like irrigation, rural electricity, research and extension, and rural credit. Basically, these reforms need to be directed towards de-politicizing and de-bureaucratizing the management by involving the farmers, so that a link can be established between the efficiency of the services delivered and charges to be collected for the services rendered.

Finally, the strategy for poverty alleviation and human resource development through the expansion of employment opportunities and provision of primary education and health services has to be revamped by involving the beneficiaries. This is necessary for achieving food security as well as for improving resource literacy, and thus for relieving pressure on common property resources.

The above reforms of institutions for the creation of infrastructure and delivery of services can yield the desired results only if the farmers' awareness and participation is enhanced at the grass-roots level. For this, the local self-governing institutions, for example, Panchayati Raj institutions need to be strengthened by delegating to them functions for socio-economic development of respective areas; devolving necessary financial resources; and entrusting to them power over the administration. Such a decentralization would contribute to proper designing and effective implementation of various development programmes including those for sustainable use of resources such as through watershed development and water users' associations.

17

Watershed Development in India

Recent Experience and Emerging Issues

Watershed development has been conceived basically as a strategy for protecting the livelihoods of the people inhabiting the fragile eco-systems experiencing soil erosion and moisture stress. The aim has been to ensure the availability of drinking water, fuel wood, and fodder and to raise the income and employment for farmers and landless labourers through improvements in agricultural production and productivity. Even as an official programme, watershed development is over three decades old in India. It has undergone periodic reviews by expert committees with a view to improving upon its strategy and components. One such committee—the latest so far—submitted its report to the Ministry of Rural Development in 1994 (GOI 1994). This technical committee had the benefit of studying and learning from the already existing cases of outstanding success in watershed development such as Sukhomajri, Ralegaon Sidhi, Adgaon, certain tribal areas of Panchmahal, Mittemari, and Jhabua, to mention only a few. Learning from these and other success stories, the technical committee recommended planning on watershed basis through the participation of the people at all stages, active involvement of voluntary organizations, and coordinated effort resulting in convergence of treatment by the concerned government departments.

Conceptually, the present strategy of watershed development is prompted by the need to protect the inhabitants of the fragile eco-systems from acute distress caused by recurring droughts. In this sense, it is a strategy for survival, even though in quite a few cases, the successful implementation of watershed development programmes has led to a substantial increase in income and employment for the people. Even the many cases of outstanding success pioneered by eminent non-governmental organizations (NGOs) reveal that such efforts were originally driven by acute distress caused by recurring droughts. Indeed, the overwhelming response from the people to the initiatives taken by the NGOs is explained by the misery to which they were subjected.

It is necessary to distinguish this strategy for protection or survival from a broader or holistic strategy for the development of agriculture in dry land or rain-fed areas. Such a strategy would involve issues of agricultural technology suited to rain-fed areas, price and credit policies, infrastructure development for processing, marketing, and transportation of agricultural produce, and trade policies to afford reasonable protection to dry land farmers. Some of these supporting measures are no doubt present in certain dry land areas, especially in the watershed areas run by some of the distinguished NGOs, where there is a sustained increase in agricultural productivity and income. But this is nowhere comparable to the policy framework and infrastructure available to the areas in the country which have experienced the green revolution. Such a wider strategy for extending the green revolution to the rain-fed or dry land areas is essential not only for deriving full benefit from soil and moisture conservation already accomplished in some areas through the watershed development programme, which Anil Shah has aptly described as 'Watershed-Plus' (Shah, Anil, 2000), but more fundamentally to provide the necessary economic incentives for turning watershed development into a truly spontaneous and demand driven movement of the people in dry land areas not covered so far, and to sustain watershed development already undertaken when the current official programme comes to an end.

Prospects for Agriculture in 2020

Let us look at the prospects for agriculture in the country in the year 2020 with the objective of maintaining self-sufficiency in the production of foodgrains. According to one estimate, in such a case, the availability of groundwater for irrigation would emerge as a critical bottleneck: The requirement of groundwater would exceed its availability for irrigation by nearly 30 per cent. Since the requirement will exceed the replenishable supplies for irrigation at the existing rate of recharge of groundwater, it will lead to over-extraction of groundwater in several states and by 2020 as much as 71 per cent of irrigated area is likely to be from groundwater sources (Chopra and Goldar 2000).

Closely related to this is the problem of degradation of land in the rain-fed or dry land areas. As it is, the rate of degradation of land in such areas in the 1990s is likely to have proceeded at more than twice the rate observed in the 1980s, basically on account of soil erosion from run-off (Reddy 2000). This is happening despite all the official and NGO interventions for soil and moisture conservation through watershed development which may not have covered more than 25 per cent of rain-fed area needing treatment. The acute famine for drinking water experienced in several parts of the country during the last few droughts, despite a series of favourable monsoons preceding them, shows that droughts are becoming increasingly severe in the recent period. Clearly, the existing interventions for drought proofing have failed to neutralize the overall processes of degradation of natural resources underway in the rural areas. This calls for a thorough reappraisal of our agricultural policies with a view to evolving an overall policy framework that provides adequate incentives and opportunities for soil and moisture conservation through watershed development as well as for judicious use of scarce water resources in rain-fed areas.

Recent Experience

Under the new guidelines as many as 10,000 watershed projects under the Drought Prone Areas Programme (DPAP) have been launched in the country since 1994 and are at various stages of implementation. Out of these, Andhra Pradesh alone accounts for as many as 24 per cent. Next comes Madhya Pradesh with around 17 per cent of projects, followed by Uttar Pradesh (10 per cent), Gujarat (8.6 per cent), Tamil Nadu (7 per cent), and others. Eight to ten years of implementation is a long enough period to justify an evaluation of a nation-wide project like this, especially when new guidelines are being experimented with. Unfortunately, however, no systematic effort has been initiated at the national level so far for undertaking evaluations either of a concurrent nature or in-depth studies by independent institutions adequately equipped for the purpose. What we have are some studies undertaken by certain NGOs and individual scholars from certain institutions on their own. Besides, we have a good deal of anecdotal information gathered by the senior officials of the concerned departments from the state and the central levels, which is authentic and useful. Much of this can be scanned from the tour notes of such officials; from the deliberations at high level meetings and seminars; and from the published papers by individuals. The inferences in this chapter are based on some such studies and anecdotal information, and on a series of useful discussions the author has had with knowledgeable persons on the subject. These are supplemented by field observations by the author in a few watersheds in Andhra Pradesh.

Before this evidence is presented in some detail, it would be useful to quickly summarize the major findings. The unmistakable impression one gets from all this information is that the overall impact of the programme has been positive and significant when compared to the period before the implementation of the new guidelines. There has been an improvement in the access to drinking water in some of the project areas even during the year of drought. Crop yields have risen and there has been a substantial increase in area under cultivation in the rabi season, leading to a rise in employment and reduction in migration of labour. Availability of fodder for animals has also improved, leading to a rise in the yield of milk.

All this might come as a pleasant surprise to many who, for understandable reasons, continued to remain sceptical about the prospects for ensuring peoples' participation on a wider scale under the government sponsored programme, even as they were convinced from the experience of success stories that when peoples' participation is ensured, watershed development leads to a substantial improvement in the livelihoods of the people.

Let us now look at the highlights from some of the available studies. 'DILASA', an NGO, selected six Drought Prone Area Programme (DPAP) watersheds in different parts of western India, to study the impact of the programme. Most of these projects were launched in 1996. After the completion of 80–95 per cent of works under the programme, a detailed survey of 15 farmers in each watershed was conducted by following the 'Before' and 'After' method. In most cases, the crop yields after the implementation of the programme were higher by over 60 per cent. The cropping intensity increased by 40–60 per cent. As a result, the total output from crops registered a big increase, ranging from 150–250 per cent in most cases. As much as two-thirds of this increase in output came from *rabi* crops indicating improved stability in output and increase in employment. Dairying and other economic activities have also shown a marked improvement. Migration of labour has been reduced; enrolment of children (especially girls) in schools, has increased; and there is increased participation of women in decision making. However, the study has highlighted the need for the development of roads for deriving full benefit from the programme.

Development Support Centre (DSC) headed by Anil C. Shah has carried out a study of impact of watershed development in May–June 2000—a year of very severe drought—in 8 drought affected districts of Gujarat (Shah, Anil 2000). The study compares drought in a village in each district with the benefit of watershed programme for the last 4 to 5 years, utilizing at least 70 per cent of the total budget allocated under the programme, with an adjoining village without the benefit of watershed development programme. The study investigates the position regarding access to drinking water, area under crops in kharif and rabi seasons, yields of main crops, fodder and animal husbandry, milk yield, local employment and migration, and food security. The findings are revealing in that they show the incidence of drought to be much less severe in watershed villages when compared to the adjoining non-watershed or 'control' villages. The study comes to the conclusion that the 'overall impact is not only positive but also impressive...to a large extent the participatory watershed scheme launched in 1995–6 by Ministry of Rural Development has been found to mitigate the impact of drought'. However, the study points out that the activities and enterprises which specially affect women such as drinking water and dairying tended to receive less attention. Further, the study observes that the expenditure on drought relief being incurred now can be spent more productively by allocating it for watershed development with very little extra expenditure.

Amita Shah and Gani Memon in a quick review of watershed development projects (WDPs) being implemented since 1995–6 in Gujarat, examine their initial impact at the household level based on a primary survey covering 120 households in 4 micro watersheds selected from Rajkot, Surendranagar, Amreli, and Bharuch (Shah and Memon 1999). Even though the project had barely completed 4 years of its implementation, irrigated area had almost doubled since the project intervention. Since increased irrigation has been used mostly for growing cotton during kharif which gets extended up to rabi season, there is, in effect, an increase in cropping intensity. Increased irrigation has led to a substantial rise in average yield or productivity per hectare from all crops combined. Thus the total net returns from all crops increased by 63 per cent. As many as 87 per cent of the households reported that the project created direct benefit in terms of drinking water facility, such proportion being nearly 100 per cent in Surendranagar and Bharuch. Majority of the landless households (71 per cent) reported increase in the availability of employment mainly on the project activities, even though it has not yet led to reduction in migration.

Unfortunately, evaluations like the above for the western part of the country are not available for states like Andhra Pradesh and Madhya Pradesh which are on the top in respect of the number of watershed projects undertaken. However, the success story of Jhabua in Madhya Pradesh in the early 1990s is too well known to need any repetition. Political and administrative will and spontaneous response from the tribal population changed the face of Jhabua within a period of a decade. Although less than 10 per cent of the problem area in Madhya Pradesh is now covered by the watershed development programme under DPAP, anecdotal evidence points to good performance in qualitative terms.

In Andhra Pradesh, the area where watershed development work has been done for 5 years accounts for about 10 per cent of the problem area designated for DPAP. According to an evaluation by the State Water Conservation Mission, between October–November 1998 and October–November 1999, out of nearly 2000 watersheds evaluated, in as many as 90 per cent of the watersheds, water levels increased to varying levels despite a decline in rainfall by 28 per cent; nearly 1.7 lakh hectares of additional area had been brought under irrigation; and, as a result, migration of labour declined by 10–40 per cent in different watersheds. It is pointed out further that none of the villages experiencing acute drinking water shortage during the summer of the year 2002 belonged to any of the watersheds under the programme. Another evaluation made by the State's Groundwater Department for 51 watersheds in 10 districts in 1999 showed an increase of over 70 per cent in irrigated area in the post-project period.

The two highly drought prone districts of Kurnool and Mahabubnagar, which are on the top in the state in respect of the number of watershed projects launched, showed some encouraging pictures for the three year period, 1995–8, when the new guidelines were implemented, as compared to the period 1992–5. District-wise aggregate data show that there was a significant increase in gross irrigated area (11 per cent in Kurnool and 34 per cent in Mahabubnagar) between these two periods—mostly from tanks and wells—which was allocated mainly to rice. As a result, the yields of rice improved by around 15 per cent. However, there was an increase in rainfall between the two periods in both the districts. But, close observers of the scene attribute a good part of the improvement in irrigation and crop yields in these districts to watershed development. This is substantiated by the latest evaluation by the State Water Conservation Mission: within one year, that is, between October–November 1999 and August–September 2000, the number of watersheds rated as 'A', on the basis of various indicators of performance, doubled in Mababubnagar while the number of such watersheds rose by 60 per cent in Kurnool. Discussions with several officials involved in the implementation of the programme and other independent observers—connected with training and evaluation—who are in constant touch with the field situation in the state reveal that the overall impact of the programme is very positive.

From all these evaluations, one does not get a direct indication of soil conserved through watershed development except indirectly in so far as it is reflected in the increase in crop yields. Even though, to a large extent, soil and moisture conservation are positively correlated, it would be useful to develop indicators and methodologies for capturing separately the improvements in soil status.

Factors Accounting for Good Performance

The position across the country in respect of performance of this programme is highly uneven. While Gujarat which has a long tradition of highly dedicated NGOs working in this field continues to be on top in respect of quality in performance, states like Orissa, Bihar, and Uttar Pradesh seem to be way behind in regard to the number of watersheds selected as well as manner of implementation. Despite this, on the whole, the performance of the programme in the country shows a distinct improvement in the last few years. The single most important factor accounting for the positive impact of watershed development under the government sponsored programme in different parts of the country enumerated above is the community participation and decentralization of programme administration made possible under the new guidelines. This has come about on account of political and bureaucratic commitment to the new strategy. This encouraging experience points to the large potential for extending such participatory programmes under the sponsorship of the government.

In Madhya Pradesh, the encouraging performance of the recent period is attributable largely to the positive response from the people, especially in tribal areas, owing to their tradition of community participation, and to political and administrative will for decentralizing administration, and strengthening of Panchayati Raj institutions. In Andhra Pradesh too, informed opinion attributes the encouraging performance basically to political and administrative will which made possible a large coverage by the programme. Andhra Pradesh has made an innovation by providing for a separate project director at the district level for the implementation of watershed projects in DPAP areas. Even though grass roots democracy through Panchayati Raj institutions is yet to be consolidated, the state is known for the empowerment of the rural poor, especially women, through the active functioning of self-help groups (SHGs). According to the latest estimate, as many as 100,000 such groups were registered in the state, their total savings reaching Rs 2 billion. The National Bank for Agriculture and Rural Development (NABARD) has guaranteed to provide credit to 40,000 of these SHGs who constituted 40 per cent of such refinance linked SHGs in the country at the end of June 2000. The performance of watershed projects is found to be better where there is greater empowerment on account of SHGs, although these groups have yet to be closely integrated with watershed development so as to ensure equitable sharing of benefits.

Emerging Issues

Despite the noticeable improvement in performance, the experience outlined above raises a number of important issues which have a bearing on the sustainability of watershed development when the official programme comes to an end. It is proposed to pick up for the present discussion the following five major issues: (i) Institution-building and leadership formation for ensuring effective participation of people on a sustained basis; (ii) Capacity building through training at various levels; (iii) Expert and independent evaluation of the programme; (iv) Convergence of agriculture development programmes with watershed development; and (v) According high priority to the strategy for the development of rain-fed farming in the country.

Institution-building and Leadership Formation

Ironically, it appears that the very same factor, viz., people's participation and decentralization of programme administration, which accounts for the success achieved so far, is highly inadequate for sustaining this development, especially in areas where the programme has proceeded too fast by fulfilling the targets for completion of works without waiting for the required institution-building and leadership formation at the grass roots level (Yugandhar *et al.* 1999). This is not surprising given the entrenched bureaucratic ethos and the nature of our social structure. Even with the best of intentions, it requires quite some time for the bureaucracy, especially at the lower levels, to undergo the necessary motivational and attitudinal transformation for plunging wholeheartedly in the task of empowering people by delegating authority. Again, owing to the mutually conflicting interests of different groups constituting our rural society, building up institutions and evolving leadership for rallying the rural community around common interests with adequate stake for weaker sections and sustaining the momentum is a painstaking and time-consuming task. The performance in this respect needs a review for initiating remedial measures with highest priority.

Capacity Building through Training

Capacity building for watershed development through training encompasses wide ranging tasks such as awareness building or imparting resource-literacy; development of technical skills; and reorienting motivations and attitudes of officials and political functionaries at all levels towards the need for empowering the people through decentralization. Those who administer the programme, and who themselves need such training, are not best fitted to oversee these training programmes. While a number of measures have been taken for strengthening training at various levels since the adoption of new guidelines, experience so far strongly suggests the need for (a) broadening these programmes with a view to imparting training to bureaucracy at all levels as well as to political functionaries from Panchayat level to parliament; (b) improving the content and quality of training programmes with due priority given to the processes of empowerment of the people and of decentralization; (c) intensifying training by adequately taking care of the changing requirements in the field; and (d) ensuring the autonomy of training institutions and their uninterrupted functioning on the required scale by entrusting this task to an independent nodal agency at the national level and by guaranteeing adequate funding.

Evaluation

Despite wide coverage of the programme in the country launched in 1994–5, there is virtually no institutional mechanism put in place at the national level for evaluation or for undertaking studies of basic and long-term nature. A programme like watershed development, which involves a hierarchy of administration and communities at the grass roots level in highly varying agro-climatic and socio-economic conditions, invariably requires mid-course corrections of varying degree in the light of ongoing experience. Typically, an implementing agency would see greater value in spending an extra few crores of rupees for undertaking works in the field rather than spending this money for research and evaluation. However, according to some observers, mid-course corrections can improve the programme benefits substantially, in some cases up to 100 per cent. But, even if we consider the improvement to be very modest, say, 10 per cent, then a 1 per cent of programme outlay on meaningful research and evaluation would have a very high pay-off in terms of achieving the programme objectives. It is of utmost importance, therefore, to put in place an institutional mechanism for research and evaluation in this field by involving reputed institutions in the country for upgrading the quality of evaluation, for example, by evolving methodologies for capturing the participatory processes and convergence of complementary interventions; by guaranteeing to them adequate funding on a long-term basis; and by ensuring for them autonomy in the pursuit of research and evaluation.

Integration with Agriculture Development Programmes

The integration of watershed work with Joint Forest Management is being attempted following the decision by the Ministry of Rural Areas and Employment with the concurrence of the Ministry of Environment and Forests: forest lands forming part of such watersheds are also to be treated simultaneously as per the guidelines. Several state governments have taken the necessary steps in this direction. However, at the moment there is little presence of the agriculture department in the DPAP watersheds by way of promoting locally relevant research and extending suitable technologies, inputs and other necessary support to farmers. The Ministry of Agriculture has adopted the DPAP guidelines in respect of the National Watershed Development Project for Rain-fed Areas (NWDPRA) watersheds under its purview. This is a welcome move, as it would raise the productivity from the Agriculture Department's own measures for raising agricultural production, already in place in these areas. The convergence of services from the Agriculture Department in the watersheds managed by the Ministry of Rural Development would contribute to raising the productivity of land and water resources conserved and augmented through watershed development and would thus induce the farmers to sustain their effort towards watershed development in these areas. An early integration of the interventions by the two departments in such areas is very much called for.

Strategy for Rain-fed Farming

However, such a convergence, though necessary, would not be sufficient for optimizing the benefits from soil and moisture conservation through watershed development and for sustaining the interest of dry land farmers in such efforts in the long run, unless there is a major shift in the existing policy for dry land agriculture. To appreciate this, it is necessary to understand the basic differences between the conditions faced by dry land farmers and those in the green revolution areas.

In the irrigated or favourable areas, given the technology, the decisions and efforts of farmers as individuals were central to the spread of the green revolution, whereas in the dry land areas such individual farm-level decisions have to be preceded by community effort for soil and moisture conservation which is a painstaking and time consuming process. Besides, dry land areas are characterized by greater agro-climatic diversity than the traditional irrigated areas, necessitating location-specific research for evolving viable technologies and practices. However, dry land areas have not received so far the priority they deserve in respect of agricultural research: the Green Revolution was characterized by land-saving but water-using technologies whereas dry land areas need water-saving enterprises and practices which optimize output per unit of scarce water. In the absence of such technologies, the farmers in the dry land areas go in for water-intensive crops like rice when water resources are conserved giving rise to conflicts on water and scarcity of drinking water. Unlike irrigated crops like wheat and rice, crops under dry land conditions face yield uncertainty as well as price uncertainty, in addition to being less remunerative, as price support and procurement operations are highly inadequate in these areas. Further, pricing of electricity for pumping water at a flat rate or even supplying it free instead of on a volumetric rate has led to the over-exploitation of scarce groundwater resources. Infrastructure like roads and marketing is also inadequate in dry land areas. However, given the necessary shift in the policy framework in respect of agricultural research, extension and supply of inputs like seeds, infrastructure development, and price and credit policies, dry land areas hold considerable promise for the development of agriculture. Indeed, the returns on investments in inputs as well as research at the margin are now higher for such areas than for irrigated areas, which so far have received greater attention (Fan and Hazell 1997). Consumer demand is shifting fast towards water-saving enterprises like dairying, animal husbandry, horticulture, and floriculture in which rain-fed areas have a comparative advantage. Also, such products have a good potential for export. Agro-processing, therefore, holds a great promise in dry land areas. All of this combined can be expected to provide the necessary incentives for the conservation of natural resources and indeed for easing pressure on such resources. Watershed development can certainly become more manageable under such a scenario.

18

Sustainable Use of Water for Irrigation

Indian Experience and Areas for Reform

Growing Water Scarcity

Water resources are becoming extremely scarce. According to the projections made by the National Commission for Integrated Water Resource Development Plan, the requirement of water for irrigation in India will grow by more than 50 per cent in the next 50 years. The water requirements for household consumption and for industry would rise even faster. In view of this, even after fully exploiting the usable water resources, the balance between the supply and demand for irrigation water can be achieved only by improving the level of irrigation efficiency in a big way from about 36 per cent efficiency in 1993–4 to 60 per cent in the year 2050 (Government of India 1999). A 10 per cent improvement in the efficiency of water use would be equivalent to adding some 14 million hectares of gross irrigated area (Saleth 1996). A model of water supply and demand for 118 countries accounting for 93 per cent of world population, built by the International Water Management Institute (IWMI), shows that around 50 per cent of the increase in demand for water by the year 2025 can be met by increasing the effectiveness of irrigation. Most of this gain in irrigation effectiveness would be in countries with a high percentage of irrigated rice. India and China together would account for as much as one-half of the world's total estimated water savings from increased irrigation effectiveness. Therefore, the capacity of large countries like India and China to efficiently develop and manage water resources is likely to be a key determinant of global food security in the 21st century (Seckler *et al.* 1998).

Usable water supplies are highly unevenly distributed across the globe and across regions within a large country like India. Therefore, notwithstanding the balance achieved at the national level between the demand for and supply of water, shortage of drinking water would pose a serious problem in the drought-prone regions of the country, especially because over 90 per cent of rural population depends on groundwater for drinking purposes. The poor who depend upon dug wells, which dry up fast, are the first to suffer. Under such circumstances, the only way to ensure local food security and water security to meet the basic needs for drinking and cooking, is by undertaking rainwater harvesting and groundwater recharge on a large scale through the participation of the community, including especially the women and the landless. This should be possible because, unlike in regions of high rainfall, land area per head is larger in the low rainfall or drought-prone areas where 10 tiny dams with a catchment of 1 ha each can collect more water than one larger dam with a catchment of 10 ha (Agarwal 2000). Augmentation of groundwater through artificial recharge, including watershed development, by harnessing surplus monsoon run-off can raise the irrigation potential from groundwater sources substantially over and above the existing potential of 64 million ha (Chada 2000).

Variations in Water Productivity

In the last two decades, we have been faltering in our efforts to augment water resources, even as the use of the available water resources has become increasingly unsustainable. Public investment in major and medium irrigation schemes has been declining, in real terms, throughout the 1980s and the 1990s, even though as much as 40 per cent of the potential still remains to be exploited. We have not taken significant steps so far for improving water-use-efficiency through modernization/renovation of existing systems which have deteriorated over the years. According to the Mid-term Appraisal of the Ninth Five Year Plan, the progress achieved so far in participatory irrigation management (PIM), designed to improve water-use-efficiency, is rather slow. The irrigated area transferred to water users associations (WUAs) in India is only about 7 per cent as against 45 per cent in Indonesia, 66 per cent in Philippines, and 22 per cent in Thailand (Government of India, Planning Commission 2000). As regards groundwater, the rate of extraction has been far above the rate of recharge. As a result, the number of over-exploited and dark blocks has increased by nearly 70 per cent over the last 14 years (Government of India, Planning Commission 2000).

Ultimately, savings in irrigation water can be achieved only by raising the productivity of water, defined broadly as the volume or value of crop output per unit of water used. Definition of water productivity varies in the literature depending on how the denominator in this ratio is specified. When, at one extreme, water released from the system is used as the denominator, water productivity becomes all-inclusive subsuming water-use-efficiency, that is, the ratio of consumptive use of water to the water released. At the other extreme, when the denominator consists of water lost as evapotranspiration by plants in any particular season, then improvement in water productivity can arise basically from the improvement in yields.

Interestingly, water savings in crop production the world over in the last few decades have accrued indirectly from the rise in crop yields, and very little directly from improvement in water-use-efficiency (CGIAR 2001a). This is particularly true in developing countries like India where the improvement in irrigation efficiency has been very slow. For one thing, a clear focus on water productivity, that is, productivity per unit of water used is new for the international agricultural research system (CGIAR 2001b). Nearly two hundred years ago, Thomas Malthus focused on the fixity or scarcity of land in relation to population growth as the cause for recurring famines. This perception prompted the evolution and use of land-saving technologies and practices which substantially raised productivity per unit of land. Until recently, irrigation water has seldom been regarded as a scarce resource in the favourable rain-fed areas of Europe, North America, and Japan, where water losses on account of evaporation and evapotranspiration are also lower because of cooler climate. In the last century, major breakthroughs in crop yields per unit of land were witnessed in these countries, from where such technologies were transferred to the developing countries. Recently, however, the growing competition for water from industry, urban areas for household consumption, and for environmental purposes in these developed countries has been exerting pressure to save water allocated to irrigation. Besides, the rising level of water pollution is accentuating the scarcity of fresh water in all the sectors.

The green revolution has substantially raised yields in irrigated areas in India, resulting in a rise in the productivity of irrigation water. Such an increase in water productivity on account of land-saving technological changes can eventually ease pressure on water for irrigation, even when there is no change in water-use-efficiency. Since irrigated area under foodgrains accounts for the bulk of the increase in foodgrains output, growth of foodgrains output in relation to the growth of irrigated area under foodgrains would give a good measure of the changes in the productivity of irrigation water. Despite the green revolution, which was confined largely to wheat in the north-western region in the 1970s, foodgrains output grew at about the same rate as gross irrigated area. Thus there was no growth in productivity of irrigation water for foodgrains in the country in this decade (Table 18.1). During the 1980s, however, the green revolution was broad-based, covering rice in the central and eastern regions of the country where high rainfall supplements irrigation. Thus foodgrains output grew at a higher rate than irrigated area resulting in a positive growth in the productivity of irrigation water. However, in the post-reform decade of the 1990s, there was a deceleration in the growth of foodgrains output leading to a significant decline in the productivity growth of irrigation.

Table 18.1: Productivity of Irrigation for Foodgrains in Indian Agriculture

(growth rates)

	1970–1 to 1980–1	1980–1 to 1990–1	1990–1 to 1996–7
Gross Irrigated area	2.31	1.72	1.70
Output	2.30	2.90	2.00
Productivity of Irrigation	–0.01	1.18	0.30

Sources: 1. Government of India, Ministry of Agriculture, *Indian Agricultural Statistics*, 1992–3, 1997.
2. Government of India, Central Statistical Organization, *Statistical Abstract—India*, 2000–01.

The decline in water productivity growth in the foodgrains sector of Indian agriculture in the last decade may be attributed partly to the loss of momentum in the development of yield-increasing technologies and partly to the political economy of irrigation from groundwater sources. For example, there was a sharp decline in agricultural growth in east Uttar Pradesh on account of severe cuts in the supply of power for pumping water, which was diverted to west Uttar Pradesh to satisfy the powerful farm lobby (Shah 2001). The known potential from the green revolution is yet to be fully realized in the eastern states where productivity of irrigation water can be raised significantly both on account of high precipitation which supplements irrigation water and the controlled nature of irrigation from groundwater sources which are abundant in this region: whereas eastern India has over one-fourth of India's usable groundwater resources, less than one-fifth of this is developed.

Sources for Raising Water Productivity

Although research focused on water productivity is relatively new, the gap between the available knowledge to increase water productivity and its beneficial application appears quite large (CGIAR 2001a). In the case of India at present, such a gap between knowledge and its application is greater in respect of water productivity than for land productivity. Unlike irrigation water, property rights for land are well-defined and protected which is the single most important factor providing incentives for farmers to successfully participate in the green revolution. Second, the green revolution has been facilitated by institutional support such as the provision of extension services, credit, and marketing. Third, agricultural price policy, whether for output or for inputs, has provided the necessary stimulus for stepping up output per unit of land through input intensification. So far as irrigation is concerned, the failures have been massive on all the three fronts, viz., property rights, institutions, and public policy. It would be instructive, therefore, to identify the major problems afflicting irrigation in each of these areas.

But, what are the major sources for raising the productivity of irrigation water? An understanding of these would help to see the problems afflicting irrigation in a proper perspective. We have seen that technological changes which raised crop yields per unit of land have so far been the major source of the rise in productivity per unit of irrigation water. Since genetic improvements for raising the productivity of land further are very much in the realm of possibility, they can, at the same time, significantly raise water productivity, especially if such genetic improvements are targeted towards saving water. These improvements include the development of crop varieties with better tolerance to drought, cool seasons which reduce evaporation and evapotranspiration, and saline conditions. Biotechnology is considered to have a great potential for raising yields and imparting stability in adverse environments (CGIAR 2001 b). In India, technological changes to improve water productivity by raising crop yields seem to hold a better promise in the short- and medium-term than the attempts to improve water-use-efficiency, which can be expected to yield significant results only in the long-run, owing to the severe political constraints, and managerial and institutional bottlenecks besetting these efforts.

Second, productivity of irrigation water can be raised by skillfully supplementing it with rainwater, especially in the high rainfall areas, despite the possible losses on account of evaporation and evapotranspiration. Because of this, agricultural development strategy that accords greater priority to high rainfall areas like the central and eastern regions in the country may result in significant savings on high-cost surface irrigation.

Third, water losses occur from the point of delivery from the system to the farmer's field due to evaporation, flow of usable water to sinks, pollution, salinity, and water logging. Such losses cannot eventually be recovered at the basin level. These can be minimized with appropriate management practices, provided there are adequate incentives to farmers for adopting water-saving practices. Fourth, farmers are known to re-allocate land and water to high value crops in response to the changing demand. As incomes rise, consumer demand shifts away from some of the water-intensive crops like rice to water-saving horticultural products. However, trade and price policies and policies on input subsidies, including on irrigation water, would determine whether farmers would be induced to switch over to water-conserving enterprises.

Finally, globalization opens up opportunities for countries faced with water scarcities to specialize in the production and export of water-saving crops and import water-intensive ones. Favourable rain-fed areas of Europe, North America, and parts of South America may gain comparative advantage in the export of water-intensive crops (Seckler 1996). A country like India, faced with water scarcity, can safeguard its food security by entering into collaborative arrangements with certain countries, which have abundant land and water resources but are short of labour and capital and do not have enough domestic demand, for production and exchange of foodgrains and other water-intensive products like sugar. Such arrangements are already working in the case of fertilizers and petrochemicals (Hashim 2000).

Government versus Market Failure in Water Management

Well-defined and secure or enforceable property rights on irrigation water and volumetric pricing of surface water as well as electricity for pumping water, are necessary to induce farmers to adopt water-saving practices. However, under the existing system of public management of irrigation, we have failed to ensure these pre-conditions for the efficient use of water. The well-known explanation for government failure in respect of irrigation is the lack of accountability of its management to the user-farmers, and its growing politicization. The most worrisome manifestation of this politicization in the recent period is the political rent-seeking by offering free electricity for pumping water which has led to the over-exploitation of groundwater resources.

Therefore, a question that arises in this context is whether privatization of irrigation can provide the necessary correctives. But market failure is as endemic in irrigation and water management as government failure. Market failure is caused, in the first place, by the widespread prevalence of externalities defined as uncompensated costs or benefits accruing to some, owing to the activities of some others. Then, there are high transaction costs, for example, costs of infrastructure for setting volumetric pricing and its enforcement. Third, property rights for irrigation water are insecure and ineffective. This is commonly manifested in the farmers at the head-reaches of the system appropriating much more water than they are entitled to, at the expense of those at the tail-end (Perry *et al.* 1997). Full-scale privatization of irrigation under such circumstances, in the absence of necessary institutional mechanisms for correcting the distortions arising from market failure, can lead to serious inequities and inefficiencies in the use of water.

Irrigation management transfer (IMT) to the user-farmers is being increasingly advocated and practised the world over to provide correctives to the distortions arising from the failure of the market as well as the state. India has embarked upon participatory irrigation management (PIM), under which the management of some of the systems is being turned over to the WUAs. Conservation of land and groundwater resources through rainwater harvesting is another area where market failure as well as government failure have been glaring. As a solution to this, participatory watershed development is being evolved and practised in many countries, including India, for the protection and sustainable use of land and water resources.

Performance of Participatory Irrigation Management

The evidence so far on IMT in several countries, and on PIM in India, shows some positive results in terms of an increase in yields, water productivity, and farm incomes. Incentives to the farmers to participate and the quality of leadership seem to be the key for the success of these ventures (Guerra *et al.* 1998). In India, the performance of PIM so far indicates that the unwillingness of the lower levels of bureaucracy to fully transfer powers and functions to the user associations is the major bottleneck in the successful working of these institutions (Brewer *et al.* 1999). Such a reluctance to delegate powers and functions, by stifling local initiative, prevents the emergence and development of leadership at the grass roots—an essential pre-requisite for the success of these institutions.

Similarly, the experience with watershed development under the new participatory approach in India shows that the immediate results are positive in terms of the rise in water table, crop yields, employment, and incomes of the participants (Rao 2000). And, where property or use rights on common property resources are well-defined and protected, there has been a significant decline in the distress migration of labour (Chopra and Gulati 1997; 2001). But there is still considerable uncertainty regarding the long-run sustainability of these institutions, that is, their ability to hold the different social groups together and mobilize resources from the community for maintenance of structures already created and for further development when the assistance under the current officially sponsored programmes ceases (Rao 2000; Reddy *et al.* 2001). This holds true even for a relatively promising experiment towards PIM in Andhra Pradesh (Raju 2000). The performance of IMT so far in several other countries points to similar uncertainties (Perry *et al.* 1997).

The present obsession of bureaucracy in India with the fulfilment of physical and financial targets has to give place, first, to greater devolution of powers and functions to the user-associations, including their involvement in the renovation and modernization of the systems as well as in their management right from the outlet level. Second, there needs to be much greater stress on building up social capital through social mobilization of different groups of user-farmers for sustainable use of land and water through conflict resolution among them and their capacity building by putting in place an autonomous and credible infrastructure for training. The institutions developed in this process need to be integrated with more formal legal or market institutions for sustaining them (Chopra 2001). Third, independent and professional evaluations of the ongoing programmes can help mid-course corrections that would greatly enhance the fulfilment of programme objectives.

Public Policy

In the area of irrigation and water management, the state should increasingly concern itself with overall public policy to create conducive socio-economic environment for the efficient and productive use of water. The state should divest itself from the tasks of managing the systems, because its failures have been conspicuous in this area which accounts for the major opportunities available for improving water productivity (CGIAR 2001a).

Governments in the states and at the Centre need to accord the highest priority to the renovation/modernization of the existing systems which account for nearly 40 per cent of the irrigated area from the major and medium irrigation projects. The rate of return from such investments would be very high when compared to the projects creating new irrigation potential. Modernization of the delivery systems and the distribution channels for the existing projects would have a high pay-off, as they would facilitate a clear definition of property rights or entitlements of farmers and their effective enforcement. They would also facilitate the adoption of measures by the water users to improve water-use-efficiency and productivity.

Price and procurement policy of the government has an important bearing on the efficiency and productivity of water use through its impact on cropping pattern. A glaring illustration of this is the price policy for rice and wheat in the recent period which has resulted in the accumulation of over 60 million tonnes of foodgrains by 2002—nearly thrice the actual requirement—with the Food Corporation of India (FCI). It has been estimated that for each hectare of paddy raised under irrigated conditions, as much as 16,000 tonnes of irrigation water is applied in the semi-arid north-western Indian states (Dhawan 2001), from where bulk of the rice is procured by the FCI. One can thus imagine how many billion tonnes of scarce water has been wastefully used over the years in the semi-arid plains of India, which could have been saved or diverted to higher productivity uses if the price and procurement policies were better aligned with the emerging domestic and export demand for foodgrains.

The experimental work backed by the Indian Council for Agricultural Research (ICAR) found that 25–40 per cent saving in irrigation water could be achieved through intermittent submergence and transplanting paddy seedlings at about the time of onset of monsoon rains. Similarly, water savings of the order of 50 per cent in the case of drip irrigation and 25 per cent in the case of sprinkler irrigation can be realized (Dhawan 2001). But, only about one per cent of irrigated area in the country is at present covered by drip and sprinkler methods of irrigation. These technologies are not adopted by the farmers because water is available at a very low cost or is even free. The incentives are in fact perverse in as much as the capital cost of drip and sprinkler irrigation is prohibitively high for the Indian farmer due to various taxes and high interest rate (Dhawan 2001).

The debate on water rates in the country so far has centred round the revenue accruing to the government for covering the operation and maintenance charges. The objective of conserving water needs to be brought into the forefront in these discussions. Given that water rates have depreciated very much in real terms, it is not certain that a significant rise in these rates within the feasible range would induce the farmers to save water under the existing system of management. On the other hand, a system of rationing water supplies in water-scarce regions even with moderate charges can induce farmers to increase water productivity, provided the supplies are reliable in terms of quantity and timings as in the case of the Warabandi system in north-western India (Berkoff 1990; IWMI 2001). In any case, raising water rates significantly would not be politically feasible unless it is linked with the performance of irrigation services and made explicit that revenues so raised would be reinvested locally to upgrade the services.

Water users' associations and panchayats should be fully empowered and induced to charge and collect water and electricity rates from the farmers on the basis of the volume of actual consumption where metering is possible, or, on the basis of the quantities of water received or electricity consumed as estimated by the farmers' associations where metering is uneconomical or otherwise infeasible. The revenues so collected should be allowed to be retained entirely by the WUAs under the aegis of panchayats for maintenance and development of irrigation services, with possible supplementation from the state governments.

It is clear from the foregoing discussion that given the technology and public policy, institutions concerning water use hold the key to raising water productivity by bridging the vast gap that now exists between knowledge and its application. Water institutions are a relatively new and challenging area of research for social scientists. Also, research in this area is highly inter-disciplinary.

Section VI

Conclusions

19

An Overview of Findings and Agenda for Further Reform

Introduction

The Setting

The incentive framework for Indian agriculture improved considerably as a result of trade and exchange rate liberalization and a significant reduction in the protection to domestic industry, following economic reforms introduced in the country in the early 1990s. The terms of trade for agriculture have improved and there has been a record rise in agricultural exports. On the whole, farmers' expectations have been raised for better prospects from the opening up of the economy. This is reflected in a big rise in private investment in agriculture in the 1990s. The full benefits for agriculture from the macroeconomic reforms introduced so far can be expected to materialize, in the course of time, when reforms directly affecting agriculture such as removal of restrictions on domestic trade and processing, stepping up public investment in agriculture, and reforms in the management of infrastructure, are put in place. Indeed, the slowing down of agricultural growth in the post-reform period, despite a favourable macroeconomic environment, is explained by the neglect of such reforms directly affecting agriculture.

The Objectives of Reforms

The basic objectives of reforms in agriculture should be: first, stepping up agricultural growth to at least 4 per cent per annum to sustain the overall growth rate in gross domestic product (GDP) at a high rate, say, 8 per cent. Second, diversifying agriculture with a view to promoting, among other things, the growth of the rural non-farm sector such as agro-processing, thus facilitating a significant shift of the labour force from agriculture to non-agriculture. Third, increasing the application of cost-reducing technologies to make agriculture competitive. Fourth, reducing rural poverty and inequality through broad-based growth of agriculture by reducing disparities between different regions and classes of farmers and by strengthening the role of women in farming. Finally, protecting the environment by reversing the ongoing degradation of natural resources such as land and water and by preventing the excessive chemicalization of agriculture.

Reforms needed for achieving these objectives, outlined in the foregoing chapters, are summarized below within the framework of a two-pronged strategy to improve the performance of agriculture: (a) to release the initiative and enterprise of farmers and the private sector in general by removing restrictions on agricultural trade, processing, etc.; and (b) to facilitate adequate supply response to the incentives so created by strengthening infrastructure, agricultural research and extension, and delivery of credit, while consolidating the food security achieved so far, reducing poverty, and protecting environment.

Removal of Restrictions on Domestic Trade and Processing

Removal of Restrictions

The prevailing restrictions on domestic trade and processing of agricultural commodities are inherited from the post-war, pre-green revolution era of shortages. With the achievement of self-sufficiency in foodgrains, increasing trend towards diversification of agriculture, globalization of trade and World Trade Organization (WTO) commitments, such restrictions on movement, storage, and processing have outlived their utility and have become counter-productive, denying fair prices to producers as well as to consumers and inhibiting much needed investments in the technological upgradation and modernization of activities like processing, storage, and marketing.

The Essential Commodities Act (ECA), Agricultural Produce Marketing Act (APMA), the Small Scale Industry (SSI) reservation, and so on, need to be thoroughly reviewed and revamped with a view to abolishing all legal impediments under these acts that restrict the entry of big private sector, including foreign direct investment (FDI), in marketing, storage, and processing. For example, agro-processing, including the processing of groundnuts and mustard oilseeds now reserved for SSIs, needs to be liberalized. Major investments in these sectors will emerge, if the legal environment provides the private sector a level playing field vis-á-vis cooperatives and public sector concerns. It is essential to facilitate the emergence of vertical integration between farmers, processors, and retailers to facilitate high value addition in agriculture. To ensure that food safety laws are duly enforced, and sanitary and phyto-sanitary (SPS) standards adopted, it is desirable to promote large processing facilities with state-of-the-art technology.

However, while revamping these acts, care has to be taken to see that some of the positive features in them are retained and strengthened. Given the unscrupulous practices by certain sections of traders and middlemen, some regulations, including regulated markets, are necessary. Further, in states such as Punjab and Haryana, markets and road infrastructure were developed through taxes collected via APMA. However, there is a need to rationalize these taxes. For example, commission agents' charges could be removed and *mandi* fees could be waived when processors buy directly from the farm gate (such as through contract farming) and commission charges are not levied.

Minimum Support Prices and Public Procurement of Foodgrains

The mounting stocks of foodgrains with the Food Corporation of India (FCI) are explained by the steep rise in procurement prices (acting as minimum support prices), and the open ended procurement by the FCI even when market conditions were adverse. A good part of the large amount of grain procured is off-loaded at a price almost half its 'economic cost'. Such market operations at huge discounts drove out the private sector from grain trade, and consequently the government is saddled with even more stocks.

In principle, since the minimum support price (MSP) is intended to provide an element of insurance against precipitous fall in prices, it should preferably be based on the average paid-out cost, while the procurement price should be set by the market conditions in competition with the private trade. However, sudden and drastic changes in the existing system of pricing and procurement of foodgrains carry the risk of undermining food security so assiduously built over a long period. In the medium term, therefore, the objective should be to consolidate the food security achieved so far and simultaneously move towards diversification of agriculture in consonance with the changing demand and resource endowments.

Towards this end, the government should, as a rule, accept the recommendations of the Commission on Agricultural costs and Prices (CACP) while deciding the level of MSP. Moderation on the price front for foodgrains, by tilting the relative prices in favour of non-foodgrains, needs to be combined with vigorous non-price interventions for making the cultivation of non-foodgrains attractive to farmers such as through research and extension, infrastructure development for agro-processing and marketing, and measures for promoting exports. Since diversification leads to risk and uncertainty for higher value added products, their risk management can be subsidized. In the meantime, the foodgrain surpluses available with the FCI provide an opportunity to generate rural employment for productive works like watershed development, afforestation, and for building up other community assets. They should also be used for providing mid-day meals to children in schools for improving their nutrition and reducing drop-out. Over and above this, the below the poverty line (BPL) families, whose children go to school, can be compensated for their children's earnings foregone by giving them 5–10 kg of free grain per month, so as to induce them to send their children to school.

A major element in the new dispensation should be to allow the private sector to operate in the market without any restrictions in terms of the movement of grain, stocking limits, levy to the government agencies, exports, etc. This necessitates that the public agencies (FCI) should not be reimbursed for their losses due to their open market operations—beyond what is absolutely necessary on account of the maintenance of buffer stocks and the operation of the public distribution system (PDS)—at a price much below their cost. Otherwise the private sector will be driven out of the market. An alternate system of storing in warehouses by providing credit to farmers, say, up to 70 per cent of the value of the stocks stored, could be considered.

It would be good to encourage vertical integration even in the foodgrain sector. The freedom to operate warehouse receipt system, direct buying from the farmers by the private companies (without recourse to commission agents), rationalizing the purchase tax on grains, mandi tax etc., would encourage private companies to invest in the development of the grain markets, storage, and processing of grain.

Trade and WTO Related Issues

There is a need to formulate a consistent policy for export of agricultural products and processed agro-products in which the country has a comparative advantage. Most agricultural commodities (cotton, onions, sugar, etc.) continue to be under severe export controls and quotas. These destroy any chance of building up a sustained international market. Exporters should have the freedom to enter into long-term contracts. They should be allowed to buy from the farm-gate or from the market at MSP and stocking and handling should be freely allowed.

India should argue at the WTO that all the subsidies need to be clubbed together, instead of being placed in separate boxes (green, blue, amber), as some of the developed countries have been claiming large exemptions by using such provisions and also by interchanging subsidies from one box to the other. India would not be adversely affected if these are clubbed together, as the aggregate measure of support (AMS) to Indian agriculture is still well below the deminimis of 10 per cent. This position would be reinforced if, as India has been arguing, the AMS is calculated as the sum of product-specific and non-product-specific support, as the former is significantly negative in the Indian case. Moreover, input subsidies to the resource poor farmers are exempt from reduction commitments even now under the WTO provisions. If India avails of this, the non-product specific support may come down to less than half of what it is today. Bound rates should not be lowered and anti-dumping and anti-subsidy duties or safeguard measures must be invoked in time. Imports should comply with standards and the Trade Related Intellectual Property Rights (TRIPS) system needs to be strengthened.

Agricultural Research and Extension

Agricultural Research

India is endowed with one of the most advanced agricultural research systems among the developing countries in terms of scientific skills as well as its reach, even though a great deal of restructuring is needed for its efficient functioning. Indian farmers, despite low literacy levels, have responded exceptionally well to the opportunities opened up by new technologies. Also, frontier technologies like biotechnologies remain under-exploited in the country. Therefore, the returns from investment in agricultural research and extension in the country can be expected to be very high, relatively quick, and assured.

The existing public outlay on agricultural research and education stagnating around 0.5 per cent of agricultural GDP in the country is too meagre and needs to be stepped up substantially. At the same time, there is considerable potential for raising the effectiveness of these outlays by reordering the priorities in agricultural research and redefining the relative roles of public and private sectors in research and extension.

There is a need for a shift away from individual crop-oriented research focused essentially on irrigated areas towards research on crops and cropping systems in dry lands, hills, tribal, and other marginal areas. In view of high variability in agro-climatic conditions in such unfavourable areas, research has to become increasingly location-specific with greater participation or interaction with farmers. Greater attention to research on horticultural products that are land-saving as well as water-saving, animal husbandry and dairying integrated with crop production, and on small ruminants can benefit resource-poor farmers and women, besides being environmentally sustainable.

Progress in post-harvest technology is essential to promote value addition through the growth of the agro-processing industry. Economies of scale can be exploited through the food park concepts. Agricultural diversification necessitates subsidizing risk management, and private sector involvement in agro-processing opens up opportunities for sharing risk with the farmers through contract farming. However, steps have to be taken to ensure contractual obligations, for example, when market prices are higher than contractual prices.

Private sector participation in agricultural research, extension, and marketing is becoming increasingly important, especially with the advent of biotechnology and protection being accorded to intellectual property. However, private sector participation tends to be limited to profitable crops and enterprises undertaken by the resource-rich farmers in well-endowed areas. Public sector research has to increasingly address the problems facing the resource-poor farmers in the less-endowed regions. There is a need to avoid overlapping between the two sectors even as the complementarities between them are fully exploited, by restructuring the existing institutions for the management of agricultural research (Alam 2002; Pal and Saxena 2003). A high-level body of scientists could be entrusted with the task of delineating the roles of public and private sectors.

Extension

The existing travel and visit (T&V) system of extension is top–down in its approach, has a narrow focus in so far as it is oriented to individual crops grown in favourable areas, offers very little scope for the initiative and participation by the farmers and is also not accountable to them. Further, the squeezing of assistance by the central government to states for extension services has led to the virtual breakdown of the extension machinery in the states. As a result, farmers are becoming increasingly dependent upon the private sector for extension services. In the absence of public regulation of such services, the resource-poor and gullible farmers are becoming victims of exploitation by the unscrupulous traders and moneylenders interested in selling spurious material.

There is, therefore, an immediate need for revamping and revitalizing the existing agricultural extension system in the country, so as to conform to the new priorities in agricultural research, with adequate financial support from the Centre and the states. The main ingredients of this reform should be: (i) Active involvement of farmers through user groups and self-help groups (SHGs), and accountability to them; (ii) Enabling participation by the private sector, farmers' associations, and the non-governmental organizations (NGOs), to complement public services, by putting in place an independent regulatory body, to which samples can be submitted for quality checks, encompassing inputs like fertilizers, pesticides, and seeds; (iii) Increasing use of media and information technology, including cyber kiosks, to disseminate knowledge on new agricultural practices and information on output and input prices for improving the effectiveness of agricultural services in general. The use of information technology will reduce the requirement of a large number of extension workers at the block level and would indeed complement, to a considerable extent, the services rendered by the extension workers in remote areas; (iv) Building gender concerns into the system, for example, by manning of extension services predominantly by women in hill and tribal areas where farming is managed essentially by women; and (v) Capacity building of extension functionaries and farmers, among other means, through distance education (Government of India, Planning Commission 2001a).

Management of Infrastructure

Exploiting the Available Irrigation Potential

Public investment in basic infrastructure, especially roads, irrigation, and power, where the private sector is still reluctant to enter, will have to be stepped up. The government programme on highways and rural roads has made some progress, but major institutional and price reforms are required in irrigation and power sectors to raise efficiency, and generate resources for the proper upkeep and maintenance of the systems.

Nearly 40 per cent of the available irrigation potential of 58.5 million hectares from major and medium irrigation projects in the country still remains to be exploited. Over 400 such projects were in the pipeline at various stages during the Ninth Plan period. When these ongoing projects are completed, bulk of the remaining irrigation potential would have been exploited. Decline in public investment and the thin spread of resources over a large number of projects are responsible for the delay in the completion of these projects. This underlines the need for stepping up public investment for the speedy completion of ongoing major and medium irrigation projects by the states, as the latter account for over 95 per cent of public investment in irrigation in the country. The resource-poor states in the eastern and central regions account for the bulk of the irrigation potential remaining to be exploited. There may, therefore, be a need for special central assistance to enable such resource-poor states to speedily execute the ongoing irrigation projects.

Due to the easy availability of power in large parts of the country for pumping water for irrigation, as much as 78 per cent of the available potential of 81.4 million hectares from minor irrigation sources, consisting predominantly of groundwater resources, has already been exploited. However, further progress towards the exploitation of the remaining potential hinges on the availability of electric power for pumping water in the eastern states where as much as 75 per cent of the groundwater potential still remains to be exploited (Government of India 2001b).

Raising Water-use-efficiency

Since water-use-efficiency for irrigation is very low in the country, achievement of water security depends not only on the exploitation of the remaining potential but increasingly on the efficient and productive use of available irrigation water. There exists a vast gap now between the knowledge available for improving water-use-efficiency and its actual application in the country. This is explained by the lack of incentives to follow improved practices under the existing system of management and pricing of water. However, reforms in management and pricing are inter-linked as farmers would be willing to pay higher charges only if the efficiency of services improves.

Involvement of user-farmers in the management of irrigation systems at various levels is accepted the world over as an effective alternative to the present system of management by the government, as well as to privatization. Participatory irrigation management (PIM) being experimented in the country towards this end has thrown up certain useful lessons.

Unwillingness to devolve adequate powers to the water users' associations (WUAs) and insufficient infrastructure for capacity building at the grass roots level have inhibited the participation of user-farmers and impeded the growth of leadership at the local level. India has been lagging behind several South-east Asian countries in respect of coverage by WUAs as well as effectiveness of their performance (Government of India, Planning Commission 2000). Therefore, there has to be a vigorous drive towards the empowerment of WUAs in the country by putting in place an adequate infrastructure for capacity building and for extending the coverage under PIM, as, at present, only about 15 per cent of the net irrigated area in the country is partially covered (Government of India 2002).

Input Subsidies and Pricing of Irrigation Water and Rural Electricity

The rising subsidies on irrigation water from canals and on electricity for pumping water have benefited the large farmers as well as the consumers at large on account of the food security achieved and the decline in the relative prices of foodgrains for quite some time. However, these subsidies caused severe deterioration of the systems due to the neglect of their maintenance in addition to becoming fiscally unsustainable. Further, they have led to the highly wasteful use of canal water, ecological degradation from water logging, salinity, and pollution, excessive consumption of electricity, and excessive withdrawal of groundwater resulting in the shortage of drinking water in several parts of the country. There is, therefore, an immediate need to reverse this process.

Awareness on the part of the farmers about the harmful consequences of rising input subsidies and their cooperation in pricing the inputs on a volumetric basis is essential for making the change-over politically feasible and sustainable. A possible solution is to evolve a system where the village communities develop a stake in the conservation of resources. As an experiment, WUAs and Panchayati Raj institutions (PRIs) can be fully empowered and induced to charge and collect water and electricity rates from the farmers on the basis of the volume of actual consumption where metering is possible, or, on the basis of the quantities of water received or electricity consumed as estimated by the farmers' associations where metering is uneconomical or otherwise infeasible. In such situations, panchayats can regulate the cropping pattern and the use of water for raising water-use-efficiency and productivity. The revenues so collected should be allowed to be retained partly or wholly by the WUAs under the aegis of panchayats for maintenance and development of irrigation and rural electricity services. Since agricultural income has not been taxed, this should be made the fiscal domain of PRIs through a land-based tax.

Where necessary, a subsidy at a flat rate, say, on the estimated consumption of electricity on holdings up to one or two hectares, can be given to all the farmers or only to the small and marginal farmers, requiring them to pay for the extra consumption. This would have the merit of providing relief to a large number of deserving farmers in a manner that is politically feasible, even as there would be an incentive to conserve electricity and water.

In situations where volumetric pricing is not practicable, farmers have to be charged for water and electricity at a flat rate, say, per horse power of electric motor, by announcing a time-frame of 2–3 years, where phased increase in tariffs would be linked to improvements in supply. However, care has to be taken to ensure that high flat rates do not result in a small number of affluent farmers cornering water and selling it to the small and marginal farmers at very high rates. Pumping and selling water by PRIs and a subsidy on investment in wells for the resource-poor farmers may promote competition by increasing the number of wells.

The prevailing heavy subsidy on nitrogenous fertilizers perpetuates inefficiencies in the domestic fertilizer industry. The benefit flowing to the farmers and consumers of food is illusory, as it is leading to the degradation of soil on account of excessive chemicalization and adverse NPK ratio. As in the case of water and electricity discussed above, a fixed quantity of fertilizers sufficient for one or two hectares may be subsidized for all the farmers, if necessary through a system of input stamps, requiring them to purchase the remaining quantities in the market at the going rates. Although income support is the best form of support for marginal farmers, perhaps routed through PRIs, it may not be administratively workable. Also, considering the incentives needed for input intensification, there is a need to continue with the present system of input subsidies for marginal farmers.

Credit Reforms

About 60 per cent of the credit requirements of farmers are now met by institutional sources, and the remaining 40 per cent by informal sources like money lenders who charge very high interest rates. However, small and marginal farmers (less than 2 ha.), including tenants, who account for nearly 80 per cent of holdings and one-third of area operated, depend far more heavily on informal sources. Among the formal credit institutions, the commercial banks have emerged as a major player in agriculture credit accounting for about 50 per cent followed by cooperatives (about 43 per cent), and regional rural banks (RRBs) to the extent of about 7 per cent (Government of India 2001c).

In the post-reform period, despite the rise in capital intensity of agriculture in the wake of its diversification, and despite broadening the definition of 'priority sector' by adding a number of activities hitherto financed outside the priority sector, the direct agriculture advances by the commercial banks declined to 11–12 per cent of net bank credit as against the original target of 18 per cent. The position is much worse in the eastern and north-eastern states, even though commercial banks are saddled with excess liquidity. The Rural Infrastructure Development Fund (RIDF), started a decade ago, presumably as a temporary measure to provide infrastructural support to agriculture in lieu of its falling share in commercial bank credit, seems to have been turned into an easier route for meeting part of the stipulated obligations. In the process, individual needs of the farmers for investment and production credit are not being adequately met. This declining priority to agriculture is apparently explained by the efforts on the part of the banks to reduce 'transaction costs' and minimize 'risks'. Nothing short of a major change in the mindset, and a new code informed by social purpose, initiated and monitored by the authorities in the banking system, can remedy the situation.

The share of cooperative banks in the institutional credit for agriculture and allied activities has declined from 45 per cent in 1996–7 to 41 per cent during 2000–01 (Government of India 2001c). Under the prevailing economic scenario of liberalization and globalization, the cooperatives have to be strong enough to compete in the open market. They may need to be assisted in recapitalization and also by substantially increasing the quantum of refinance by the National Bank for Agriculture and Rural Development (NABARD). Also, the proposals initiated by the Centre for amending the cooperative laws of the states with a view to inject professionalism, autonomy, and transparency in the functioning of these societies need to be followed up expeditiously.

Kisan Credit Scheme, aimed at providing adequate and timely support to the farmers from the banking system in a flexible and cost effective manner, does not seem to be succeeding in its avowed purpose because of various stipulations and restrictions. Its operation seems to be limited to only fertilizers from fixed shops. A more farmer-friendly credit card system needs to be operated so as to realize the objectives of the scheme (Government of India 2001a).

High value agriculture needs higher working capital and also entails higher risks. Facilitating credit through processors, input dealers, and NGOs that are vertically integrated with the farmers, including through contract farming, for providing them critical inputs or processing their produce, could increase the credit flow to agriculture significantly. These dealers/processors can act as non-banking financial intermediaries, who can get refinance from the banking sector and can give loans to agriculture, and bear the risk of default. Such arrangements would reduce transaction costs and ensure good recovery. Policy changes are needed to facilitate such intermediation by freeing interest rates within a band.

Self-help groups of women for providing micro-credit have been a success story in the country. Such households being essentially landless, credit by SHGs has been confined mainly to activities falling outside agriculture. However, their experience does point to the promise that groups comprising small and marginal farmers, especially women farmers, hold in managing credit for land-saving activities like animal husbandry, dairying, horticulture, and agro-forestry provided there are contractual arrangements with dealers and processors for the provision of inputs and services for marketing. As capital assets of these farmers are limited, community/group collateral and the produce on farmers' land, including that of tenants, should be considered as collateral in granting credit.

Rural Poverty and Inequality

Poverty

If we consider the experience over a period of a decade after the reforms, that is, 1990s, the socio-economic indicators bearing on poverty give a relatively favourable picture when compared to the immediate post-reform period. This is on account of the improvement in per capita GDP growth and also due to some recovery in public expenditure on agriculture, rural development, and social sectors.

However, the growth rate of rural employment was slow around 0.5 per cent per annum between 1993–4 and 1999–2000 as compared to 1.7 per cent per annum between 1983 and 1993–4. Despite the slow growth in employment, the growth in real wages in agriculture was significant in the 1990s, as in the previous decade, because the growth of agricultural output per head was positive and there was increasing diversification of agriculture towards high value activities for which productivity and wage rates were high. The rate of inflation relevant for the rural poor came down significantly during the latter half of 1990s when compared to the immediate post-reform period.

Per capita real expenditure on rural development (at 1993–4 prices) at the state level having declined towards the mid-1990s, rose again representing a rise of 4 per cent between 1990–1 and 1999–2000 (Chapter 14). The recovery was sharper for the poorer states, for example, Bihar, Madhya Pradesh, Orissa, Rajasthan, and Uttar Pradesh. These favourable factors resulted in reducing the incidence of rural poverty in 1999–2000 as compared to 1993–4.

The pace of poverty decline in the post-reform period seems to be more or less the same as in the pre-reform period. It appears from this that the accelerated GDP growth in the post-reform period did not translate itself into accelerated poverty reduction. Speedy reduction of poverty would require the rapid shift of the labour force now concentrated in agriculture to the rural non-farm sector comprising agro-processing and rural industries. Therefore, the growth of this sector, through the development of rural infrastructure and appropriate policies, holds the key to the eradication of poverty.

Inequalities

A striking feature of the post-reform experience is the increase in inter-state inequalities in the growth of per capita state domestic product (SDP), in the average per capita consumption expenditure (APCE) and in the rate of reduction in rural poverty. This was marked by increasing divergence, that is, the richer states in general registered a much higher growth in GDP than the poorer states.

Contrary to the experience of the 1980s, the annual rate of reduction in rural poverty in the 1990s was significantly lower in the poorer states than in the better-off states. The entire eastern region, Assam, Orissa, West Bengal and Bihar, Andhra Pradesh, and Madhya Pradesh where the growth of agricultural wages was low, experienced lower reduction in rural poverty (Chapter 14).

There is also an increase in rural–urban as well as intra-urban inequalities in per capita consumption expenditure in the post-reform period. Other things remaining the same, the rise in inequality in per capita expenditure would lead to a rise in the head-count ratio (HCR). Thus, another 13 million people (out of the population of a billion) would have been lifted above the poverty line if there was no rise in income inequalities in the post-reform period.

Poverty Among the Socio-economically Disadvantaged Sections

The incidence of poverty (HCR) continued to be higher than the average among the socially disadvantaged sections in 1999–2000. Among the population belonging to scheduled castes (SCs) in rural areas, it was 9 percentage points higher than the national average. It was even higher for the scheduled tribes (STs). Looking at the distribution of the rural poor among different socially disadvantaged sections in 1999–2000, we find that as many as 81 per cent of the rural poor belonged to socially disadvantaged sections.

The class of rural wage labour—which is socio-economically disadvantaged—constitutes over two-thirds of the rural poor. If we add to this category, the poor belonging to the class of self-employed in agriculture among small and marginal holdings who depend essentially on family labour, rural labour accounts for the overwhelming proportion of the rural poor.

Social Sector Expenditures

The growth of social expenditures in the post-reform period of 1990s decelerated greatly when compared to the pre-reform decade of 1980s. Per capita social sector expenditures (on social services plus rural development) by the Centre, at 1993–4 prices, which rose at the rate of 14.1 per cent per annum between 1980–1 and 1989–90, registered a much lower growth of 6.3 per cent per annum between 1992–3 and 2002–03. Similar expenditures by all the states together registered a decline from 9.3 per cent per annum to 6.3 per cent per annum over the same period (Chapter 14).

The above trends in public expenditures on social sectors are consistent with the slow progress in certain social indicators over this period. Although the annual rate of decline in illiteracy rate was significantly higher in the 1990s when compared to that in 1980s, this was mainly due to refocusing of expenditure on education in favour of primary education. Infant mortality rate declined by 1.5 per cent per year during 1990s, as against 2.9 per cent per year during the 1980s. The decline in total fertility rate during the 1990s was only marginally higher than that during the 1980s.

Measures to Conserve Land and Water Resources

Watershed Development

The experience from the ongoing watershed development programme for drought proofing of rain-fed agriculture by conserving land and water resources has been encouraging. The single most important factor accounting for the positive impact of this programme is community participation and decentralization of programme administration made possible under the new guidelines. Yet, the present level of participation is inadequate for sustaining this development, especially in areas where the programme has proceeded too fast by fulfilling the targets for completion of works without the required institution-building and leadership formation at the grass roots level. The coverage has, nevertheless, to expand through increased outlays, as only about 25 per cent of around 107 million hectares of degraded land in the country is estimated to have been treated so far (Government of India, Planning Commission 2000).

Certain policy changes are needed for the movement to become self-sustaining as and when the assistance under the current officially sponsored programme ceases. The foremost amongst these requirements being institution-building and leadership formation, it calls for empowering the people who inhabit the watersheds by delegating authority to their committees and user-groups. Mobilizing adequate contribution from the land owning households on a regular basis for the maintenance of assets created, and ensuring equitable benefits to weaker sections, especially the landless poor, are essential for sustaining the movement. The second major task is creation of awareness and capacity building through training at various levels by entrusting this to an autonomous nodal agency at the national level and by guaranteeing adequate funding. Third, a major shift is needed in the existing policy for dry land or rain-fed agriculture by according greater priority to agricultural research and extension, supply of inputs, infrastructure development like roads and marketing and price and credit policies. Because of the emerging shift of consumer demand towards water-saving products which also have a good export potential, greater priority to dry land agriculture can provide the necessary incentives to the local communities to sustain their interest in the conservation of land and water resources and indeed for easing pressure on such resources (Rao 2000).

Joint Forest Management

Joint forest management (JFM) is a programme for the regeneration and conservation of forest resources in partnership with the local people consisting largely of tribal population. This programme has, on the whole, made a much better impact in a relatively short period when compared to the watershed development programme. Apart from the absence of problems arising from individual property rights as in areas under watershed development, the returns to the participating farmers from the regeneration of forests are quick and assured. Also, the institutions of forest dwellers, especially of tribals, are conducive to community participation.

For these reasons, JFM, as the centrepiece of forest development funded by the Government of India and the donors, holds a great promise. Some of the major problems still to be addressed are: permitting JFM in good or high productivity forest areas, encouraging profitable enterprises like agro-forestry, increasing the participation of women, greater security to the poorer segments of the participants, recognizing self-initiated or spontaneously formed groups, and clarifying the use rights of the dwellers so that those living nearer the forest area develop a greater stake in protecting the forests. Relaxation of existing restrictions on marketing and processing of forest produce will increase the returns to the participating farmers by ending the privileged position now enjoyed by the government and the industry (Government of India 2001d).

Hill and Tribal Areas

The protection of the fragile ecology of hills requires a major shift from short duration crops like foodgrains to forestry, animal husbandry, pasture management, and horticulture. This calls for effective interventions by way of research and extension, and development of transport and marketing infrastructure. Since farming is done essentially by women in hill areas, greater interaction with them would be necessary for developing technologies and programmes suited to these areas (Krishnaraj and Shah 2002). Also, access to technology, inputs, and credit has to be ensured predominantly through women extension workers.

Although tribal areas in general are endowed with high rainfall and plentiful groundwater resources, agricultural productivity is very low on account of traditional technology and low input use. Further, even though the incidence of poverty among tribals is much higher than the average, they have a better access to land when compared to the poor in general. There is, therefore, considerable potential for raising agricultural productivity and reducing poverty in tribal areas through the development of well irrigation and provision of appropriate technology and inputs. As in hill areas, women play an important role in agriculture in tribal areas. Direct access to inputs and services for them needs to be ensured through women extension workers. Tribal and hill areas including the North-east have a comparative advantage in organic farming because of lower use of chemical inputs. This profitable avenue should be exploited through appropriate policies (Government of India 2001a).

Flood-proofing of Flood-prone Agriculture

About 4 per cent of the crop area in the country, located mainly in the eastern states, is affected by recurring floods. The traditional land use and cropping patterns are closely adapted to the seasonal flooding cycle, with the emphasis being on flood management rather than on flood control. Farmers usually harvest bumper rabi crops in the post-flood season, thus compensating kharif losses to some extent. The strategy for flood proofing through embankments, dams, and sluices, combined with the use of high yielding varieties for irrigated rabi crops, has led to significant and positive changes in the farming systems, diversified employment opportunities, and better food security. In the light of this experience, research has to be designed to adjust cropping systems to the flooding cycle, to harvest flood water for irrigation in the post-flood season, and to evolve yield-raising technologies (Subbiah 2002).

Land Ceiling and Tenancy Laws

In view of the continued pressure of population on land, it may not be advisable to remove, at the present juncture, the ceiling on the ownership of agricultural land. Ceiling on the ownership of land has in general made the land market favourable to the small and marginal farmers who can augment their ownership as well as operational holdings. However, tenancy laws guaranteeing security of tenure and prescribing the rental share have led to the growth of concealed tenancy which discourages investment by the tenants and restricts the flow of credit to them. Since such tenants are in any case paying market rents, liberalization of tenancy laws can help to increase their employment and income by augmenting their operational holdings, stepping up investment and getting better access to credit and inputs.

Fiscal Trends in the Post-reform Period

The continued decline in public investment in agriculture and slow recovery in public expenditure on social sectors, including rural development, are traceable to the failure of economic reforms to mobilize public revenues by stepping up the tax–GDP ratio and reducing the subsidies, for example, on irrigation and electricity for pumping water. Also, fiscal reforms have not been able to reign in inessential public expenditure such as unusual hikes in salaries of government employees.

Despite the rise in taxable capacity, as indicated by the rise in per capita GDP, the tax–GDP ratio has declined significantly in the post-reform period. This is explained, among other things, by the failure to tax income from services—a sector responsible for the acceleration of GDP in the post-reform period.

The growth of revenues from income tax and union excise duties which are shareable with the states, was lower in the 1990s by about 2.5 percentage points when compared to the 1980s. Since the devolution or shares from these revenues for states were fixed by the finance commissions, the decline in the growth of these revenues led to a decline in the growth of revenues for the states, especially for the poorer ones, as the per capita devolution recommended for them is higher than that for the better-off states.

On the expenditure side, the pay hike for the employees at the centre led to similar hikes at the state level resulting in the rise in fiscal deficits at both the Centre and the states, despite the slow growth of expenditures on agriculture, rural development, and other social sectors.

It is clear from the above that fiscal reforms both for raising revenues and reducing inessential expenditures are a prerequisite for protecting and raising the social expenditures for reducing poverty. It is also clear that the Centre has a greater responsibility for raising revenues and for containing inessential expenditure.

Conclusion

The role of the government by way of public policies, programmes, and investment is going to be extremely important. Success depends crucially on effective governance at the grass roots level, as many of these programmes are going to be location specific. Interaction with farmers is essential for ensuring relevance and quality of the programmes designed, and accountability to them is necessary for effective implementation. The key to the success is the effective functioning of the Panchayati Raj institutions as enjoined by the 73rd and 74th amendments to the Constitution. As it is, most state governments have been reluctant to transfer functions, finances, and functionaries to the panchayats, as indicated in the Eleventh Schedule to the Constitution (Rajiv Gandhi Foundation 2000). Major initiatives are needed from the Centre to persuade the states to devolve these powers and, if necessary, bring about consensus for directly transferring from the Centre to the panchayats resources allocated to schemes falling under the subjects listed in the Eleventh Schedule.

Appendix A9

Objective and Findings

The purpose of this note is to illustrate: (i) the higher per capita consumption of cereals in rural areas on account of greater manual labour requirements; (ii) the higher cost of obtaining urban goods of consumption in rural areas; and (iii) consequently, higher per capita consumption of cereals in rural areas attributable to the cross elasticity of demand with respect to the prices of urban goods of consumption.

The main findings are: (a) The higher cereal intake in rural areas, on account of higher manual labour put in, is the single largest component of the rural–urban difference in per capita consumption of cereals. Although this component has been declining over time, it still constituted nearly 50 per cent of the rural–urban difference in per capita consumption of cereals in the early 1990s (Table A9.1); (b) Although the cost of obtaining urban goods of consumption in rural areas, when compared to their urban prices, has declined over a period of time, it is still quite high in the early 1990s—over 50 per cent higher when compared to their urban prices; and (c) Consequently, nearly 25 per cent of the higher per capita consumption of cereals in rural areas can be attributed to this cross elasticity of demand (Table A9.1).

Methodology

It is difficult to arrive at an estimate of the rural–urban difference in per capita consumption of cereals due to manual labour independently on the basis of any extraneous information. We have, therefore, assumed that the rural–urban difference in the consumption of cereals pertaining to the bottom three as well as the middle four expenditure groups contains this component apart from that arising from the difference in price and per capita expenditure. We also assume that the urban goods of consumption demanded by these lower expenditure groups are available in rural areas and that the rural–urban difference in the prices of such goods is the same as that for cereals, albeit, in the opposite direction. This assumption may not be unreasonable because the urban goods entering into the consumption basket of such groups are necessities having a long-standing market in rural areas.

On the basis of the findings from the existing studies on the demand for foodgrains, we have assumed an expenditure elasticity of 0.33 and price

Table A9.1: Shares of Different Components of Rural–Urban Difference in Per Capita Consumption of Cereals (All Expenditure Groups)

(per cent)

	1972–3 (1)	1993–4 (2)
Per cent Difference in Rural Per Capita Consumption of Cereals over Urban Consumption:		
Observed	35.77	26.06
After Accounting for Expenditure Differences	45.75	38.78
Per cent Share:		
1. Own Price	11.7	20.7
2. Cross Price	39.6	25.1
3. Manual Labour	48.7	54.2
	100.0	100.0

elasticity of –0.50. We do not have widely accepted empirical estimates of the cross elasticity of demand for foodgrains with respect to the prices of urban goods of consumption. However, we know from the Slutsky-Schultz' relation that the algebraic sum of income, price, and cross elasticities of demand for any commodity equals zero (Srinivasan and Bardhan 1969), which gives us the cross elasticity of 0.17.

The component of cereals demand due to manual labour in rural areas has been estimated as the residual after accounting for expenditure, price, and cross elasticities of demand for the lower seven expenditure groups. This relation implies the assumption that the cross elasticity of demand for cereals with respect to the prices of other rural goods and services is zero. However, this cross elasticity is likely to be positive. Owing to this omission, the cross elasticity we are using may be on the higher side. Since the prices of rural goods and services (other than cereals) can be expected to be lower than the prices of similar items in urban areas, this omission may have overestimated the component due to cross elasticity and hence underestimated the component due to manual labour. Since, for lower expenditure groups, necessities like foodgrains and clothing, account of the bulk of the budget—expenditure on other rural goods and services claiming a very small proportion—the error on account of their exclusion may not turn out to be serious.

We have arrived at the components of average (all classes) difference in per capita consumption of cereals in rural areas due to per capita expenditure differences, manual labour, and difference in price. The residual is attributable to the cross elasticity of demand with respect to the price or cost of obtaining the urban goods of consumption (Appendix Table A9.2). By using the coefficient of cross elasticity, we can obtain the rural–urban price difference

Table A9.2: Components of Rural–Urban Difference in Per Capita Consumption of Cereals

(per cent)

	Bottom 30%		Middle 30%		All Expenditure Groups	
	1972–3	1993–4	1972–3	1993–4	1972–3	1993–4
	(1)	(2)	(3)	(4)	(5)	(6)
1. Expenditure	–8.14	–9.14	–8.36	–11.21	–9.98	–12.72
2. Own price	4.96	5.80	5.68	6.87	5.35	8.02
3. Cross price	1.69	1.97	1.93	2.34	18.13	9.72
4. Manual labour	13.74	15.66	30.80	26.41	22.27	21.04

in regard to urban goods of consumption. This gives a measure of the cost to the rural consumers of obtaining urban goods of consumption in rural areas, if available, or of obtaining them from urban areas.

Since, as mentioned, we may have overestimated the cross elasticity with respect to the prices of urban goods, we would only be underestimating and not exaggerating the cost of obtaining urban goods of consumption in rural areas. These costs seem to be much higher (57 per cent) than the rural–urban differences in the prices of cereals (–16 per cent) even in 1993–4. The corresponding differences in rural–urban prices in 1972–3 were 106.6 per cent and (–10.7 per cent).

Finally, we would like to state that this exercise should be regarded as merely illustrative, as it is based on certain restrictive assumptions. One such obvious limitation is that the expenditure and price elasticities assumed are invariant over time as well as with respect to different expenditure groups.

Appendix A14

Alternative Estimates on Poverty

It is, by now, well known that the 55th round (1999–2000) National Sample Survey (NSS) based estimates on poverty are not directly comparable with earlier years because of changes in the reference period. In the 55th round, the data on consumption expenditure on food items were collected using two different reference periods—the last 30-days and the last 7-days from the same households. The second change in the reference period is that the consumption expenditure on clothing, footwear, medical (institutional), and durable goods was collected using a 365-day recall period. In the case of all other non-food items, the 30-day recall period was used as earlier.

The official Planning Commission estimates for 1999–2000 are unadjusted estimates but use 30-day estimates for food instead of 7-day estimates. According to official estimates, rural poverty declined from 45.7 per cent to 37.3 per cent in 1993–4. It declined by 8.4 percentage points (average annual decline was 0.8 percentage points) during 10 and a half years. In the post-reform period, rural poverty declined from 37.3 per cent in 1993–4 to 27.1 per cent in 1999–2000. It declined by 10.2 percentage points (average annual decline of 1.7 percentage points) during the 6-year period. Thus, according to official estimates rural poverty declined much faster in the post-reform period as compared to the pre-reform period. This is also true of urban poverty.

Even though the official estimates are arrived at by using 30-day estimates for food, they are supposed to be 'contaminated' because both 30-day and 7-day questions were posed to the same households. Moreover, many non-food items were based on 365-day questions. Official estimates do not adjust for this change in reference periods.

Deaton and Dreze (2002) provide alternative estimates of poverty. They make an attempt to 'adjust' the 55th round estimates to acquire comparability with the earlier rounds. For some items, 30-day recall period is retained in the 55th round. Deaton and Dreze use consumer expenditure of these intermediate goods for estimating poverty ratios.[1] This has the assumption of a stable relationship between intermediate goods expenditure and total expenditure. They also use improved price indices to update the poverty line over time. According to their estimates, the rate of reduction in rural poverty

[1] For more details on adjustments, see Deaton and Dreze (2002).

between 1993–4 and 1999–2000 was similar to that between 1987–8 and 1993–4. In both periods, rural poverty declined by 6–7 percentage points. Their estimates also show that urban poverty is only 12 per cent—significantly lower than the official estimates.

Sundaram and Tendulkar (November 2003) used comparable mixed reference based (MRP) poverty measures in the 50th round in order to compare with 55th round estimates. As mentioned above, till the 50th round, NSS had a uniform reference period (URP) of 30-day questions for food and non-food. In the 55th round, the NSS used mixed reference period of 30-days (leaving for the moment 7-day questions) for food and intoxicants and 365-days for other items. Fortunately, unit level data for the 50th round contains mixed reference period estimates. Sundaram and Tendulkar used these comparable measures for 50th round. Their estimates show that rural poverty declined from 49.0 per cent in 1983 to 39.7 per cent in 1993–4 (URP). Rural poverty declined by 9.3 percentage points during the 10 and a half year period indicating a 0.9 percentage point decline per annum. In the post-reform period, poverty declined from 34.2 per cent in 1993–4 (MRP) to 28.9 per cent in 1999–2000 showing 5.3 percentage points decline (0.9 percentage points per annum) during the post-reform period. Their estimates for rural poverty thus show that the rate of decline during 1990s was similar to that in the 1980s. Sundaram and Tendulkar, however, divide the average annual decline with initial values of poverty ratios and show that rate of decline was higher in both rural and urban poverty. But if we look at average annual changes only, the rate of decline was not higher in the post-reform period for rural poverty. In fact, the rate of decline in urban poverty was lower in the 1990s as compared to the 1980s.

In an unpublished study, Sen and Himanshu (2003) made several adjustments in order to compare 1999–2000 data with earlier years. Basically, they make two adjustments: (a) using 50th round comparable mixed reference period (MRP) based measures; (b) adjusting for 7-day questions for food and intoxicants in the 55th Round.[2] It may be noted that Sundaram and Tendulkar did not make adjustments for 7-day questions in the 55th round. Based on the two adjustments, Sen and Himanshu's study (2003) shows that rural poverty declined from 31.6 per cent in 1993–4 to 28.8 per cent in 1999–2000. In other words it declined by only 3 percentage points with an average annual decline of 0.5 percentage points during 1993–4 to 1999–2000. Even if we take the average annual decline as percentage of initial values, the rate of decline in poverty in the 1990s was not higher than that in the 1980s. According to Sen and Himanshu estimates, the decline in urban poverty was also similar (0.5 percentage points) during the period 1993–2000.

[2] Sen and Himanshu also question the Deaton and Dreze estimates which are based on a stable relationship between intermediate goods and total goods.

References

Abramovitz, M. (1956), 'Resource and Output Trends in the United States since 1870', *American Economic Review* (Papers and Proceedings), 46.

Agarwal, Anil (2000), 'Drought? Try Capturing the Rain', *The Asian Journal*, Vol. 7, No. 3.

Ahluwalia, Montek S. (1978), 'Rural Poverty in India', 1956–7 to 1973–4. Occasional Papers, World Bank Staff Working Paper No. 279, Washington, D.C.

—— (2000), 'Economic Performance of States in Post-Reforms Period', *Economic and Political Weekly*, 6 May.

Alam, Ghayur (2002), 'Agricultural Research and Indian Farmers: Past Performance and Emerging Issues', Ministry of Agriculture, Government of India.

Appu, P.S. (1995), 'Land Reforms in India—A Survey of Policy, Legislation and Implementation' (mimeo), Mussoorie: Lal Bahadur Shastri National Academy of Administration.

Asian Development Bank (1992), *Asian Development Review*, Vol. 10, No. 1.

Balisacan, Arsenio M. (1992), 'Rural Poverty in the Philippines: Incidence, Determinants and Policies', *Asian Development Review*, Vol. 10, No. 1.

Bandyopadhyay, Arun (1984), 'Economics of Agricultural Credit with Special Reference to Small Farmers in West Bengal', Delhi: Agricole Publishing Academy.

Bautista, Romeo M. and Alberto Valdes (1989), 'The Bias against Agriculture: Trade and Macroeconomic Policies in Developing Countries', California: ICS Press.

Berkoff, D.J.W. (1990), Irrigation Management on the Indo-Gangetic Plain, World Bank Technical Paper No. 129, The World Bank.

Bhalla, G.S. (1995), 'Globalisation and Agricultural Policy in India', Presidential Address delivered at the 54th Annual Conference of the Indian Society of Agricultural Economics, *Indian Journal of Agricultural Economics*, Vol. 50, No. 1, January–March, pp. 7–26.

Bhalla, Sheila (1998), 'Trends in Poverty, Wages and Employment in Rural India', in R. Radhakrishna and Alak N. Sharma (eds), *Empowering Rural Labour in India—Market, State and Mobilisation*, Institute for Human Development, New Delhi.

Bhalla, Sheila *et al.* (1991), 'Report of the Study Group on Employment Generation', in the Report of the National Commission on Rural Labour, Vol. II, Government of India, Ministry of Labour, New Delhi

Bharadwaj, K. (1974), *Production Conditions in Indian Agriculture*, Cambridge: Cambridge University Press.

Bhattacharya, B.B. and C.H. Hanumantha Rao (1986), 'Agriculture Industry Interrelations: Issues of Relative Prices and Growth in the Context of Public Investment', Paper presented at the Eighth World Economic Congress, New Delhi, 1–5 December.

Bhattacharya, B.B. and S. Sakthivel (2003), 'Economic Reforms and Jobless Growth in India in the 1990s', *The Indian Journal of Labour Economics*, Vol. 46, No. 4.

—— (2004), 'Regional Growth and Disparity in India: Comparison of Pre- and Post-Reform Decades', *Economic and Political Weekly*, 6 March.

Bhattacharya, B.B., R.B. Barman, and A.K. Nag (1994), 'Stabilisation Policy Options—A Macroeconometric Analysis', Reserve Bank of India, Bombay.

Binswanger, Hans and Shahidur Khandker (1992), 'The Impact of Formal Finance on the Rural Economy of India', The World Bank, WPS, 949.

Bottrall, Anthony (1991), 'Overview' in Ruth Meinzen-Dick and Mark Svendsen (eds), *Future Directions for Indian Irrigation—Research and Policy Issues*, Washington, D.C.: International Food Policy Research Institute.

Brewer, J., S. Kolavalli *et al.* (1999), 'Irrigation Management Transfer in India: Policies, Processes and Performance', IIM, Ahmedabad and IIMI, Colombo, Oxford & IBH Publishers.

Brundtland, G.H. *et al.* (1987), *Our Common Future*, Report by the World Commission on Environment and Development, New York: Oxford University Press.

Byrd, William A. and Lin Quingsong (eds) (1990), *China's Rural Industry: Structure, Development and Reform*, World Bank, Oxford University Press.

Centre for Science and Environment (1998), *Fifth Citizen's Report on the State of India's Environment*, New Delhi.

Chada, D.K. (2000), 'Ground Water Recharge: Option for Ground Water Management', *The Asian Journal*, Vol. 7, No. 4.

Chadha, G.K. (1993), 'Non-farm Employment for Rural Households in India: Evidence and Prognosis', *The Indian Journal of Labour Economics*, July–September.

Chakravarty, Sukhamoy (1993), *Selected Economic Writings*, Delhi: Oxford University Press.

Chand, Ramesh (1996), 'Ecological and Economic Impact of Horticultural Development in the Himalayas—Evidence from Himachal Pradesh', *Economic and Political Weekly*, Vol. XXXI, No. 26, June 29.

—— (2000), 'Trade Liberalization, Agricultural Prices, and Net Social Welfare in India', submitted at the Third Asian Conference of Agricultural Economists, Jaipur, 18–20 October.

Chopra, Kanchan (2001), Social Capital and Development Processes: The Role of Formal and Informal Institutions (mimeo), Institute of Economic Growth, Delhi.

Chopra, Kanchan and Bishwanath Goldar (2000), 'Sustainable Development Framework for India: The Case of Water Resources' (mimeo), Delhi: Institute of Economic Growth.

Chopra, Kanchan and S.C. Gulati (1997), 'Population, Poverty and Environmental Degradation: The Role of Property Rights', in the *Challenge of the Balance–Environmental Economics in India*, Anil Agarwal (ed.), New Delhi: Centre for Science and Environment.

—— (2001), *Migration, Common Property Resources and Environmental Degradation—Inter-linkages in India's Arid and Semi-arid Regions*, New Delhi: Sage Publications.

Chung Ki-Whan and Nae Won Oh (1992), 'Rural Poverty in the Republic of Korea: Trends and Policy Issues', *Asian Development Review*, Vol. 10, No. 1, pp. 91–124.

Commission on Agricultural Costs and Prices, CACP (2001), 'Reports of the CACP for the Crops Sown During 2000–2001 Season', Ministry of Agriculture, GOI, New Delhi.

Consultative Committee for International Agricultural Research, CGIAR (2001a), Technical Advisory Committee, Water and the CGIAR, Discussion Paper.

—— (2001b), Water Productivity Research in the Context of CGIAR, Discussion Paper.

Dadibhavi, R.V. (1988), 'Dimensions of Regional Disparities in Institutional Credit to Agriculture', *Indian Journal of Agricultural Economics*, Vol. 43, No. 3, July–September.

Dandekar, V.M. and F.K. Wadia (1989), 'Development of Institutional Finance for Agriculture in India', *Journal of Indian School of Political Economy*, Vol. I, No. 2, July–December.

Dasgupta, Partha (1993), *An Enquiry into Well-Being and Destitution*, New York: Oxford University Press.

Dasgupta, R. (1993), *Alternative Approach to Agricultural Credit*, Concept Publishing Company.

Deaton, Angus and Jean Dreze (2002), 'Poverty and Inequality in India: A Re-examination', *Economic and Political Weekly*, Vol. XXXVII, No. 36, 7 September.

Demery, David and Lionel Demery (1992), Adjustment and Equity in Indonesia, OECD, Paris.

Desai, Bhupat M. and N.V. Namboodiri (1997), 'Determinants of Total Factor Productivity in Indian Agriculture' (mimeo), Ahmedabad, India: Indian Institute of Management.

Desai, D.K. (1988), 'Institutional Credit Requirements for Agricultural Production—2000 AD', *Indian Journal of Agricultural Economics*, Vol. 43, No. 3, July–September.

Dev, Mahendra S., C. Ravi, Brinda Viswanathan, and Ashok Gulati (2003), 'Economic Liberalization, Targeted Programmes and Household Food Security: A Case Study of India', CESS–IFPRI Report (to be published), IFPRI, Washington D.C.

Dev, S.M. (1995), 'Economic Reforms and the Rural Poor', *Economic and Political Weekly*, 19 August, Vol. 30, No. 33, pp. 2085–8.

—— (2003), *Right to Food in India*, Working paper No. 50, Hyderabad: Centre for Economic and Social Studies.

Dev, S.M. and A.N. Sharma (1999), 'Economic Reforms, Employment and Poverty in India' (mimeo), New Delhi: Institute for Human Development.

Dev, S.M. and Jos Mooij (2003), 'Patterns in Social Sector Expenditures: Pre- and Post-reform Period' (mimeo), Hyderabad: Centre for Economic and Social Studies.

Dhawan, B.D. (1985), 'Irrigation's Impact on the Farm Economy,' *Economic and Political Weekly*, Vol. 20, No. 39, p. 185.

—— (1993), *Trends and New Tendencies in Indian Irrigated Agriculture*, Institute of Economic Growth, New Delhi: Commonwealth Publishers.

—— (1996), 'Relationship Between Public and Private Investments in Indian Agriculture with Special Reference to Public Canals', *Indian Journal of Agricultural Economics*, Vol. 51, Nos 1 and 2, January–June, Mumbai, India.

—— (2001), 'Technological Change in Indian Irrigated Agriculture: Diffusion of Water Economising Technologies and Practices' (mimeo), Institute of Economic Growth, New Delhi.

Directorate of Economics and Statistics (1987), Ministry of Agriculture, *Agricultural Statistics at a Glance*, Delhi.

Dreze, Jean and Amartya Sen (2002), *India—Development and Participation*, New Delhi: Oxford University Press.

ESCAP, Economic and Social Commission for Asia and the Pacific (1995), *Benefits and Challenges Facing Asia-Pacific Agricultural Trading Countries in the Post-Uruguay Round Period* (ST/ESCAP/1526), United Nations, New York.

—— (1996), *Rural Poverty Alleviation and Sustainable Development in Asia and the Pacific* (ST/ESCAP/1617), United Nations, New York.

Economic Times (2002), 5 February.

Evenson, Robert E., Carl E. Pray, and Mark W. Rosegrant (1999), *Agricultural Research and Productivity Growth in India*, Research Report 109, Washington, D.C.: International Food Policy Research Institute (IFPRI).

Fan, S. and P. Hazell (1997), 'Should India Invest more in Less-favoured Areas?', Environment and Production Technology Division Discussion Paper No. 25, Washington, D.C.: International Food Policy Research Institute.

Fan, Yuan (1990), 'Employment Problems in the Rural Non-agriculture Sector in the People's Republic of China', *ARTEP Working Papers*, New Delhi.

FAO, Regional Office for Asia and the Pacific, Bangkok (1995), *Selected Indicators of Food and Agriculture Development in Asia-Pacific Region*, 1984–94, p. 10.

Gaiha, R. (1993), 'Design of Poverty Alleviation Strategy in Rural Areas', FAO Economic and Social Development Paper 115, Rome: FAO.

Government of India (1991a), *Report of the National Commission on Rural Labour*, Vol. II, Ministry of Labour, New Delhi

—— (1991b), *Interim Report of the Tax Reforms Committee*, New Delhi.

—— (1994), *Report of the Technical Committee on Drought Prone Areas Programme and Desert Development Programme*, New Delhi: Ministry of Rural Development.

—— (1995a), *Economic Survey 1994–95*, New Delhi.

—— (1995b), *National Accounts Statistics*, New Delhi.

—— (1996), *Economic Survey 1995–96*, Ministry of Finance, New Delhi.

—— Planning Commission (2000), *Mid-Term Appraisal of Ninth Five Year Plan (1997–2002)*, New Delhi.

—— (2001), *Economic Survey 2000–2001*, New Delhi.

—— (2001a), Report of the Steering Group on Agriculture and Allied Sectors for the Tenth Five Year Plan, New Delhi: Planning Commission.

—— (2001b), 'Report of the Working Group on Minor Irrigation for Formulation of the Tenth Plan (2002–2007) Proposals' (mimeo), New Delhi: Ministry of Water Resources, Minor Irrigation Division.

—— (2001c), 'Report of the Working Group on Agricultural Credit, Cooperation, and Crop Insurance for the Formulation of the Tenth Five Year Plan (2003–2007)' (mimeo), New Delhi: Planning Commission.

—— (2001d), 'Report of the Working Group on Watershed Development, Rain-fed Farming and Natural Resources Management for the Tenth Five Year Plan' (mimeo), New Delhi: Planning Commission.

—— (2002), *Economic Survey 2001–2002*.

—— (2002), Ministry of Finance, *Indian Public Finance Statistics*, 2001–02.

—— (2002), *Tenth Five year Plan 2002–2007*, Vol. II, Planning Commission, New Delhi.

—— (2003), *Economic Survey 2002–2003*, New Delhi.

—— Department of Agriculture, *All India Report on Input Survey, 1981–82*, New Delhi.

—— *Economic Survey 1992–93*.

—— *Economic Survey 1993–94*.

—— Ministry of Chemicals and Fertilizers (1998), *Fertilizer Pricing Policy-Report of the High Powered Review Committee*, March, New Delhi.

—— Ministry of Finance, *Economic Survey 1993–94*, New Delhi.

—— Ministry of Labour (1991), *Report of the National Commission on Rural Labour*, Vol. 1, New Delhi.

—— (1991), 'Report of the Study Group on Women and Children' in the *Report of the National Commission on Rural Labour*, Vol. II.

—— Ministry of Rural Development (1994), *Report of the Technical Committee on Drought Prone Areas Programme and Desert Development Programme*, New Delhi.
—— Ministry of Water Resources (1999), *Report of the National Commission for Integrated Water Resources Development Plan*, Vol. 1, New Delhi.
—— Planning Commission (1992), *Eighth Five Year Plan*, Vol. II, New Delhi.
—— (1992), *Report of the Committee on the Pricing of Irrigation Water.*
—— *Ninth Five Year Plan, 1997–2002*, Vol. II, New Delhi.
—— (2000), *Mid-term Appraisal of the Ninth Five Year Plan (1997–2002)*, New Delhi, October.
—— (2003), E*conomic Survey 2002–03*, New Delhi.
Guerra, L.C., S.I. Bhuiyan, T.P. Tuong, and R. Barker (1998), 'Producing More Rice with Less Water from Irrigation Systems, SWIM Paper 5, International Water Management Institute (IWMI).
Guhan, S. (1995), 'Social Expenditures in the Union Budget', *Economic and Political Weekly*, Vol. 30, Nos 18–19, 6–13 May, pp. 1095–101.
Gulati, Ashok (1990), 'Fertilizer Subsidy: Is the Cultivator Net Subsidized?' *Indian Journal of Agricultural Economics*, Vol. XVL, No. 1, January–March.
—— (2001), 'Trade Liberalization and Food Security: Challenges to Indian Policy Makers' (mimeo), Washington, D.C.: International Food Policy Research Institute (IFPRI).
Gulati, Ashok and Gary Pursell (1991), 'Trade Policies, Incentives and Resource Allocation in Indian Agriculture' (mimeo), Washington, D.C.: The World Bank.
—— (1993), 'Trade Policy, Incentives and Resource Allocation in Indian Agriculture' (mimeo), Working Paper No. 1172, The World Bank.
Gulati, Ashok and Kathleen Mullen (2003), 'Responding to Policy Reform: Indian Agriculture During the 1990s and After', Paper presented at the Fourth Annual Conference on India: Economic Policy Reform, The Centre for Research on Economic Development and Policy Reform, Stanford University, Palo Alto, California, 5–7 June 2003.
Gulati, Ashok and Rajni Katula (1992), 'Input Subsidies in Indian Agriculture: Concepts and Quantification' (mimeo), March.
Gulati, Ashok and Pradeep K. Sharma (1991), 'Government Intervention in Agricultural Markets: Nature, Impact, and Implications', Journal of Indian School of Political Economy, April–June.
Gulati, Ashok and Seema Bathla (2002), 'Capital Formation in Indian Agriculture: Trends, Composition and Implications for Growth', Mumbai: National Bank for Agriculture and Rural Development (NABARD).
—— (2002), 'Institutional Credit to Indian Agriculture: Defaults and Policy Options', Mumbai: National Bank for Agriculture and Rural Development.
Gulati, Ashok and Sudha Narayanan (2003), *The Subsidy Syndrome in Indian Agriculture*, New Delhi: Oxford Publishing House.

Gulati, Ashok, Mark Svendsen, and Nandini Roy Choudhury, (1994), 'Major and Medium Irrigation Schemes: Towards Better Financial Performance', *Economic and Political Weekly*, 25 June.

Gupta, Anil K. (1991), 'Banking for Rural Transformation: Issues for the Nineties' in Surjeet Singh (ed.), Institute of Development Studies (IDS), Jaipur, *Rural Credit—Issues for the Nineties*, New Delhi: Oxford & IBH Publishing Co. Pvt. Ltd.

Gupta, S.P. (1994), 'Recent Economic Reforms and Their Implications on the Poor and Vulnerable Sections of the Society', Paper presented at the IDPAD Seminar on 'Structural Adjustment and Poverty in India: Policy and Research Issues', The Hague, 29 November.

—— (1995), 'Economic Reform and Its Impact on Poor', *Economic and Political Weekly*, Vol. 30, No. 22, 3 June, pp. 1295–313.

—— (1996), 'Recent Economic Reforms in India and Their Impact on the Poor and Vulnerable Sections of Society', in C.H.H. Rao and Hans Linnemann (eds), *Economic Reforms and Poverty Alleviation in India*, New Delhi: Sage.

Haque, T. and Sunita Verma (1988), 'Regional and Class Disparities in the Flow of Agricultural Credit in India', *Indian Journal of Agricultural Economics*, Vol. 43, No. 3, July–September.

Hashim, S.R. (2000), 'From Food Security to Water Security', *The Asian Journal*, Vol. 7. No. 4.

Hicks, J.R. (1932), *Theory of Wages*, London: Macmillan Company.

Hirway, Indira *et al.* (1991), 'Report of the Study Group on Anti-Poverty Programmes' in the *Report of the National Commission on Rural Labour*, Vol. II, New Delhi.

Hoekman, Bernard and Kym Anderson (1999), 'Developing Country Agriculture and the New Trade Agenda', The World Bank, Development Research Group, May.

ICAR, Indian Council of Agricultural Research (1997), *Draft Ninth Five Year Plan 1997–2000*, Ministry of Agriculture, Government of India, New Delhi.

IWMI, International Water Management Institute (2001), 'Basin-Level Use and Productivity of Water: Examples from South Asia', Research Report 49.

Jain, H.K. (1993), *The GATT proposals of Agriculture: Their Scientific Implications*, New Delhi: National Institute of Science, Technology and Development Studies.

Jayaraman, B. (2001), 'Micro-finance: Retrospect and Prospects', Occasional Paper 20, National Bank for Agriculture and Rural Development, Mumbai.

Jodha, N.S. (1989), 'Dry Farming Research: Issues and Approaches', in N.S. Jodha (ed.), *Technology Options and Economic Policy for Dryland Agriculture: Potential and Challenges*, The Indian Society of Agricultural Economics, Mumbai, New Delhi: Concept Publishing Company.

Johansen, Frida (1993), 'Poverty Reduction in East Asia—The Silent Revolution', World Bank Discussion Paper, 203.

Johansson, Sara and Per Ronnas (1996), *Rural Industrialization: A Review of Selected Asian Experiences*, ILO, SAAT, New Delhi.

Jose, A.V. (1988), 'Agricultural Wages in India', *Economic and Political Weekly*, Vol. 23, No. 26, 25 June.

Joshi, P.K. and Ashok Gulati (2003), From Plate To Plough: Agricultural Diversification in India, Paper presented at the JNU–IFPRI Workshop on 'The Dragon and the Elephant: A Comparative Study of Economic and Agricultural Reforms in China and India', New Delhi, 25–26 March.

Kalirajan, K.P. and R.T. Shand (1997), 'Sources of Output Growth in Indian Agricullture', *Indian Journal of Agricultural Economics*, Vol. 52, No. 4.

Keyzer, M.A. and M.D. Merbis (1999), 'CAP-Reform in Agenda 2000: Logic and Contradictions', in *The External Economic Dimensions of the European Union*, G. Faber and P. van Dijek (eds), Kluwer.

Khan, Azizur Rahman (1994), 'Stabilisation, Structural Adjustment and the Labour Market: Issues and Evidence from Asia, in Rizwanul Islam (ed.), *Social Dimensions of Economic Reforms in Asia*, ILO, New Delhi.

Khoshoo, T.N. (1986), 'Environmental Priorities in India and Sustainable Development', Presidential Address to the Indian Science Congress Association, New Delhi, January.

Killick, T. (1994), 'Structural Adjustment and Poverty Alleviation', Standing Committee on Poverty Alleviation, UNCTAD/PA/7, 18 May.

Krishna, Raj (1982), 'Some Aspects of Agricultural Growth, Price Policy and Equity in Developing Countries', *Food Research Institute Studies*, Vol. XVIII, No. 3.

Krishnamurty, K. (1985), 'Inflation and Growth: A Model for India' in K. Krishnamurty and V. Pandit (eds), *Macro-Econometric Modeling of the Indian Economy: Studies in Inflation and Growth*, India: Hindustan Publishing Corporation.

Krishnaraj, Maithreyi and Amita Shah (2002), *Women Farmers of India: Declining Options—Future Possibilities*, Ahmedabad: Gujarat Institute of Development Research.

Kumar, Hemendra (2001), 'Investment in Land and Water: India's Experience' in Proceedings of the Regional Committee, FAO, Bangkok, 3–5 October.

Kumar, Praduman (2002), *Economic Analysis of Total Factor Productivity of Crop Sector in the Indo-Gangetic Plain of India by District and Region*, Division of Agricultural Economics, New Delhi: Indian Agricultural Research Institute.

Kumar, Praduman and Mark W. Rosegrant (1995), 'A 2020 Vision for Food Supply and Demand in India', Paper presented at the Workshop on a 2020 Vision for Food, Agriculture, and the Environment, organized by the International Food Policy Research Institute and the Institute of Integrated Development Studies, Kathmandu, Nepal, 27–29 March.

Kumar, Praduman and V.C. Mathur (1996), 'Structural Changes in the Demand for Foodgrains in India', *Indian Journal of Agricultural Economics*, Vol. 51, No. 4, October–December, pp. 664–73.

Kundu, Amitabh (1996), 'New Economic Policy and Urban Poverty in India', in C.H. Hanumantha Rao and Hans Linnemann (eds), *Economic Reforms and Poverty Alleviation in India*, New Delhi: Sage.

Kuznets, S. (1966), Modern Economic Growth, New Haven, CT: Yale University Press.

Lipton, M. (1995), 'Liberalisation, Poverty Reduction and Agricultural Development in India', in R. Cassen and V. Joshi (eds), *India: The Future of Economic Reform*, Oxford University Press, Mumbai, Kolkata, Chennai.

Mellor, John W. and Gunvant M. Desai (1986), 'Agricultural Change and Rural Poverty—Variations on a Theme', by Dharm Narain, Delhi: Oxford University Press.

Minhas, B.S. (1991), 'On Estimating the Inadequacy of Energy Intakes: Revealed Food Consumption Behaviour Versus Nutritional Norms (Nutritional Status of Indian People in 1983)', *The Journal of Development Studies*, Vol. 28, No. 1, October, pp. 1–38.

Minhas, B.S., L.R. Jain, and S.D. Tendulkar (1991), 'Declining Incidence of Poverty in 1980s: Evidence Versus Artefacts', *Economic and Political Weekly,* Vol. XXVI, Nos 27 and 28, July, pp. 6–13.

Mishra, S.N. and Ramesh Chand (1995), 'Public and Private Capital Formation in Indian Agriculture: Comments on Complementarity Hypothesis and Others', *Economic and Political Weekly*, Vol. XXX, No. 25, 24 June, Mumbai.

Misra, V.N. and Peter B.R. Hazell (1996), 'Terms of Trade, Rural Poverty, Technology and Investment: The Indian Experience', 1952–53 to 1990–91, *Economic and Political Weekly*, Vol. XXXI, No. 13, 30 March, Mumbai.

Mujumdar, N.A. (2001), 'The New Architecture of the Rural Credit System', Professor M.L. Dantwala Monograph Series, Monograph No. 1, Department of Economics, University of Mumbai.

Murty, K.N., 1998. 'Foodgrain Demand in India to 2020—A Comment', *Economic and Political Weekly*, 14 November, pp. 2943–44.

—— (1999), 'Decomposition of Changes in Cereals Demand into Its Components in Semi-arid Tropical Area', Paper presented at the 35th Indian Econometric Society Meeting held at the Department of Economics, University of Rajasthan, Jaipur, 11–13 March.

Narain, Dharm (1976), 'Growth of Productivity in Indian Agriculture' in K.N. Raj, Amartya Sen, and C.H. Hanumantha Rao (eds), *Studies on Indian Agriculture*, Delhi: Oxford University Press.

Narasimham, M. (Chairman) (1991), Report of the Committee on the Financial System, New Delhi.

—— (1993), 'Economic Reforms: The Unfinished Agenda', Rajiv Gandhi Institute for Contemporary Studies, New Delhi.

Natarajan, I. (1995), 'Trends in Firewood Consumption in Rural India', *Margin*, National Council of Applied Economic Research, October–December, New Delhi.

National Bank for Agriculture and Rural Development (NABARD) (2001a), *Report of the Expert Committee on Rural Credit*, Mumbai, July.

—— (2001b), 'Recovery Management in Rural Credit', Occasional Paper 21, Mumbai.

National Council of Applied Economic Research (1991), Study of Fertilizer Consumption and Quality of Seeds, Vol. 1 (mimeo).

Navalawala, B.N. (1994), 'Planning Perspective of Farmers' Participation in Irrigation Management in India' (mimeo).

Nayyar, Rohini (1996), 'New Initiatives for Poverty Alleviation in Rural India', in C.H. Hanumantha Rao and Hans Linnemann (eds), *Economic Reforms and Poverty Alleviation in India*, New Delhi: Sage.

Nickel, William, and Shamima Khan (1993), 'Rural Credit—Towards A Sustainable System for the Twenty-first Century', Seminar on Agricultural Reforms, Bombay: Indira Gandhi Institute of Development Research.

Pal, S., D. Jha, and A. Singh (1997), *Agricultural Research and Extension in India: Institutional Structure and Investments*, New Delhi: National Centre for Agricultural Economics and Policy Research.

Pal, Suresh and Raka Saxena (2003), 'Agricultural R&D Reforms in India: Policy and Institutional Imperatives', in Suresh Pal, Mruthyunjaya, P.K. Joshi and Raka Saxena (eds), Institutional Change in Indian Agriculture, New Delhi: National Centre for Agricultural Economics and Policy Research.

Pant, Niranjan (1991), 'Ground Water Issues in Eastern India' in Ruth Meinzen-Dick and Mark Svendsen (eds), *Future Directions for Indian Irrigation—Research and Policy Issues*, Washington, D.C.: International Food Policy Research Institute.

Papola, T.S. (1992), 'Rural Non-farm Employment: An Assessment of Recent Trends', *The Indian Journal of Labour Economics*, July–September.

—— (1993), 'Anti-poverty and Special Employment Programmes in India: Their Role and Effectiveness under the Structural Adjustment Programme', Working Papers, World Employment Programme Research, ILO, Geneva.

Parikh, Kirit S., N.S.S. Narayana, Manoj Panda and A. Ganesh Kumar (1995), 'Strategies for Agricultural Liberalization: Consequences for Growth, Welfare and Distribution' (mimeo), Bombay: Indira Gandhi Institute of Development Research.

Peacock, James W. (1991), 'Key Elements of Modern Biotechnology of Relevance to Agriculture', Plenary Address at the International Association of Agricultural Economists, 22 August–9 September, Tokyo, published in the Proceedings Volume of the IAAE.

Perry. C.J., Michael Rock, and D. Seckler (1997), 'Water as an Economic Good: A Solution, or a Problem?', Research Report 14, IIMI.

Planning Commission, GOI (2001), 'Report of the Working Group on Public Distribution System and Food Security for Tenth Plan'.

Prabhu, Seeta K. (1996), 'The Impact of Structural Adjustment on Social Sector Expenditure: Evidence from Indian States', in C.H. Hanumantha Rao and Hans Linnemann (eds), *Economic Reforms and Poverty Alleviation in India*, New Delhi: Sage.

Prasad, T. and I.D. Sharma (1991), 'Groundwater for Agriculture in Eastern India: Problems, Prospects and Issues' in Ruth Meinzen-Dick and Svendsen, Mark (eds), *Future Directions for Indian Irrigation—Research and Policy Issues*, Washington, D.C.: International Food Policy Research Institute.

Puhazhendhi, V. and K.J.S. Satyasai (2000), 'Micro-finance for Rural People: An Impact Evaluation', National Bank for Agriculture and Rural Development, Mumbai.

Quibria, M.G. and T.N. Srinivasan (1994), 'Introduction', in M.G. Quibria (ed.), *Rural Poverty in Asia: Priority Issues and Policy Options*, New York: Oxford University Press.

Radhakrishna, R. and K. Hanumantha Rao (1995), 'Food Security, Public Distribution and Price Policy', in N.S.S. Narayana and Anindya Sen (eds), *Poverty, Environment, and Economic Development* (Festschrift for Kirit S. Parikh), Interline Publishing Pvt. Ltd.

Radhakrishna, R. (1996), 'Food Trends, Public Distribution System, and Food Security Concerns', *Indian Journal of Agricultural Economics*, Golden Jubilee Number, Vol. 51, Nos 1 and 2, January–June.

Radhakrishna, R. and Shovan Ray (Project Directors) (2003), 'South Asia Poverty Alleviation Progamme: Poverty Inventory Study for India', Report Submitted to UN Office for Project Series, Kaula Lumpur, Indira Gandhi Institute of Development Research.

Radhakrishna, R. and Subbarao, K. with Indrakant, S. and Ravi, C. (1997), 'India's Public Distribution System: A National and International Perspective, The World Bank, Discussion Paper No. 380, November, Washington, D.C.

Radhakrishna, R. and C. Ravi (1992), 'Effects of Growth, Relative Price and Preferences of Food, and Nutrition', *The Indian Economic Review*, Special Number in Memory of Sukhamoy Chakravarty, Vol. 27, pp. 303–23.

Rajiv Gandhi Foundation (2000), *Panchayati Raj in India: Status Report 1999*, New Delhi: Rajiv Gandhi Foundation Task Force on Panchayati Raj.

Raju, K.V. (2000), 'Participatory Irrigation Management in Andhra Pradesh: Promise, Practice and a Way Forward', Working Paper 65, Institute for Social and Economic Change.

Rakshit, Mihir (2000), 'Post-Uruguay Round Negotiations: A Developing Country Perspective', *Artha Vijnana*, March.

Rao, C.H. Hanumantha (1989), 'Technological Change in India Agriculture: Emerging Trends and Perspectives', *Indian Journal of Agricultural Economics*, Vol. 44, No. 4, October–December.

—— (1991), 'Implications of Modern Biotechnology for the Structure of Agriculture in the Less Developed Countries', invited paper presented at the Conference of the International Association of Agricultural Economists, Tokyo, 22 August–9 September; published in the Proceedings Volume of the IAAE.

—— (1991), 'World Development Report, 1991: An Appraisal', *Indian Economic Review*, Vol. XXVI, No. 2, pp. 253–6.

—— (1994), 'Agricultural Growth and Rural Poverty in India: Emerging Trends and Perspectives', *Indian Economic Review*, Vol. XXVIII, No. 2.

—— (1994), Agricultural Growth, Rural Poverty, and Environmental Degradation in India, New Delhi: Oxford University Press.

—— (1994a), '*Economic Liberalization and Agriculture*: Requirements of Agricultural Research and Technology', *Yojana*, August, New Delhi.

—— (1995), 'Attack on Poverty and Deprivation: Role of Structural Change and Structural Adjustment', Presidential Address at the 36th Annual Conference of the Indian Society of Labour Economics, *The Indian Journal of Labour Economics*, Vol. 38, No. 1, January–March.

—— (1995), 'Budget: Welcome Social Focus', *The Economic Times*, 26 April.

—— (1996), 'Economic Reforms, Agricultural Growth, and Rural Poverty: Some Reflections on the Relevance of East and South-east Asian Experience for India', Sukhamoy Chakravarty Memorial Lecture at the 78th Conference of the Indian Economic Association at Chandigarh, *The Indian Economic Journal*, Vol. 43, No. 4, April–June.

—— (2000), 'Watershed Development in India: Recent Experience and Emerging Issues', *Economic and Political Weekly*, Vol. XXXV, No. 45, 4 November.

—— (2001), 'Changing Economic Structure of the Rural Economy in Asia and the Pacific' in *Rural Transformation in Asia and the Pacific*, Asian Productivity Organization, Tokyo.

—— (2003), 'Rural Non-farm Sector and Lessons from Asian Experience', in Rohini Nayyar and Alakh N. Sharma (eds), *Rural Transformation in India: The Role of Non-farm Sector*, New Delhi: Institute for Human Development.

Rao, C.H. Hanumantha and Ashok Gulati (1994), 'Indian Agriculture: Emerging Perspectives and Policy Issues', *Economic and Political Weekly*, 31 December, Vol. 29, No. 53, pp. A-158–69.

—— (1997), 'Price Policy Reforms for Irrigation Water in India' (mimeo), Washington, D.C.: International Food Policy Research Institute, October.

Rao, C.H. Hanumantha and R. Radhakrishna (1997), 'National Food Security: A Policy Perspective for India', presented at the 23rd International Conference of Agricultural Economists, Sacramanto, California, 10–16 August.

Rao, C.H.H. (1969a), 'Resource Prospects from the Rural Sector—The Case of Indirect Taxes', *Economic and Political Weekly*, Review of Agriculture, March, pp. A-53–58.

—— (1969b), 'Reply', *Economic and Political Weekly*, Vol. 4, No. 26, Review of Agriculture, June, p. 5.

—— (1975), *Technological Change and Distribution of Gains in Indian Agriculture*, New Delhi: Macmillan.

—— (1992), 'Integrating Poverty Alleviation Programmes with Development Strategies—Indian Experience', *Economic and Political Weekly*, Vol. XXVII, No. 48, 28 November.

—— (1994), 'Policy Issues Relating to Irrigation and Rural Credit in India', in G.S. Bhalla (ed.), *Economic Liberalisation and Indian Agriculture*, Institute for Studies in Industrial Development, New Delhi.

Rao, C.H.H. (1996), 'Economic Reforms, Agricultural Growth and Rural Poverty', *The Indian Economic Journal*, Vol. 43, No. 4, April–June.

—— (1997a), 'Sustainable Development with Special Reference to India: An Economist's Perspective', Keynote Address in the Challenge of the Balance-environmental Economics in India: Proceedings of a National Environment and Economics Meeting, Anil Agarwal (ed.), New Delhi: Centre for Science and Environment.

—— (1997b), 'Agricultural Growth, Sustainability, and Poverty Alleviation in India: Recent Trends and Major Issues of Reform', IFPRI Lecture Series 5, Washington, D.C.: International Food Policy Research Institute.

—— (2001), 'Declining Demand for Foodgrains in Rural India: Causes and Implications', *Economic and Political Weekly*, 22 January.

Rao, C.H.H. and P. Rangaswamy (1988), 'Efficiency of Investment in IRDP: A Study of Uttar Pradesh', *Economic and Political Weekly*, 25 June.

Rath, N. (1989), 'Agricultural Growth and Investment in India', *Journal of the Indian School of Political Economy*, Vol. I, No. 1, January–June.

—— (1989), 'Institutional Credit for Agriculture in India', *Journal of Indian School of Political Economy*, Vol. I, No. 2, July–December.

Rath, Nilakanth (1985), 'Garibi Hatao: Can IRDP Do It?', *Economic and Political Weekly*, 9 February.

Ravallion, Martin and Gaurav Datt (1996), 'India's Checkered History in Fight against Poverty: Are There Lessons for the Future?', *Economic and Political Weekly*, Vol. XXXI, Nos 35, 36, and 37, September.

Ravi, C. (2001), 'Complete Demand System, Welfare and Nutrition: An Analysis of Indian Consumption Data', Ph.D. thesis submitted to Dr B.R. Ambedkar Open University, Hyderabad

Ray, S.K. (1992), 'Development of Irrigation and its Impact on Pattern of Land Use, Output Growth, and Employment Generation', *Journal of Indian School of Political Economy*, 4 (No. 4), pp. 677–700.

Reddy, Ratna V. (1991), 'Under-utilization of Land in Andhra Pradesh: Extent and Determinants', *Indian Journal of Agricultural Economics*, Vol. XLVI, No. 4, October–December, pp. 444–7.

—— (2000), 'Land Degradation in India: Extent, Costs, Determinants and Trends' (mimeo), Hyderabad: Centre for Economic and Social Studies.

Reddy, Ratna V., M. Gopinath Reddy, S. Galab, and Oliver Springate-Baginski (2001), 'Watershed Development and Livelihood Security: An Assessment of Linkages and Impact in Andhra Pradesh, India' (mimeo), Centre for Economic and Social Studies, Hyderabad and School of Geography, University of Leeds, UK.

Reddy, Y.V. (2001), 'Indian Agriculture and Reform Concerns, Issues and Agenda', *Reserve Bank of India Bulletin*, May, Mumbai.

Repetto, Robert (1986), 'Skimming the Water: Rent-seeking and the Performance of Public Irrigation Systems', Washington, D.C.: World Resources Institute.

Reserve Bank of India (1989), *A Review of the Agricultural Credit System in India, Report of the Agricultural Review Committee*, Bombay.

—— (2001), *Handbook of Statistics on Indian Economy, 2001*.

—— (2002), *Report on Currency and Finance*, 2000–2001.

—— (2003a), Annual Report 2002–2003.

—— (2003b), *Handbook of Statistics on the Indian Economy*, 2002–2003.

——(2003c), State Finances: A Study of Budgets of 2002–2003.

—— (2003). Report on Currency and Finance 2001–2002.

Ricardo, David (1817), 'On the Principles of Political Economy and Taxation, London, in *The Works and Correspondence of David Ricardo*, edited by Piero Sraffa with the Collaboration of M.H. Dobb, Cambridge University Press, for the Royal Economic Society, 1966.

Rosegrant, M. and Hans Binswanger (1994), 'Markets in Tradable Water Rights: Potential for Efficiency Gains in Developing-Country Water Resource Allocation', *World Development Report*, Vol. 22, No. 22, pp. 1613–25.

Rosegrant, Mark W. and Peter B.R. Hazell (2000), *Transforming the Rural Asian Economy: The Unfinished Revolution*, Asian Development Bank, New York: Oxford University Press.

Ruth, Meinzen-Dick, Meyra Mendoza, Loic Sadoulet, Ghada Abiad-Shields, and Ashok Subramanyan (1994), 'Water-users Associations: Review and Best Practices Study', Washington, D.C.: International Food Policy Research Institute.

Saha, Anamitra (2000), 'Puzzle of Declining Rural Foodgrains Consumption', Discussion, *Economic and Political Weekly*, Vol. XXXV, No. 27, 1 July, pp. 2453–4.

Saith, Ashwani (1993), 'From Collectives to Markets: Restructured Agriculture—Industry Linkages in Rural China—Some Macro-level Evidence', *ARTEP Working Papers*, New Delhi.

—— (1993), *Chinese Rural Industrialization; Some lessons for Reforming and Developing Economies*, ARTEP Working Papers, New Delhi.

Saleth, Maria R. (1996), 'Water Institutions in India—Economics, Law, and Policy', New Delhi: Commonwealth Publishers.

—— (1999), *Strategic Linkages in Rural Diversification—Empirical Analysis and Policy Issues*, New Delhi: Commonwealth Publishers.

Sarap, Kailas (1991), *Interlinked Agrarian Markets in Rural India*, New Delhi: Sage Publications.

Schiff, Maurice and Alberto Valdes (1992), *The Political Economy of Agricultural Pricing Policy, Vol. 4–A, Synthesis of the Economics in Developing Countries*, A World Bank Comparative Study, Baltimore and London: The Johns Hopkins University Press.

Seckler, David (1996), The New Era of Water Management: From 'Dry' to 'Wet' Water Savings, *Issues in Agriculture*, 8, Washington, D.C.: CGIAR.

Seckler, David, Upali Amarasinghe, David Molden, Radhika de Silva, and Randolph Barker (1998), 'World Water Demand and Supply, 1990 to 2025: Scenarios and Issues, Research Report 19, International Water Management Institute (IWMI), Colombo, Sri Lanka.

Sen, Abhijit (1993), 'Agriculture in Structural Adjustment', paper presented at the Seminar on Agricultural Reforms in India, Indira Gandhi Institute of Development Research, 11–12 January.

—— (1996), 'Economic Reforms, Employment, and Poverty: Trends and Options', *Economic and Political Weekly*, Vol. XXXI, Nos 35, 36, and 37, September.

—— (2000), 'Estimates of Consumer Expenditure and its Distribution: Statistical Priorities after NSS 55th Round', *Economic and Political Weekly*, 16 December.

Sen, Abhijit and Himanshu (2003), 'Poverty and Inequality in India: Getting Closer to the Truth', Centre for Economic Studies and Planning, Jawaharlal Nehru University (mimeo), New Delhi.

Shah, Amita (1998), 'Watershed Development Programmes in India: Emerging Issues for Environment-Development Perspectives', *Economic and Political Weekly*, 33 (June 27) pp. A-66–A-79.

Shah, Amita and Gani Memon (1999), 'Watershed Development Project in Gujarat: A Quick Review' (mimeo), Ahmedabad: Gujarat Institute of Development Research.

Shah, Anil, C. (2000), 'Eloquent Silent Revolution', Ahmedabad: Development Support Centre.

Shah, Tushaar (1993), 'Groundwater Markets and Irrigation Development—Political Economy and Practical Policy', Bombay: Oxford University Press.

——(2001), 'Wells and Welfare in the Ganga Basin: Public Policy and Private Initiative in Eastern Uttar Pradesh, India', Research Report 54, IWMI.

Shankar, Kripa (1992), 'Water Market in Eastern UP', *Economic and Political Weekly*, Vol. 27, No. 18, 22 May.

Sharma, Anil (1994), 'Electricity for Minor Irrigation', *SEMINAR*, 418, June, New Delhi.

Shetty, S.L. (1990), 'Investment in Agriculture: Brief Review of Recent Trends', *Economic and Political Weekly*, Vol. XXV, Nos 7 and 8, 17–24 February.

—— (2003), 'Credit Flows to the Poor: Vulnerable Sections, Sectors and Regions of the Indian Economy—A Review', in R. Radhakrishna and

Shovan Ray (Project Directors) (2003), *South Asia Poverty Alleviation Pogamme: Poverty Inventory Study for India*, Report Submitted to UN Office for Project Series, Kuala Lumpur, Indira Gandhi Institute of Development Research.

Siamwalla, Ammar (1991), *Labour-abundant Agricultural Growth and Some of its Consequences: The Case of Thailand*, Bangkok: TDRI.

Singh, J.P. (1985), 'Some Aspects of the Strategy of Agricultural Development in Eastern Region of India' in Report of the Study Group on Agricultural Strategies for Eastern Region, Planning Commission.

Solow, R.M. (1957), 'Technical Change and the Aggregate Production Function', *Review of Economics and Statistics*, 39.

Srinivasan, T.N. and P.K. Bardhan (1969), 'Resource Prospects from the Rural Sector—A Comment', *Economic and Political Weekly, Review of Agriculture*, Vol. 4, No. 26, June, pp. 1–4.

Stuijvenberg, Piter A. Van (1996), 'Structural Adjustment in India—What about Poverty Alleviation?', in C.H. Hanumantha Rao and Hans Linnemann (eds), *Economic Reforms and Poverty Alleviation in India*, New Delhi: Sage.

Subbiah, A.R. (2002), *Natural Disaster Management*, Millennium Study on the State of the Indian Farmer, New Delhi: Ministry of Agriculture, Government of India.

Sundaram, K. (2001), 'Employment and Poverty in 1990s: Further Results from NSS 55th Round Employment—Unemployment Survey, 1999–2000', *Economic and Political Weekly*, 11 August.

Sundaram, K. and S.D. Tendulkar (2003), 'Poverty in India in the 1990s: Revised Estimates', *Economic and Political Weekly*, Vol. 38, No. 46, 15 November.

Subbarao, K. (1985), 'Regional Variations in Impact of Anti-Poverty Programme: A Review of Evidence', *Economic and Political Weekly*, 26 October.

Tendulkar, S.D. and L.R. Jain (1995), 'Economic Reforms and Poverty', *Economic and Political Weekly*, 10 June, Vol. 30, No. 23, pp. 1373–77.

Thorbecke, E. (1992), *Adjustment and Equity in Indonesia*, Paris: OECD.

Tjondronegoro, Sediono M.P., Irlan Soejono, and Joan Hardjono (1992), 'Rural Poverty in Indonesia: Trends, Issues and Policies', *Asian Development Review*, Vol. 10, No. 1, pp. 67–90.

Tyagi, D.S. (1990), *Managing India's Food Economy: Problems and Alternatives*, New Delhi: Sage.

UNDP (1993), 'India: Employment, Poverty and Economic Policies', ILO, ARTEP, New Delhi.

Vaidyanathan, A. (1991), 'Critical Issues Facing Indian Irrigation', in Ruth Meinzen-Dick and Mark Svendsen (eds), *Future Directions for Indian Irrigation*, Washington, D.C.: International Food Policy Research Institute.

—— (1993), 'Proper Pricing of Irrigation Water', *The Hindu*, 21 March.

—— (1999), *Water Resource Management—Institutions and Irrigation Development in India*, New Delhi: Oxford University Press.

Valdes, Alberto, and Joachim Zietz (1995), 'Distortions in World Food Markets in the Wake of GATT: Evidence and Policy Implications', *World Development Report*, Vol. 23, No. 6.

Varshney, Ashutosh (1999). 'Mass Politics or Elite Poltics? India's Economic Reforms in Comparative Perspective' in J. Sachs, A. Varshney, and N. Bajpai (eds), *India in the Era of Economic Reforms*, New Delhi: Oxford University Press.

Veeraiah Ch. and N. Madankumar (1994), 'Waste of Irrigation Water under Major Irrigation Projects in Andhra Pradesh and its Prevention', Paper Presented at the Seminar on Wastages of Irrigation Water under Major Irrigation Projects, Department of Economics, Sri Venkateswara University, Tirupati, September.

Vyas, V.S. (1994), 'Agricultural Price Policy: Need for Reformulation', in G.S. Bhalla (ed.), *Economic Liberalisation and Indian Agriculture*, New Delhi: Institute for Studies in Industrial Development.

Wing Thye Woo, Bruce Glassburner and Anwar Nasution (1994), 'Macroeconomic Policies, Crises, and Long-term Growth in Indonesia', 1965–1990, Comparative Macroeconomic Studies, World Bank.

World Bank (1983), *Thailand: Rural Growth and Employment*, Washington, D.C.

—— (1990), 'Indonesia: Strategy for a Sustained Reduction in Poverty', Washington, D.C.: A World Bank Country Study.

—— (1992), 'China: Strategy for Reducing Poverty in the 1990s', World Bank Country Study, Washington, D.C.

—— (1990), *World Development Report 1990: Poverty*, Washington, D.C.

—— (1991), *World Development Report, 1991*, Washington, D.C.

—— (1993a), 'The East Asian Miracle—Economic Growth and Public Policy', Oxford University Press.

—— (1993b), 'Sustaining Rapid Development in East Asia and the Pacific'.

—— (1992), *World Development Report, 1992*, Washington, D.C.

—— (1995), *World Development Report*, Washington, D.C.

—— (1997), 'India: Achievements and Challenges in Reducing Poverty', Washington, D.C.

—— (1999), 'India, Foodgrains Marketing Policies: Reforming to Meet Food Security Needs', Vol. II, Report No. 1829-IN.

World Development Indicators 2000, The World Bank, March 2000.

World Trade Organization (2001), 'Negotiations on WTO agreement on Agriculture: Proposals by India in the areas of: (i) Food Security, (ii) Market access, (iii) Domestic Support, and (iv) Export Competition', 15 January.

Yugandhar, B.N., J. Venkateswarlu, and Vijay Kochar (1999), 'Watershed Based Development in Arid and Semi-Arid Areas of Andhra Pradesh', *Journal of Rural Development*, Vol. 18, No. 3, NIRD, Hyderabad.

Zeeuw, De Aart (1997), 'International agricultural trade negotiations under GATT/WTO: Experiences, future challenges and possible outcomes', *European Review of Agricultural Economics*, Vol. 24.

Annexure

List of Papers by the Author used as Basic Source Material

1. 'World Development Report, 1991: An Appraisal', *Indian Economic Review*, Vol. XXVI, No. 2, pp. 253–6.
2. 'Integrating Poverty Alleviation Programmes with Development Strategies: Indian Experience', Keynote Address at the Commonwealth Consultation on Rural Poverty Alleviation, Colombo, Sri Lanka, 5–9 October 1992, published in *Economic and Political Weekly*, Vol. XXVII, No. 48, 28 November 1992.
3. 'Economic Growth and Social Justice: Changing Roles of Planning and Markets', Ravi Narayan Reddy Memorial Lecture, Hyderabad, 7 September 1994.
4. 'Policy Issues Relating to Irrigation and Rural Credit in India', in G.S. Bhalla (ed.), 1994, *Economic Liberalization and Indian Agriculture*, Institute for Studies in Industrial Development, New Delhi.
5. 'Agricultural Growth, and Rural Poverty in India: Emerging Trends and Perspectives', Dharm Narain Memorial Lecture, Institute of Economic Growth, Delhi, published in *Indian Economic Review*, Vol. XXVIII, No. 2, 1994.
6. 'Economic Liberalization and Agriculture: Requirements of Agricultural Research and Technology', Keynote Address at the Mid-term Meeting of the Consultative Group on International Agricultural Research (CGIAR), 23 May 1994, New Delhi, published in *Yojana*, Annual Number, August 1994.
7. 'Economic Reforms and the Prospects for Rural Labour', V.V. Giri Memorial Lecture, 35th Conference of the Indian Society of Labour Economics, Ahmedabad, 22 January 1994, published in the *Indian Journal of Labour Economics*, Conference Number 1994.
8. 'Liberalisation of Agriculture in India: Some Major Issues', Keynote Paper, *Indian Journal of Agricultural Economics*, July–September, 1995.
9. 'Attack on Poverty and Deprivation: Role of Structural Change and Structural Adjustment', Presidential Address at the 36th Annual Conference of the Indian Society of Labour Economics, *The Indian Journal of Labour Economics*, Vol. 38, No. 1, January–March 1995.

10. 'Economic Reforms, Agricultural Growth and Rural Poverty: Some Reflections on the Relevance of East and South-East Asian Experience for India', Sukhamoy Chakravarty Memorial Lecture at the 78th Conference of the Indian Economic Association at Chandigarh, *The Indian Economic Journal*, Vol. 43, No. 4, April–June 1996.
11. 'Agricultural Growth, Sustainability, and Poverty Alleviation in India: Recent Trends and Major Issues of Reform', IFPRI Lecture Series 5, December 1997, Washington D.C: International Food Policy Research Institute.
12. 'Sustainable Development with Special Reference to India: An Economist's Perspective', Keynote Address, in The Challenge of the Balance-environmental Economics in India: Proceedings of a National Environment and Economics Meeting, Anil Agarwal (ed.), 1997, New Delhi: Centre for Science and Environment.
13. 'Sustainable Agricultural Development in India: An Economist's View on Performance and Perspectives', Keynote Speech at the First Asia-Pacific High Level Conference on Sustainable Agriculture, Beijing, China, 4–8 October 1998.
14. 'Sustainable Development of Agriculture', presentation at a Plenary Session of the First Biennial Conference of the Indian Society of Ecological Economics, Bangalore, 20–22 December 1999.
15. 'Declining Demand for Foodgrains in Rural India: Causes and Implications', Presidential Address at the 13th National Conference on Agricultural Marketing, NIRD, Hyderabad, 12 October 1999, published in *Economic and Political Weekly*, 22 January 2000.
16. 'Watershed Development in India—Recent Experience and Emerging Issues', Lovraj Kumar Memorial Lecture (SPWD), published in *Economic and Political Weekly*, Vol. 35, No. 45, 4 November 2000.
17. 'Changing Economic Structure of the Rural Economy in Asia and the Pacific' in *Rural Transformation in Asia and the Pacific*, 2001, Tokyo: Asian Productivity Organization.
18. 'WTO and Viability of Indian Agriculture', 6th Foundation Day Lecture at the National Academy of Agricultural Sciences, IARI, New Delhi, 5 June 2001, published in *Economic and Political Weekly*, Vol. XXXVI, No. 36, 8 September 2001.
19. 'Sustainable Use of Water for Irrigation in Indian Agriculture', Presidential Address at the Second Biennial Conference of the Indian Society of Ecological Economics, Bhopal, 19–21 December 2001, Published in *Economic and Political Weekly*, Vol. XXXVII, No. 18, 4 May 2002.
20. 'Foodgrain Surpluses: Causes and Policy Implications', C.D. Deshmukh Memorial Lecture, Council for Social Development, Hyderabad, March 2002.
21. 'Reform Agenda for Agriculture', Rajiv Gandhi Foundation, 2003, published in *Economic and Political Weekly*, 15 February 2003.

Index